Knowledge will forever govern ignorance,
and a people who mean to be their own governors
must arm themselves with the power
knowledge gives.

A popular government without popular information,
or the means of acquiring it is but a
prologue to a farce
or a tragedy… or perhaps both.

Ray v Turner, supra, p 304, fn. 10 (Wright, J., concurring)

[redacted]

redacted

jeni decker

ISBN-13: 978-1508491491
ISBN-10: 1508491496

[redacted]

MICHIGAN DEPARTMENT OF
Supplementary Complaint
Additional Complaint Page
NATURE OF COMPLAINT
Prosecutor J
CRIME LAB:
MEDICAL EXAMINER
Scene of the crime
Gambles
Murdered clerk had received calls
Police probe Reed City murder
Reporting Officer

[redacted]

There are things known
and there are things unknown,
and in between are the doors of perception.
~ Aldous Huxley

INTRODUCTION

The thing to remember is that I'm not a true crime writer. If you are familiar with the genre, if there's a standard cookie-cutter way those types of books are written, this probably won't be that book. This is about my experience researching a decades-old murder that remains unsolved.

I never intended to write this book, but one day I woke up, had my morning coffee, went through my emails and private messages, and suddenly realized I'd become invested on a daily basis; taking calls, doing interviews, bothering the city and county clerks for documents—all of whom were extremely helpful—and for the record, I put the patience of a few to the test. Computers had to be consulted, files had to be rifled through, stairs had to be climbed, and in more than a few cases, dank basements had to be negotiated by way of steep cement stairs, even during ongoing repairs to keep the ancient leather-bound volumes safe from the elements. Having said that, I owe a quick shout-out to the gals over at the Osceola County building. You know who you are. I appreciate your tolerance. Jackie Beam with Reed City—you're a mensch, too. I probably owe you more baked goods.

Now don't get me wrong. I'm not saying public records *shouldn't* be readily available and handed over by a clerk with a smile on his (or her) face, and a song in his (or her) heart. They *should*. Public records are *our* records. They are not the property of the entity doling them out, despite what they may tell you or how persnickety they get when you request them. They are but the gatekeepers to said records, and if they are doing their jobs correctly, they are not in any way obstructing your ability to retrieve information, nor are they giving you a hard time for asking questions.

Alas, I like to deal in reality. After having typed the acronym FOIA (Freedom of Information Act) more times this year than I care to calculate, often using it as a verb, I can tell you with swift certainty that not every municipal entity is equal when it comes to handing out records. We'll leave the disparity in how charges are calculated for later. Maybe grab some Tums® and have them ready.

At some point I realized there were things the public should know. Stuff to which we should all be paying more attention. Like the rate of unsolved homicides in this country, or maybe just your area. Check it against national averages when you get a second, if you're able to locate that information. If your State Police keep that kind of information readily available, you're lucky. Now check to see where your state falls in the homicide clearance rate category. Are a healthy number of those murders getting solved? *Excellent*.

If you answered no, ask yourself why that might be. What could hinder cops from solving a case? I'd venture to say that if the record keeping is abysmal, the clearance rate might reflect that. If evidence is not being processed in a timely manner, that could also play into things. For your consideration, I'd propose the following: All case files should at this point be digitized. That means if you have, for instance, a thirty two year old murder that remains unsolved, and you think you might consider re-working it at some point, (never mind referring to it in the press as "open and ongoing") you'd better have that case file completely digitized, indexed, and I certainly hope you are regularly submitting prints (if you have them) to AFIS in the hopes of locating the perpetrator, should said perp ever do anything naughty again for which he will be fingerprinted.

From *The Restless Sleep – Inside New York City's Cold Case Squad* (Stacy Horn, 2005): "There are three reasons a case goes cold. Either they couldn't solve it (no evidence or witnesses), they didn't want to solve it, or someone screwed up."

That's pretty broad but accurate, nonetheless.

Sometimes they don't have enough evidence. Cops could even know who did it, but don't have that one little thing they need to put the monster away. To make matters more complicated, they better have collected enough of those little things along the way to satisfy the prosecutor because those guys and gals aren't interested in taking something to court if they don't think they can win. They have their own numbers to think about, and there's double jeopardy to consider. This combination of circumstances is the reason for the vast majority of unsolved homicides in this country.

It's a numbers game when you start talking about cases that have gone cold. The departments want arrests. Period. Frankly, *We the People* do as well. We don't want jerks out there making meth and driving drunk and kidnapping kids and doing all manner of horrible crap because the manpower in the area has all been assigned to a single homicide. In most cases, the percentages of cold cases climb because they have a growing number of cases with no new leads.

Okay, so maybe there are places where the guys working these tough cases are just... average. Maybe even not so good at their jobs. But I think it's important to labor under the assumption that we haven't got a glut of incompetent detectives. Cases get solved. *Lots of them*. And for every one of them—from burglary to mass murder, and everything in between—there's more minute to minute, hour to hour legwork and research than any of us would care to ponder. Cases don't get solved in an hour (minus commercial breaks) in real life. DNA doesn't get tested and provide a *Voila!* moment quickly in the real world. Some labs have a backlog of years on evidence testing. We won't even go into the devastating backlog of rape kits Detroit has of this writing—some that go as far back as the 1980s.

You know what? Maybe we *will* get into it. I think it bears mentioning.

In 2009 over 11,000 sexual assault kits were found abandoned in a Detroit Police storage facility. *Eleven thousand*. After years of hacking away at red tape and budgetary restraints, in the first 1,600 kits that were processed (very recently, mind you), approximately 100 serial rapists were identified, and ten convicted rapists. According to Wayne County Prosecutor Kym Worthy, just from this 1,600 tested, "Perpetrators have moved on from Michigan to commit similar crimes in 23 other states."

I'll pause for a minute and let that sink in—or you can beat your head up against the wall for a bit. Whatever you need.

Rape. Let me repeat that. *Rape*. A woman is sexually assaulted. The violation goes unpunished and justice is delayed because someone can't keep track of where rape kits are. *Are you kidding me?* Do you know how hard it is for rape victims to summon the strength to come forward? Let's pretend it's *your* daughter or mother or sister or grandma or auntie or niece who was sexually assaulted, but shoddy recordkeeping and apathy keeps this woman who has suffered from *at least* knowing the person who hurt her isn't out there hurting someone else.

Nope, sorry. They're out there, alright, doing it in twenty-three other states.

Sweet baby Jesus.

I'm going to say this about those 11,000 rape kits that were allowed to languish for years, and then we'll move on. That fiasco is <u>*criminal*</u> and whoever at the State Police and/or associated labs that are responsible for thousands of tests having not been processed is responsible for every victim raped by those repeat offenders. Someone should be held liable for that. That's not just a clerical error. That's a *crime*.

Now, the same kind of thing can occur with homicides if the DNA isn't properly tested and re-tested when new technology comes available. Also, if prints on old cases aren't re-checked in the system to see if the unknown bad guy may have reoffended in the interim and finally gotten printed. There's no *Great and Powerful Oz* sitting in a booth somewhere at every police department who rings a little bell and announces over the intercom when a predator who committed a crime for which there is no fingerprint match suddenly does something bad and finally gets printed.

"Attention! May I have your attention please? You know the guy who brutally assaulted that woman in that case you guys were working thirty years ago? Well he just did it again in Virginia. Go get 'em!"

That's not how it works. These things have to be checked regularly. The older the case, the less likely they will get re-checked. And here's the rub: for a lot of these perpetrators, once isn't enough. If they can do it once and get away with it, why not again? Maybe even again. And then maybe they evolve and get better at doing the bad stuff so that at some point their MO doesn't even look like it did with crime number one, and now they are a lot better at not leaving evidence behind.

As I write this, I don't know if Janette Roberson will ever get justice and that makes me angry. I feel as though I've been mad about it for a long time now, and these are just some of the questions I started asking myself after I stumbled across a discussion thread about an unsolved murder that occurred thirty years ago in the small town I'd moved to a few years earlier.

With regard to the research and preparation for this book, there are too many people to thank. Also a couple I'd like to slap. I'll leave the latter to your imagination, but suffice to say that sometimes we take on ventures of this magnitude because a person or two acts like *you're* the bad guy for asking questions at all. *Screw those people*. If you have questions, *ask*. And *keep asking*. If they try to make you feel bad about it, ask them *What about a woman getting slaughtered in her place of business and nobody paying for it after thirty years doesn't deserve further inquiry*? Maybe ask if they have a vested interest in people *not* asking, because when folks don't want you asking questions, that should send up red flags.

To the people who said, *Go get 'em!* and various similar things, *Thank you*. You guys know who you are and YOU ROCK. To the folks who spoke to me about elements of this case, I appreciate you for sharing your memories of events. Because there are a good number of you who wouldn't benefit from a public thank you, I'm going to stifle the urge to jot out a complete list. But if I sat with you, perhaps in your living room, or bar, or car, maybe we spoke on the phone while my kids made way too much noise in the background—you guys helped me do this, and I'll be forever grateful.

I spoke to a lot of fine people while writing this book and I can tell you that the citizens of Reed City are good humans. Downright salt of the earth folks. If Janette Roberson's case gets solved, it will be because of these people speaking up, asking questions, and telling things they remember. I truly believe it will be the Reed City community that does it. You guys have the answers, and I know that because you have asked all the right questions.

To the one person who went with me through every bit of information we could track down, argued every point, repeatedly bothered people neither of us knew, asked questions, got equally irritated when certain entities weren't as forthcoming with public documents as we knew they lawfully should have been, and kept at it with me, toe to toe, thank you Jen Carlson. My trusty "research assistant" is really a woman who was once a girl who lived in Reed City when Janette Roberson was killed, and it stuck with her all these years later. We did this together and I'm glad I wasn't alone in my outrage. There were days I needed someone else to shoulder it, and you were always there to do so. Also, you're as pigheaded as me, and that seemed to work for what we needed to get done. *Thank you, Jen*.

I do think it would be remiss of me not to extend my warmest thanks to Detective Sgt. George Pratt (MSP, Osceola County), Assistant District Commander Cam Henke (MSP), Detective Sgt. Mike Stephens (MSP), and Reed City Police Chief Chuck Davis—all of whom have, at some point, patiently dealt with my (or my assistant's) questions, and for that we are extremely grateful.

Finally, to Janette Roberson: *I'm so sorry*. Sorry about everything you lost, sorry for the loss of your family and friends, and sorry for the physical pain you must have endured. But most of all, I'm sorry he's still out there.

I hope they get him one day.

[redacted]

Author's Note

In most cases, I have used actual names of people found in public documents generated by Michigan State Police, Reed City Police Department, Osceola County Sheriff's Department, Cadillac Police Department, and Wexford County, among others.

All true names of law enforcement officers and municipal workers have been used. Those who choose to work for city, county, and state governments, as well as law enforcement do so at the pleasure of the taxpayer, and because their duty to the people (and power over them) requires a great deal of trust, their actions while in the course of performing their job should always be transparent, particularly in a situation where any question of their performance is at issue.

In a few instances (either at the request of the person I interviewed, or at my own discretion, based on my interaction with the interviewee) I have chosen to use a pseudonym. In these cases, the name will appear as such: "*Name*" in full quotes.

Also, in certain cases I have further redacted documents supplied to me by the above law enforcement entities, or redacted sections of interviews I did with witnesses (which will be noted as [**REDACTED**] within the text) in the interest of respecting the ongoing investigation.

If you told me your story but do not find it retold on these pages, it is likely because you were the only person who offered that information and I could not corroborate it. There are quite a few of those stories—some rather intriguing—that still rattle around in my white matter, and will continue to do so for years to come. The absence of such stories within this book speaks only to a concerted effort to withhold leads passed on to me that I, in turn, passed on to police, as well as a personal rule to include nothing that could not be corroborated by law enforcement or attributed to multiple sources. Rest assured that anything I found which could even remotely be of investigative value was turned over to Michigan State Police, as I had no way of knowing, in most cases, whether it was new information to them or not, except in the case where the person who relayed the information specified they had never spoken to police. In those circumstances, I passed the information along, as well as encouraged the individual to contact MSP directly.

This book is based upon multiple police reports, news articles, witness accounts, and other public documents I was able to track down. There is (I'm told) a great deal of information I do not have access to, so the absence of something within these pages should not be interpreted by the reader to indicate that it does not exist.

Finally, as with any crime that has yet to be solved, there is a great deal of gossip, innuendo, and misinformation that continues to swirl around the murder of Janette Roberson. I did my best within these pages to dispel or correct as much of that as possible. You will note as you read that there are sometimes differences and/or inconsistencies between the statements given by witnesses. I have, in all cases, relayed what was told to me, even if it seemed to contradict the statement of other witnesses, and left it up to the reader to decide what they believe.

Three decades is a long time. Memories fade; perceptions of time are stretched or shortened. Details are forgotten or remembered differently, years later. Read each witness statement with that in mind. How accurate would you be if asked to remember the details of an event over thirty years ago?

I was not privy to any of the original witness statements, and those would be the best source for a clear picture of what happened to Janette Roberson on January 19, 1983. Those will likely never be released, so their integrity remains intact, should a prosecution ever be possible.

HOMICIDE

Some people get away with murder, literally. Not Kardashian literally—*literally*, literally. The statistics are staggering. As of this writing, in the state of Michigan there are [**insert number here**] unsolved homicides.

That's how I *wanted* to start this opening, with an actual verifiable number, but then I found out this information isn't readily available to the public. You can't call and have someone print out a list of open homicide cases under the jurisdiction of the Michigan State Police. Apparently, how they keep track of open homicide cases is a mystery second only to the construction of Stonehenge.

Once I was told there was no list that Michigan State Police kept of all unsolved homicides, I submitted a records request for the District 6 homicides because that includes the area in which Janette Roberson was murdered. I figured I'd narrow it down a bit to see if that helped.

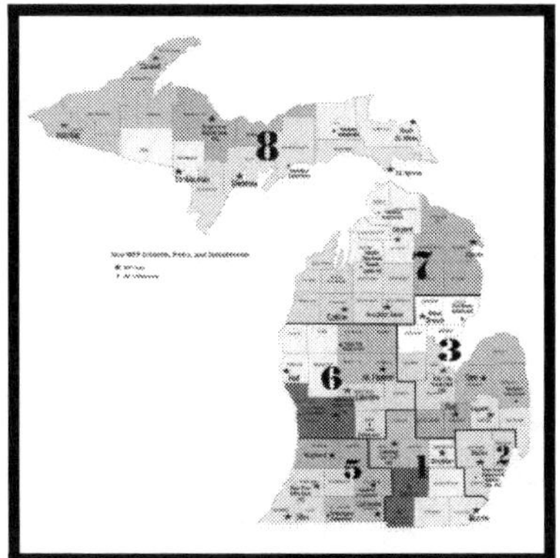

My request was granted in part and denied in part, the denial portion stating *"A master list of statewide unsolved homicides does not exist."* Wait, really? How do you keep track of them all in a way that would easily illustrate any similarities or possible serial offenders? Particularly really old cases where the original investigators are no longer attached to the case? You know, some sort of system like the drug store has to alert when you try to fill two prescriptions that would cause drug interactions. Maybe a digitized spreadsheet that notes similarities in crime scenes, possible serial perpetrator MO comparisons, for when Detectives retire and the new guys need to be brought up to speed.

Nothing? *Nada*?

After I received the District 6 list, it was clear Michigan State Police *could* get me the information, it would just have to come piecemeal and I'd have to bother them a little more to get it. So I sent another request to Michigan State Police, this time for Districts 1, 2, 3, 4, 5, 7 & 8.

Meanwhile, I studied the District 6 list. From 1970 to 2014—including Janette Roberson—there were 31 unsolved homicide cases in this district. Seven of those were attributed to the Reed City area. I began researching those cases and submitted document requests to the crack MSP FOIA team. Eventually I got a letter that requested I send them $103.49 to get those other District numbers.

Huh? They had more than that of my money sitting on someone's desk at that time for a request they had asked me to cancel. So I emailed the gal I was working with, prepared her an annotated list of the FOIA requests and charges I had outstanding, as well as the amount of my money they had floating around Lansing somewhere—which was, by the way, more than the amount requested for that District information. I got this response:

Renee,

Please let Ms. Decker know that after a review of our emails and files, the agreement was that the 2 requests that she paid half on and then cancelled (CR-93318 $117.37 and CR93687 $53.15), those monies would have been credited to the request that was replacing those two (CR95886, billed estimate of **$5,828.73**). If they don't intend to pay the balance on CR98556 and complete that request, a request for the refund of those 2 payments should be made to us in writing. We do not have the ability to keep a "balance" and deduct fees for each request. Also, any unpaid requests would still be due at this time. Please let her know she can contact me with any questions.

Thank you.

Jessina Beckner

We'll talk about the $5,828.73 in a bit. That's a fun story! I knew they had the ability to keep a "balance" and deduct fees because they had already done so for other requests of mine, early on. At another point, I had received a refund for a document request they approved, changed their minds, and decided not to send me, months after the initial request. Needless to say, by this time—just shy of New Year's, 2015—I'd had enough of the Michigan State Police FOIA Department. A root canal sans anesthesia while being forced to listen to Rush Limbaugh blather on about Obama's shortcomings sounded more pleasant than writing even one more document request.

The problem is <u>that's what they're counting on</u>. I learned from my research that it's common practice to charge exorbitant fees and make it as uncomfortable as possible for the public to get certain information if they didn't think you should have it. Go ahead, Google it. Look for court cases related to FOIA claims. They reach all the way up to the Supreme Court. It won't be a productive day, but you will come out the other end enlightened, if not really irritated. I should note that it's not just Michigan State Police. It's common practice. Even NASA was on the receiving end of some testy questioning by Congress over dragging their heels on FOIA requests.

So, as much as I would love to tell you how many unsolved murders Michigan State Police has on the books for the entire state, I can't. I should be able to, but I can't because as a citizen, I don't have unlimited funds to throw around in order to get information that should be freely accessible. I only know that in the area of Michigan where Janette Roberson was killed, District 6, I was given a list that has 31 names on it. That's one district, and we'll take their word that Michigan State Police gave me all the names, although I have no facts to back that up.

Now let's multiply 31 (unidentified killers) by eight (for 8 districts) and get a pretend number that will stand in place of the accurate number Michigan State Police is unable to supply us in anywhere close to a timely and reasonable manner, and we'll call it *Unsolved Homicides for Dummies*.

248. The number is probably much higher than that, given District Six likely has less unsolved homicides than some of the southern areas. They're really murdery down south—or so I've heard.

Let's stop for a minute and think about it, though, using our fake number that's probably way lower than the real number. 248 people who killed someone—give or take a few who may have died in the interim in a manner nowhere close to befitting their crimes—so, 248 killers walking free, eating stuff they like to eat, today a Whopper, maybe tomorrow a sandwich from Panera, and they're watching their favorite TV shows, Facebooking about their kids' accomplishments, or online gambling, maybe spending a Friday afternoon contacting their local congressman with a detailed list of gripes. Perhaps they're at Walmart arguing with the deli manager, or getting an oil change at Jiffy Lube.

248 people going on with their daily lives as if nothing untoward occurred. You know, like them slashing up the body of another human being before dinner. Stuff like that.

One thing's for certain. The person who killed Janette Roberson has issues. You don't do what was done to her and then go on to be a productive member of society. Oh, it might *look like that* on the surface, but the type of rage required to do that sort of thing doesn't go away. It's constantly on simmer. You don't want to be anywhere around when it boils over. Whoever this person is, they are not a nice person. This person is a monster. This person slaughtered a twenty-seven-year-old woman, then gathered his weapons and got the hell out of dodge like the coward that he is.

Here's the thing about Janette that gets me. You haven't really come into yourself as a woman in your twenties. That comes later, mid-life, when you've learned how to separate the worries that matter from the rest of the crap. It's when you innately come to realize the small crap mustn't be sweated. You're the most *you* that you've ever been in your forties, fifties, and beyond, and for that reason, you're more confident. You finally understand how all the pieces fit, so life begins to move more smoothly around you, rather than feeling like you're running directly into oncoming traffic.

This is a generalization of course, but that's how it feels to me, having travelled from birth through my mid-forties. It's something I've earned. I've *earned* every bit of the woman I am, and my wish for each woman out there is that she can say that, too. That's why it's called "coming into yourself."

Janette Roberson was cheated out of that chance. It was stolen from her. She left this world while still in her twenties, feeling around in front of her, trying and make things fit. I wish I could go back and have a cup of coffee with her now. Just fifteen minutes, I'd take it. I don't know enough about her to adequately relate all the uniqueness she brought to the world in the twenty-seven years she had here. I don't believe I've spoken to a single person who does. I'm not sure if any of the people I talked to *really* knew who Janette was in January of 1983. Her kids were too young, still in elementary school. Her mother is gone as I write this, and probably took the largest volume of Janette's memories with her to the grave. The family members I've spoken to weren't part of her day-to-day life at the time she was murdered, so it's hard to say if anyone really knew who Janette Roberson was when she died. There's a whole world that goes on inside you at that age when you're doing all that puzzling. She wasn't given the chance to be become the woman she was meant to be.

Then there was the town. *Reed City, Michigan*.

Lots of drama plaguing Reed City in January 1983, I tell you what. An embezzlement scandal was brewing in the city clerk's office.

(Incidentally, Janette's mother was the City Clerk and Treasurer.) Threatened litigation over a business owner who'd opened a Tool and Die, but alleged he'd been purposely misled about the property and it was going to cost him a pretty penny to fix. The State Police were still smarting from a failed attempt at getting a proposition passed on the 1982 ballot—one that was summarily voted down after months of mudslinging between the local cops (city/county) and State Police. Speaking of cops, one of them got himself tossed in the pokey after assaulting two state troopers and a bar customer, just a few weeks before Janette's murder. It's not clear if the assaults had anything to do with the aforementioned ballot proposal, though the officer did have an awful lot to say about it to the press after his firing. It may have just been plain old drunken stupidity and anger. It's clear he had the latter, based on the amount of f-bombs that were tossed around in ALL CAPS in the police report. Let's see, what else? *Oh!* The city was about $80 thousand dollars in debt at the time, the council itself got along about as well as a group of caged tigers fighting over the last hunk of meat, and they did it on TV in the form of live broadcasts.

It was an interesting time to be a denizen of Reed City in the 1980s. But little did they know, there was a killer in their midst, one who'd prove capable of indescribable violence.

The first time I cried in relation to this case was when I viewed a photocopy of the Reed City Police department's property sign-out log. For a time, RCPD had items stored, which were eventually turned over to Michigan State Police. As of this writing, according to Reed City Police Chief Chuck Davis, he maintains a full copy of the first responders report, crime scene photos, and an evidence locker—although it is unclear what evidence Reed City PD maintains. According to him, everything else was forwarded to the Michigan State Police.

The copy of the property log, dappled with what looks like spots of mold, with its handwritten WHAT, WHERE, WHEN, & WHO scrawled at the top, does not inspire confidence with regard to record keeping in the 1980s. I'd like to think if I were murdered today, someone would at least type the label of my evidence box, and not have to draw any lines by hand. I think my blood, hair, and fibers have at least earned that much for their collective time here on Earth. I've tried to be a decent citizen.

Prop. Sign out

What	Where	When	Who
Photo's + Negatives	Phil's Desk	8-4-83	Phil [illegible]
[illegible] Tapes (2)	Chief's Office	8-4-83	Phil [illegible]
Photos	MSP		D/Sgt [illegible]
[illegible]	[illegible]	[illegible]	[illegible]
Entire [illegible] Hair Etc. Box [illegible] Hair Samples Etc.	[illegible]	9-10-84	[illegible]
Video Tape. (2)	Geo. Pratt MSP #62		
Neg. Tives To →	Geo Pratt MSP #62	10-27-85	[illegible]

Reed City PD Property Sign Out Log

There was something sad about it, this half-page that made up what appears to be six years, during which time some of the items associated with the Roberson case were stored in a box and accounted for by a hastily-scrawled chart. To me, it doesn't seem to show the appropriate level of respect if you consider the severity of what occurred in the basement pet department of the Gambles store on January 19, 1983. Second only to reading the gruesome details outlined with painful specificity in the Medical Examiner's report, looking at the property sign-out sheet left me with a nagging feeling of uneasiness. Add to that sadness and anger, because for over three decades, some truly horrible person has been allowed to go about their life, living, breathing, eating, maybe singing along with their favorite radio station, when all that's left of Janette Roberson are scant memories and according to the Michigan State Police, approximately five-thousand pages documenting the investigation into her murder.

I wish I could go back there, you know? Jump into that proverbial time machine and click the vacuum-sealed door closed. I think if you would have asked me where I wanted to take the time machine, let's say, ten years ago, I would have said something like, "Back to wherever I can go to kill Hitler—or maybe drop me on the sidewalk in front of *The Dakota* early enough on December 8, 1980 that I can shove Mark David Chapman into the bushes or something."

Today there would be no hesitation. "Reed City, Michigan; Upton Avenue; January 19, 1983. Let's say, eleven-thirty." That's the time Gene Johnson remembers being there. He's the only customer I was able to track down who'd actually seen or spoken to Janette Roberson that day.

Gene was the Director of Maintenance at the hospital in Reed City at the time of the murder. He frequented the store to get supplies, they'd write out a receipt and he'd stick it on the "spike" for hospital billing. On the day of the murder, Gene says he went into the store at around 11:30. He remembers meeting Janette in the middle of the store near the stairs that led down to the basement. He walked toward her after entering the front door, and she was heading toward him from the back of the store. He says he doesn't remember her carrying anything.

"Can I help you?" Janette asked, pleasantly.

"I know this store better than you!" Gene chided.

This was the first time he'd met Janette, she hadn't worked at Gambles that long. He heard they hired someone to work downstairs, but never went down to the pet store, only shopped upstairs. In fact, he'd only been in the basement twice, both with David Engels, the store owner. First when the old *Men's Store* (the business next door) had been acquired and David was getting ready to expand. The second time, according to Gene, "...was when Dave was setting up the pet store."

From the Michigan State Police report: "The original Gambles Store is located at 114 W. Upton Ave., which is in the main business block of the city of Reed City, just to the west of US-131, was separated from adjacent buildings by brick/block walls, however after the present owner purchased the business in 1980, the building to the east, 112 W. Upton Ave., was also purchased and in the wall separating these buildings, doorways were installed, both on the main (street level) floor and the basement to give access between them."

Essentially two stores became one, with holes cut in the walls between them. In the basement today, the archway that was cut to join the two basements remains as it existed then—rough, jagged rock cut into a door-sized archway, glossed over lightly to temper the surface of the craggy rocks.

On January 19, 1983, Gene asked where everyone was. Janette told him they were all unloading the truck. He says he saw employees unloading into both back doors, which would have been the Gambles back door, as well as the side expanded into. Gene said he was maybe in the store fifteen minutes, total. He says he saw Dave and Bonnie unloading. (David and Bonnie Engels, the owners). According to Gene, they were coming in and out stacking totes. On delivery days, Gene remembers, "Bonnie would come in, but she wasn't there every day. Seems like Dave was there every day, from the day he opened the place."

Gene told Janette he could find what he needed, and remembers her saying she had to take care of something in the pet department.

She went downstairs. Gene never saw her again. It was the first and last time he ever interacted with Janette Roberson.

You know what? Scratch eleven-thirty. Let's go back to 8:00am. If I've got a time machine at my disposal, I'd like to stand across the street and watch the employees filter into their businesses on Upton to begin their workdays. January 19, 1983 was a Wednesday, the middle of the week, and I'm told it was a fairly typical day, if perhaps a tad warmer than usual for that time of year.

What I'd be doing is scanning everyone's faces, looking for any indication of what I knew was to come. Every person that passed me on the sidewalk would be scrutinized as I waited for the Gambles store owner—or his brother, the manager—to unlock the front doors and let the waiting employees inside. I'd be watching for anything that foretold the events to follow, trying to get a handle on when it might have spun out of control. I wouldn't be able to do that, of course, even if I *could* travel back in time. I'd need a lot more information than the faces of a few co-workers and passers-by to figure out how, later that day, at approximately 3:50 in the afternoon, the body of Janette Roberson would be found brutalized in the basement pet department of the store where she worked.

I want to make something very clear. The word *brutalized* does not accurately reflect the condition of Janette Roberson's body. There is no single word in the English language to adequately describe what was done to her. Law enforcement officers and profilers would technically categorize her injuries as "overkill." Multiple weapons; multiple wounds.

If I were standing across the street from Gambles that day, Flossie Earnest—a surname that does not belie her personality—would have been one of the employees arriving for a busy workday. It was truck day, all hands on deck, so when she and Angie Tillie weren't ringing up customers, they'd be stocking shelves from the boxes and totes being disgorged from the truck by other employees, including the owner and manager, who were—according to multiple witnesses—both present that day.

In 1983, Flossie and Angie were in their 50s and 60s respectively, and by the time I began researching this story, Angie was in her 90s, living in a nursing home. I learned this from Flossie, who was one of the first people I spoke to in any formal way about the murder. She helped me get in contact with a relative of Angie's, but as it turned out, I wasn't able to speak directly with her. The woman's family felt it would be too upsetting. I couldn't fault them for it. Over three decades later, the mere mention of Janette's name still brings Angie Tillie to tears.

It's no wonder. Angie saw Janette Roberson's body. I'm certain it was something she never expected to encounter at work that day, and in the days and years to come, she'd certainly wish she never had.

The weather was cold and the roads icy; winter had her last tenacious grip on Reed City in the early spring of 2014 when I spoke with Flossie Earnest. After initially passing the house, then sliding all over the road in my Chevy Tahoe while making my way back, I finally parked, walked down the driveway, up to the front door of the well-tended-to home, and knocked.

My stomach lurched. You have no idea how much I hate this part—bothering people. It's not in my nature to nudge myself into someone's space and start asking questions. It makes me uncomfortable. But in this case, my desire to know was much stronger than any hope I had of letting it go. I could have taken the easy route and left it alone. It had certainly taken more time, money, and cheer from my life in the year I'd spent researching this story than any single thing has a right to take.

By that point, though, I'd read too much. I'd seen the ME report, read three years of city council meeting minutes, flipped through endless volumes of leather-bound record books, spoken to family, read newspaper accounts—of which there were precious few considering the enormity of the crime. I'd assimilated too much information to go back and pretend I didn't know there was once a beautiful young mother who walked into work one day and ended up leaving on a stretcher, slaughtered in the middle of the day, and nobody was paying for that crime.

That's... well, that's *gross*. That's completely unacceptable. And t*hat's* the part that didn't sit well with me. Who do we see about these things? These injustices we stumble upon and realize need to be righted. How are we judged in the long run if we just let them go?

That's where I was, emotionally, when Mrs. Earnest answered the door. When her husband—who later introduced himself as

Norm—rolled up next to her in his wheelchair, I swallowed the sudden lump in my throat. It was such a lovely gesture, this man who probably couldn't have done much if I'd been an intruder with malice aforethought, but that didn't stop the instinct to protect his wife.

I introduced myself and asked if I could have a few minutes of her time, explaining to them both who I was, and why I was there. Flossie stepped aside and let me in, graciously leading me into the living room. I took a seat across from her, and Norm rolled up next to us, his manner having relaxed considerably once he realized the short, chubby redhead had no unseemly motives.

They were such a sweet couple, often finishing each other's sentences. Flossie sometimes turned to Norm for confirmation when answering a question. It was as if they'd discussed Janette's story many times, and she wanted to make sure she was relaying the information to me in the way she had shared with him over the years. It was clear that he knew the story as well as she, some three decades later, and a few times she looked at him in a very telling way, an exchange that felt like there was a bit more that I would never get to hear. Very likely their opinions on suspects, which neither seemed eager to share. I didn't ask because you kind of know. You can feel it. Some people *want* you to ask, or at least want to tell you what they think. Most people, in fact. Not the Earnests. They weren't the gossipy type. They stuck to the facts and answered each question as best as both could cobble together in recollection.

ME: I talked to Gene Johnson last night on the phone. Apparently he was in the store that day. He said he was there at 11:30 and that when he walked in, nobody was up front but Janette. She said to him, "Can I help you?" and he said, "I know this store better than you!" because apparently he was in the store a lot.

FLOSSIE: Yeah, he was in there a lot.

ME: And so he said, "Where's everybody at?" and she said, "They're unloading the truck." He then he said he was going to go get something he needed and she said she needed to take care of something downstairs. And that was the last time he saw her. He did not see anyone there when he came in but Mr. and Mrs. Engels, they were unloading. He said those were the only people he saw and they were unloading through both back doors. So you had two back doors at the time, is that correct?

FLOSSIE: Um-hmm.

ME: And one of those was the old Golvidis' back door? [The old Men's Store which the Gambles store expanded into was previously owned by a man named Golvidis.]

FLOSSIE: Um-hmm.

ME: Were you already at work at that time, at 11:30?

FLOSSIE: Yeah, I was there.

ME: Did you guys have a break room? Maybe you guys were on lunch at the time.

FLOSSIE: We always went upstairs for break.

ME: In the office, or further upstairs?

FLOSSIE: No, further upstairs.

ME: What was further upstairs? Nobody seems to know.

FLOSSIE: There was furniture up there.

ME: To sell or just—

FLOSSIE: Yeah.

ME: So customers could go up there?

FLOSSIE: Uh-huh, yeah.

ME: Nothing else but furniture?

FLOSSIE: No, just furniture.

ME: And I assume to get up there you had to go up that stairwell that was above the basement, past Mr. Engels' office, is that where he had his office at the time?

FLOSSIE: Yes, right at the top of the stairs is where he had his office.

ME: Upstairs, was there a bathroom?

FLOSSIE: No.

ME: A sink?

FLOSSIE: Uh-uh. No.

ME: Was 11:30 around the time you used to have lunch?

FLOSSIE: I don't remember. I really don't.

ME: Do you remember who was in the store when she was found?

FLOSSIE: Well, John Engels... and Angie Tillie. Me. And Dave and Bonnie. And that's all I can remember.

ME: So, would you have worked the register? Were you the person who checked people out?

FLOSSIE: Yes.

ME: Gene told me he didn't usually get checked out. He would come in, get what he needed, write it down on a receipt and put it on a peg, does that sound right?

FLOSSIE: Yeah, who'd he work for? I can't remember.

ME: The hospital. Head of maintenance.

FLOSSIE: (nodding) He came in all the time.

ME: Right, and I think that's why he said that to her. "I know this store better than you!"

FLOSSIE: Right. He just left the bill there, whatever it would be.

ME: I guess what I was wondering—and I should call him back and ask—he said that was the first time he had met Janette because he had never been down in the basement before. But if that was the first time he had met her, how would she know he wouldn't have needed to be checked out? If she was covering the front of the store, would she check customers out upstairs, or were you only allowed to run the register? Or Angie?

FLOSSIE: No. I mean we all ran it.

ME: So everyone ran the register?

FLOSSIE: Um-hmm. Yeah. There was two registers. One at the front door and there was one in the middle of the store.

ME: Oh, okay. I didn't know that. And the one in the middle was right by the entrance to the basement, correct?

FLOSSIE: Um-hmm.

ME: Would you and Angie have been unloading the truck?

FLOSSIE: No.

ME: Okay. I didn't think so but I thought, let me check, because I wondered why he didn't see you. So I'm guessing you were probably on lunch break?

FLOSSIE: I don't remember. I think I was putting stuff up (on the shelves) because—I'll tell ya, Angie came running—she went down in the basement for something, because our storeroom was to the left of where Janette's place was, you know... So, she went down to the basement for something, evidently, 'cause she came running up, and she put her head on the desk that we had right at the basement door there, and we thought—I thought she was having a heart attack. I said, "What's a matter, Angie?" So I called John—and John was upstairs, John Engels. He was upstairs having his lunch—and he come down the steps two at a time, because I said, "I think Angie's having a heart attack!" And then she just pointed to the basement. She couldn't talk, she just pointed to the basement. So then John ran down to the basement and he come up and he said, "Close all the doors!"

ME: Now, that—I have a question about that. He ran down there, he saw her, he came up and said, "Close all the doors!" But, had he checked to make sure nobody... the killer wasn't in the store—I mean, it's a pretty big store. I would have been afraid because—

Flossie shrugged here and put her hands up, questioningly.

FLOSSIE: I don't know.

ME: So you don't know—

FLOSSIE: No, I mean...

ME: But it was quick, you didn't see him checking?

FLOSSIE: No, we were just all so—(exasperated sigh)

ME: I can imagine. So are those the only two people that went down there before the police came or was there anyone else, any other store person that went down there?

FLOSSIE: I don't think so. I don't think there was. In fact, Lana (Janette's sister) called me yesterday from South Carolina, she said, "Were those coal chutes where we used to get coal, were they open all the way down the line?" and I said I really don't know. But when the owner that used to own Ben Franklin, when he gets home from Florida, I'm gonna ask him 'cause he might know.

ME: Right. At one time they were all connected.

FLOSSIE: That's what I thought.

There was some discussion of which basements may have been accessible to one another at that time. Back in the day, beneath the sidewalks that ran up and down each side of Upton Avenue there were "tunnels" that ran below the front of the businesses with coal chutes that came off at different places, as well as sections below ground where coal was stored. One of the many rumors attached to Janette's case was that the killer may have gotten in and out underground, though I found no evidence of this during my research. In fact, the crime scene technician I spoke to told me that there was no evidence collected "beyond" the back room, and he was not even aware of any possible exits from the basement to other underground areas.

FLOSSIE: You know, I think when you get down in the basement there, I think there was about this much room... [Flossie held her hands a couple feet apart here] It seemed like a person could crawl around...

ME: Crawl around where?

Norm, who had been listening throughout the conversation, interjected here, "You mean where they found the [**REDACTED**]?"

ME: What [**REDACTED**]?

FLOSSIE: Well, the one that the found.

ME: They found a [**REDACTED**]?

FLOSSIE: Well, that's what supposedly killed her.

ME: Where did they find the [**REDACTED**]?

(**NOTE:** There was a lengthy discussion about where the item in question was found, but I have redacted this section completely to preserve the integrity of the investigation.)

FLOSSIE: I heard that there were still crates down there with straw in it and stuff.

ME: The (fish/animal) tanks are still down there.

NORM: *Now*? [incredulous]

ME: Um-hmm.

FLOSSIE: (disgusted) Yeah, after thirty years.

ME: Yeah, they're still—

FLOSSIE: I mean, that place is such—it never was like that. It was a *clean* store.

ME: I don't think he's [the current owner] done much with it. [CHUCKLING]

ME: Who was the manager of the Gambles store?

FLOSSIE: Dave was. He was the owner and he was the manager. I don't know if we even *had* a manager. I managed it for a while.

NORM: Dave would be the owner and manager of the whole works.

FLOSSIE: Yeah, yeah. I wouldn't think we had any manager.

ME: So it was pretty much Dave and everyone else was an employee.

FLOSSIE: [nods]

ME: When the body was found, was David Engels there?

FLOSSIE: Uh-huh.

ME: The problem here is we have a letter from Janette's father. And he spoke with, he said, the store manager. And the store manager told him he was not there when the body was found, someone called him to the store. So I'm trying to find out, either somebody's lying, or that's not true, and these are things—I mean, it's been thirty years and—

FLOSSIE: Well, Dave was there. 'Cause I can still see him sitting on a crate, sayin', "Oh my gosh," he said, "I just came from..."

NORM: [interjects when Flossie pauses] Saginaw.

FLOSSIE: "...Saginaw, to get rid of all this stuff like murders, and here I am in my own little store and I got a murder on my hands."

ME: Yeah, and not just any murder.

FLOSSIE: So he was there. I remember that. But when he c—[exasperated sound] I don't know when in the heck he came in, but how people knew so *quickly*, 'cause the front of that store, we went and locked the door, John did, there was people out there that you wouldn't believe. How did they know?

ME: You mean they were on the sidewalk looking around?

FLOSSIE: Yeah.

ME: Wow.

FLOSSIE: It was just something else.

ME: I wondered how quick it got—you mean it was daylight and there were already people there?

FLOSSIE: Yeah, yeah. I mean, it just seemed like they just all of a sudden flocked in front of that store.

ME: Okay then, let's discuss what customers might have been in the store. Do you remember which customers were in the store when the body was found?

FLOSSIE: I don't.

ME: In the newspaper Herald articles, they said Janette was getting obscene phone calls in the days before. Did you know anything about that?

FLOSSIE: No.

ME: Did Janette talk about Alvin (her husband) a lot?

FLOSSIE: No.

ME: Was he there that day?

FLOSSIE: [shaking her head no.] Uh-uh.

ME: You don't remember seeing him at all that day?

FLOSSIE: Huh-uh, no. The only thing I know is that the school must have called her and told her to come pick up one of the kids, because she left, you know, before noon. And she went to school to pick up her kids and she must have took 'em someplace and then she come back.

NORM: How do you know it was the school that called her? Why couldn't somebody else—

FLOSSIE: Because she said, she come up and said, "I gotta go pick up my kids."

NORM: Okay.

FLOSSIE: Or, one of the kids—I think it was the little girl—from school.

ME: Maybe she was sick or something?

FLOSSIE: Yeah.

ME: So she went and picked her up, brought her to the babysitter and came back. Sound about right?

FLOSSIE: Yep.

ME: So you never saw Alvin in the store at all that day?

FLOSSIE: Nope.

ME: Where did Janette usually eat her lunch?

FLOSSIE: She went home or...

ME: She left the store, then?

FLOSSIE: Yeah.

ME: Did she leave that day? In addition to the time she went to get her child, or did she maybe grab food while she was out?

FLOSSIE: Well, I think—I don't think she left again. I mean, she went and picked up the kids.

ME: So maybe she grabbed something to eat when she was at home?

FLOSSIE: Yeah.

ME: Was there a coat rack for employees? Where did you hang your coats, do you remember?

Flossie's eyes widened as she tried to grab hold of the three-decade-old memory.

ME: I know, I'm asking silly questions, but all of them have a reason.

NORM: (trying to jog her memory) Same place, probably, where you put your purse.

ME: Hats, gloves?

FLOSSIE: I don't... Hmm.

I reminded her that they probably wouldn't have had all the coats and personal items at the register. She thought about it for a few seconds.

FLOSSIE: Well, you got me. I don't remember that at all.

ME: Let me refresh your memory and see if this sounds right. Gene Johnson said that he thought when you come in the back door there was a bathroom, and a row of pegs...

FLOSSIE: Yep. That was the *only* bathroom.

ME: That was the only bathroom?

FLOSSIE: Yes.

ME: Okay.

FLOSSIE: That must be where we hung our coats but I don't think our purses. I think those we took up and put under that counter that faced the door going down to the basement. I think that's where we put our purses.

ME: So that would have been at that second register.

FLOSSIE: Uh-huh.

ME: That makes sense.

FLOSSIE: I don't think we left our purses in the bathroom.

ME: Do you happen to know what Janette's winter coat looked like? Do you have a visual of what she looked like when she came in dressed?

FLOSSIE: [shaking head] No.

ME: Do you know of any coats or hats or anything that were missing that day? Employee's stuff.

FLOSSIE: No.

ME: So, Janette worked for David Engels. He hired her, right?

FLOSSIE: Uh-huh.

ME: Who serviced the animals? Did they purchase the animals? Who brought them in?

FLOSSIE: They were brought in from Freeland, that's where Bonnie had her shop, in Freeland—little town there by Saginaw. And, uh, Bonnie brought all those animals in, and she worked down there for a while and then they hired Janette.

ME: So she didn't work there regularly after they hired Janette?

FLOSSIE: No. But she, I mean, I think she was more or less Janette's boss. Bonnie's the one who set up the pet store and got everything all set up.

ME: In a news article, it said she was seen in front of the Animal House in Big Rapids, Janette was, eight days before the murder, and again in Gambles on the 12th giving a gentleman gerbils. Two brown gerbils and one black one. Do you remember anything about that?

FLOSSIE: No.

ME: Would she have been sent to Big Rapids to fetch stuff for the pet store that you were aware of?

FLOSSIE: Not that I know of.

There was some discussion about gerbils and the possibility of Janette selling them, but Flossie was unaware of anything like this.

ME: Who was the first officer on the scene?

FLOSSIE: [unsure]

NORM: Probably city, wouldn't you think?

FLOSSIE: I have no idea.

ME: Do you remember any of the police that were eventually there? That you remember seeing. I'm sure at that moment it was like a big crisis moment. I mean, you're not thinking about anything other than what's downstairs.

FLOSSIE: [unsure]

ME: Do you remember who called police?

FLOSSIE: I think John did.

ME: Right away, when he came upstairs?

FLOSSIE: Um-hmm. I don't know whether he called the city police or the state police. I don't even know who the city police were then.

NORM: It was Phil down there, wasn't it?

ME: I think Rathbun was out of town, that's what I was told.

FLOSSIE: I remember them coming in, but I don't know who they were.

ME: Did they have any instructions for you before they went downstairs?

FLOSSIE: No. They just went right downstairs.

ME: Do you know if anyone went down with them or if they went down by themselves?

FLOSSIE: I don't know. I don't remember that. My memory isn't that good.

ME: Actually, you're doing great. Do you know if there were any customers in the store that left after the body was discovered, but before the police got there?

FLOSSIE: [shakes head no like she's unsure]

ME: Do you know of anyone that was there at all that day, whatever time?

FLOSSIE: Well, I know—I can't think of his name but he's dead now. Big, heavy-set guy.

ME: Was he a business man?

FLOSSIE: Well, kind of. He's got a son that's on the council.

ME: Now?

FLOSSIE: Roger, his name is.

After a time, she came up with the name.

FLOSSIE: Tom Meinert. He was in Gambles that day. But he went out. He's the only one I can remember being in there.

ME: And it was before she was discovered?

FLOSSIE: Yeah.

ME: Do you remember anything that Angie said about what she saw... the body, where it was found... where in the basement?

FLOSSIE: No. She could probably tell you. She's in a home up in [**REDACTED**]. Her name is Angie Tillie. I talked to her in January on her birthday. She's ninety-some years old, but she remembered a lot more than I did because she saw her, you know?

ME: Do you remember anything that she said she saw? I'm trying to find out if... did she say it looked like there was a struggle or—

FLOSSIE: Uh-uh, nope.

ME: I'm glad you didn't go down there that day.

FLOSSIE: (closes eyes) Me too.

ME: How many truck deliveries did you have that day, do you remember?

FLOSSIE: Probably just one.

ME: Was that normal? Just one truck delivery?

FLOSSIE: Um-hum. One big truck, yeah.

ME: Were they always on Wednesdays?

FLOSSIE: Um, probably. I imagine they were 'cause they always, they had a routine, so...

ME: And so you think it was a once-a-week type thing?

FLOSSIE: Yeah.

ME: Do you know who the delivery drivers were?

FLOSSIE: No. They weren't from around. I don't know where they come from, but they weren't from around here.

ME: Was the truck there when the body was discovered, or was it already gone?

FLOSSIE: I think it was already gone.

ME: Okay, do you know what time Detective Pratt arrived?

FLOSSIE: Uh-uh.

ME: Did they separate you all and question you that night?

FLOSSIE: Mmmm, the next day, I think. Yeah, I think the next day we all went up the state police post. Yeah because we had appointments to go up there.

ME: But they didn't question you that night?

FLOSSIE: No, huh-uh. I don't think they did.

ME: What time did you all leave? Did they let you go right then, or did you have to hang around a while?

FLOSSIE: Uh, I think we hung around a little bit. I mean, we closed the store up and then we all just kind of [throws hands up] ...were baffled, you know?

ME: What time did the store usually close?

FLOSSIE: Six o'clock.

ME: So Detective Pratt got there before you closed, you remember seeing him that night?

FLOSSIE: I don't remember seeing him. He probably was there, but we were all so... [indicates confused, upset]

ME: I can imagine. So you know that all of the employees were questioned that were there that day?

FLOSSIE: Uh-huh. Uh-huh. We were all questioned separate. We all went up to the state police post.

ME: And what kind of questions did they ask you? Did you feel like it was a thorough questioning?

FLOSSIE: Yeah, it was a thorough... Well, he started out with like your family, and I was like "What's goin' on here, you know?"

ME: He was asking about your family?

FLOSSIE: Yeah.

ME: Who questioned you?

FLOSSIE: Detective Pratt.

ME: Do you know him at all? Did you know him at the time?

FLOSSIE: No. I mean I knew who he was, but that was all. I mean, he'd ask me personal questions like, "Are you and your husband getting along alright?" you know, and all that crap.

ME: What?

FLOSSIE: Yeah!

ME: Right away he was asking you those questions?

FLOSSIE: Uh-huh. I remember *that*.

ME: I'm pretty sure you wouldn't have been at the top of my suspect list. [laughing]

We discussed Pratt's questioning and I told Flossie I wasn't sure why he started questioning that way, but I did read that police have ways they do things as far as interrogations and gauging honesty, so it might have been a technique to get a feel for her before he started asking pertinent questions. Flossie thought about that and agreed.

NORM: [interjecting into conversation] I tell you, you wanna commit a crime, come to Reed City. They'll never solve the thing!

Flossie chuckled, as did I.

NORM: You know, back then I don't know if they had DNR* or not... (*he meant DNA)

ME: They didn't. They could do hair and fibers, I think, but they didn't do a lot of the same testing, so I think there's a chance they could—but even if they have DNA, they have to match it to someone in the database. If it's someone they haven't caught killing again or doing anything, they have to look at their suspects, you know?

I consulted my list to get back on track.

ME: Alright, let's see, so out of the employees that day, you were working register, you and Angie?

FLOSSIE: Uh-huh.

ME: And stocking?

FLOSSIE: Uh-huh.

ME: How long did Janette work there before this happened?

FLOSSIE: Not very long.

ME: Months, weeks?

FLOSSIE: Months, probably. Yeah, she didn't work there very long.

ME: Did any of the employees work earlier in the day and then leave?

FLOSSIE: No. We all came in at the same time.

ME: Always? Every day everyone came in together and left together?

FLOSSIE: Uh-huh.

ME: So nobody worked like half shifts?

FLOSSIE: No.

ME: Well, you'd think with that few people, not too hard to keep track of. Do you have an idea... She was last seen, according to information we have, around 1:25. I assume that was based on a register receipt? Her last sale, perhaps? Do you know?

FLOSSIE: No, I don't.

NORM: Here's Vicki, dear...

At this time, a relative was arriving, so I quickly finished up my questions.

ME: There was a period around 1:30, then when she was found around ten to four—is that normal for her to have been down there that long by herself without anyone having seen her? Is that typical?

FLOSSIE: Yeah. Uh-huh.

ME: Was she working down there alone that day?

FLOSSIE: Yes. She always—there wasn't ever anyone else.

ME: Never anyone with her?

FLOSSIE: Huh-uh, no.

I asked about the storage area but she didn't know anything about the set up back there.

ME: How often was she upstairs? Did she often cover breaks?

FLOSSIE: No. I can't imagine her being up there because I don't remember her being up there. Usually it was downstairs.

ME: The boy from the sketch. I believe that sketch was based on someone that you had described?

FLOSSIE: Well, yeah. The curly, blonde hair. He was in there, too.

ME: He was in there that day?

FLOSSIE: Uh-huh. He was in there that day, yeah.

ME: Close to the time of the murder, or way earlier?

FLOSSIE: Earlier, I think.

ME: You don't know his name?

FLOSSIE: Huh-uh.

ME: Did he ever buy supplies while he was there?

FLOSSIE: Yes, I think so.

ME: So he must have had a pet and that's why he was there regularly.

FLOSSIE: Yeah, I think, yeah.

ME: Do you know of any other townspeople that shopped down there regularly?

FLOSSIE: I can't remember any of them.

ME: Did she ever say anything about anyone bothering her?

FLOSSIE: No, huh-uh.

At this point we discussed the possibility of me talking to Angie

Tillie. The guest that had arrived while we were speaking came and introduced herself and since she was friends with Angie's daughter, we exchanged emails and she said she would contact them for me. Later on, I prepared questions for Angie Tillie and passed them along, but it was decided by the daughter with conservatorship that being questioned about it would upset her too much. I was told that after she and Flossie spoke in January around the time of the memorial walk for Janette, Angie cried for days.

Clearly the murder had made an impact that haunts her to this day.

What to Expect When You're FOIAing

We've all heard it before, how important those first twenty-four to seventy-two hours are after a crime has been committed. The possibility of a case being solved diminishes exponentially with each hour that passes.

Lansing City Pulse did an article in March of 2013 which began as a piece intended to profile Lansing's cold-case homicides and missing-persons cases over the past decade. The plan was to put the pictures of each victim in the article, hoping to garner new leads for the unsolved cases. Instead, what they got was some frightening insight into how unorganized Lansing is with regard to recordkeeping of unsolved homicides.

They began their research with a FOIA (Freedom of Information Act) request—the legal means by which the average citizen can obtain public records. Their request was as follows:

> "The names of all unsolved murder victims in cases investigated by the Lansing Police Department between the years 2000 and 2012. This includes the date of the murder and the address at which the crime was committed."

They also requested the same information regarding missing persons during that time period. Seems fairly simple, right? Boot up your computer and print off that list you use to keep track of your outstanding unsolved homicides—which probably has some indexing options so you can easily keep track of things that are similar in each case. Print off the pages for the dates in question, slap it in an envelo—

I'm sorry, what's that? my inner monologue asked. *You don't keep an organized accounting of the missing persons and unsolved murders in your city? Okay. What would it take to get that information?*

According to Lansing's city attorney, what it would take would be somewhere around $613.00 – and that didn't include "mailing costs and/or other miscellaneous expenses."

Needless to say, *The Lansing City Pulse* was flummoxed. All they wanted was some sort of list, or spreadsheet with names, dates, and addresses. What they were told is that list does not exist.

> An email exchange between City Pulse and LPD Sgt. Chris Baldwin on Dec. 10 portrays right from the start a cavalier attitude by the city to getting any information in the hands of the public, who could have potential tips.
>
> "We have a list somewhere. I really don't have time to help you on it. I don't even know where the list is," Baldwin wrote.
>
> In another email that same day, Baldwin contradicted himself, saying: "Anything before 2002 is going to be tricky and expensive, as we went to computer based reports about that time. Anything really old is in storage somewhere, and it costs $$$ just to have them pull file boxes."

So what they're *really* saying is, 'In addition to not being able to solve the cases in question, we're shitty record-keepers, we're kind of apathetic about it as well, so if you want public documents, you're gonna have to pay us *a lot*—on top of what you already pay as a taxpayer—and then maybe we'll pull the boxes out of a dusty closet somewhere and go through them.'

My fellow Michiganders, how confident does this make you about the homicide clearance rate (not to mention locating missing persons) in Lansing, if this was just a back-and-forth about cases from 2000 to 2012? Now let's pretend you're the family member of someone who was murdered in Lansing sometime in the 1980s and their case remains unsolved. How confident are you about ever getting justice?

One more question... How many municipal workers and lawmakers do you want to slap right now? Don't answer that, it's rhetorical. Also, don't slap municipal workers and lawmakers because if you do that, you'll get taken to jail and we really don't need to give them any more work because it appears they can't even get a single list of unsolved murders compiled. No need to further burden the rusty cogs in the wheels of justice any more than they already are.

When asked about the ridiculous fees Lansing wanted to charge, their Public Information Officer had this to say:

> "We can't just have one of our data people (do it), they don't have the status to go into each of these secured cases. What happens is we would have to pull our Detective Sergeant Baldwin, pull him from his normal duties... I think that's where they came up with the dollar amount. Is it possible? Yeah, it's definitely possible for him to collect all of that for you, problem is: him and maybe two other people would be pulled from their normal duties to do that, and that's just where they came up with their figure. It's just a matter of our data support people don't have the access to those sensitive cases. It would be very time consuming and they based the prices on having a Detective Sergeant pulled from his job to do the work."

Oh, is that so? Time consuming, you say? I'm sorry to trouble you in an effort to TRY TO GET MORE LEADS ON THE COLD CASES YOU HAVE BEEN UNABLE TO SOLVE.

Clearly the City Pulse reporter was much more even-keeled than my inner monologue.

What's wrong with these people? my inner monologue continued. *How are they supposed to keep track of whether any of these cases have similarities that might suggest multiple unsolved cases around a single suspect if they're NOT EVEN COMPILED TO A*

SINGLE LIST OR DOCUMENT OR SPREADSHEET OR WHATEVER THE HELL IT WOULD TAKE TO—

Settle down, inner monologue. Settle down.

In 2014, under public pressure due to that article, the department assigned a detective to handle cold cases. As of this writing, only one case had been submitted to the Ingham County Prosecutor's office seeking charges. Baby steps, I guess. From a *Detroit Free Press* article dated June 9, 2014, "He [cold case detective McCallister] assigns a solvability rating to each case, determining how best to deploy resources. McCallister's focus, for now, is cases that are most likely to be solved."

Again, my inner monologue is having trouble rising to the level of giddy enthusiasm I'd like to feel on hearing resources are being thrown at unsolved cases, mainly because I heard the same thing from Michigan State Police regarding "solvability" and "resources" and "we don't keep those kinds of lists..."

In my inner monologue's defense, the reason it's so testy is because our experience was similar to that of *The City Pulse* after sending an email to Michigan State Police's Manager of Public Affairs, Shannon Banner, when requesting MSPs list of unsolved murders dating back to 1970. I should note that the reason I was asking was because there was a huge chunk redacted from the Reed City Police Department report on the Janette Roberson that read as follows:

> "85 pages is redacted from [this portion of] the Reed City first responder's report which contain a MSP report that was appended to the RCPD report... concerns unsolved homicides between 1983 and 1984, including that of Janette Gale Roberson. The report contains copies of the investigating agency and lab reports... also lists of suspects, crime scene layouts, and various internal memoranda concerning investigators' theories of the crime, and persons of interest."

So of course my inner monologue thought, *Okay, we need to get more information on any outstanding unsolved crimes, because what* *if there <u>are</u> some that might have been committed by the same perpetrator that killed Janette?*

What I got in response from the MSP Manager of Public Affairs when I asked for a list of Michigan State Police's unsolved homicides from 1970 to present was the following:

> "We do not maintain such a list. There may be a way to obtain this information by querying our records management system; however, I'm not sure it would date back to 1970. If you are interested in pursuing this, you can send a Freedom of Information request to MSP-FOI@michigan.gov and the technicians there can determine if these records exist and are releasable."

My inner monologue barked out the kind of laugh usually associated with the clinically insane. The Michigan State Police FOIA Department "technicians" and I had already tangoed—repeatedly, masochistically, much to both of our chagrin. It really didn't end well for anyone involved. I never got the rest of the paperwork I wanted on Janette's case file because I was told it would cost about <u>six thousand dollars</u> to get it, and I don't have six thousand dollars lying around. I'm fairly certain I didn't make any new friends, either. Michigan State Police may or may not have five thousand pages associated with the Janette Roberson murder investigation, (they said *approximately*) but I cannot verify that as fact because I don't believe people just because they tell me something, considering I have been told many things in relation to this case that turned out to be untrue, and some of those things came straight from municipal employees.

I was told I was getting the Roberson file, for example, after I paid about five-hundred bucks to get it. That was FOIA # 1. Today I have a 1½ inch thick binder that is completely full of FOIA response letters. I'd count them but I'm not a masochist. When I received the fruits of my first FOIA request, the paperwork only covered up to 1986 on the investigation into the murder of Janette Roberson. After a bit of back-and-forth with MSPs FOIA department, I was told it would take about 16 to 18 hours for the local MSP Post—who had the rest of the file, which the first FOIA coordinator had failed to send me—to search, retrieve, redact, and copy the items. Why thirty years' worth of work product on an old, cold case was never turned over to Lansing to put on microfilm in the first place was not something anyone had an answer for, either.

So I waited a few weeks after being told it would take 16 to 18 hours at $55.00 bucks a pop, only to find out that *Whoopsie*, we miscalculated. Did we say 18 hours? We meant 84 hours. *Our bad.*

This letter does a better job of summarizing my concerns in a formal complaint sent to Colonel Kriste Kibbey Etue (director of the Michigan State Police) after my assistant and I had exhausted all appeals to MSP. Oh yeah, Trusty Assistant did her share of FOIAing, too. It was a bloodbath of primarily blank pages with chunks of information thrown in here or there to whet our appetite before the next wave of nothing arrived, for which we were being charged by the page *and* by the hour.

> Col. Etue,
>
> We would like to lodge a formal complaint with you regarding the FOIA process and some concerns we have. In April we began submitting requests for materials related to the Janette Roberson murder in 1983, a case that remains unsolved. Jeni Decker is researching this for a true crime book she is writing, and I am her research assistant, tasked to keep all of our FOIA requests from multiple entities organized, as well as provide assistance tracking down other information.
>
> Our first FOIA was for the file on the Janette Roberson murder on January 19, 1983. What we finally received, after being quoted one price and then charged almost triple that after a very long wait, was a partial file, only up to 1986, and only what Carla Jones was able to find on microfiche.
>
> We learned this later from Jessina Beckner, who called Ms. Decker in an effort – we thought – to assist us getting our

problem resolved. According to Ms. Beckner, Carla did not look in the other areas file information is stored, nor did she seek information from the local MSP Post, which is where, it appears, most of the file remains, three decades later. Not indexed, not organized, not digitized.

We believe if there is any hope in solving these decades-old homicides, the information should already have been input into a computer system so that officers can easily access it, if and when new information comes in. With a file that is not digitized or organized, there is almost no hope of solving the caseload of unsolved murders. Secondly, in order to bring these very old files up to date, taxpayers are, essentially, footing the bill for work that should have been done all along, in an organized, efficient manner, during downtime. For people requesting materials, it could be argued that we are now paying MSP employees to do this tedious work twice. Once on the job, and then again when we request it. It is our contention that we are being double billed, and at a pretty high hourly rate, compared to other law enforcement entities we've worked with.

We paid over $500 for about 200 blank pages. It appears that Carla started separating the exempt from non-exempt material, and then began redacting everything. We later learned that there may have been intervention by a former Detective on the case. Since then we have had trouble getting any information, and are either denied flat out, or sent estimates for exorbitant fees, even for items we have told them exactly where they can be found, by page number.

When we sought relief from MSP to try to find out why we got nothing after 1986 on a file that certainly must have been worked on in the following 28 years, Jessina Beckner asked us by email to provide digital copies of every one of the redacted documents Carla Jones provided us. I complied and scanned them all, finally sending ten digitized PDF files to Ms. Beckner. I hope those have been maintained for the next person who may request the information. I would hate to think MSP would have digitized copies yet still charge someone else the fees I incurred when those could have been stored easily.

Ms. Beckner told Ms. Decker by phone that she really wanted to help us and that there was a great deal more of the file at the local Post we were entitled to have redacted and supplied to us. Weeks passed and when we finally heard back, we were told that the Post estimated between 16 and 18 hours of work (which would have been at the $45 to $55 an hour of work price). Jessina told Ms. Decker over the phone she thought it would be closer to 12 hours. Then, sometime later, we received an estimate by mail which stated it would take MSP approximately 84 hours and just under $6000.000 dollars to furnish our request.

I am not sure where the breakdown occurred, why the Post told Ms. Beckner one thing, and then decided it would take six times longer than the original estimate, but we feel this is concerning and questionable. If the information is so disorganized that it would take that many hours to copy and redact the materials, it is probably not organized in a way that is conducive to being worked, never mind solved.

We have now begun submitting smaller, very specific FOIA's in order to determine specific exemptions, because some of our questions were either going unanswered or being ignored. It is our plan to formally appeal the original appeal at the court level, since we have exhausted our appeals on that FOIA with MSP. We were advised by council to begin submitting smaller FOIA requests from the original in order to establish specific exemptions that can be argued against in court – for example how times of police officers arriving may not be redacted, nor can every witness statement be legally redacted it its entirety, but must be gone through and the exempt and non-exempt material separated and the non-exempt materials provided to us.

Having begun this process, we have now established that we are basically being charged a flat $295 fee for even a one page report search based on page count, because we are told this file comes to over 5000 pages. Items cannot be easily found, so MSP FOIA department maintains that each time they do a search, they must search the entire document for single items, no matter where they are, apparently.

We maintain the public should not be penalized for seeking public documents because MSP is does not have the file indexed, organized, and digitized. This does not seem to go to what the Freedom of Information act intends to do, which is supply the public with records that help give a greater understanding of how government works. Right now, it appears to only be an effort to obstruct getting anything at all by overcharging for every item.

Col. Etue, we ask that you look into this matter and provide us with some relief with regard to our complaint. I have copied/pasted the relevant emails below, which will help to explain what I have outlined here. Many of the problems that occurred prior to my interaction with Ms. Beckner were with Carla Jones, which included being sent information under someone else's name, and being charged for items, then getting letters saying they had being denied and monies being returned. Why Carla left and Jessina stepped in, I am not sure, but we continue to have issues around this so we now seek your assistance.

We look forward to hearing from you and thank you in advance for your time and attention,
Jennifer Carlson / Jeni Decker

As you read that, I bet I know what you're thinking. *Man, she better not even go one mile over the speed limit for the foreseeable future, and obey every law, traffic or otherwise, for as long as she continues to draw breath.*

Yes I obey the law, and no, I don't speed. So far, so good. But if I ever end up missing, go ahead and check the MSP Post janitors' closets, evidence storage units, and assorted outbuildings. Look for oil drums or containers large enough to hold a 5-foot tall girl with a little more meat on her bones than she'd like.

The most disturbing thing about my phone conversation with Ms. Beckner was that before I offered to send her digital copies of what MSP had already sent me, she asked if I might meet her somewhere to see what the first FOIA coordinator, Carla Jones, had already sent me.

"Really? Aren't you all the way in Lansing? I don't get up there much." *Or ever.*

"Oh, well I thought I could meet you half-way, maybe."

Wait. Hold the phone... Me hopping in a car and lugging a couple hundred pages of information *your department* sent to me so you can refresh your memory as to what *your department* sent to me sounds like an idea that lives within the realm of complete mental health to you? Because it doesn't to me. It sounds like the plot of a couple unfortunate after school specials I've watched, though.

I didn't say that. Instead, I suggested maybe I could scan the pages and email them, which I ended up spending the better part of a day doing, because, among other things, it had to be broken into ten separate files in order to email. I did this as a *courtesy*, a term the FOIA department would begin using when we asked them why they did one thing for one FOIA we sent, and then later something different for another. *Oh, we did that first one as a courtesy.*

But it begs the question: Exactly what did Ms. Beckner hope to accomplish in person? Why would the Michigan State Police Supervisor of the Freedom of Information Unit ask me to get in my car and drive an hour (because Lansing is two hours from me) so she could *See what Carla gave you so I don't send you the same stuff.* Are they that unorganized up in Lansing that they don't know what they're mailing out?

I've never been afraid to point at something and go, "Um, no..." and I'm not going to start now. Michigan is not exactly a shining example of transparency and full disclosure, and it isn't like I'm the only one saying it. The State Integrity Project, sponsored by *The Center for Public Integrity* gives Michigan an overall *F* rating on its Corruption Risk Report Card, ranking it #44 out of the fifty states.

That's F, short for f*cked up. Yay, Michigan, for not being the absolute worst! That honor goes to Georgia. In the category of public access to information, Michigan got graded a *D*. When I was a kid, a *D* on my report card would get me into a whole heap of trouble.

Remember that rape kit deal? At the risk of getting re-chafed, I'll just say this: If you aren't even processing evidence in a timely, efficient manner, how can you expect to catch predators before they prey on someone else? Backlogs on evidence testing of anything more than a few weeks shouldn't be acceptable. *Period*. End of story. Getting processed evidence back to use for investigative purposes is how cops do their jobs. They can't effectively do their job if they aren't supplied the tools to do it, and those tools are things like timely processing of evidence, and records being easily available for comparison. All information on *all cases*, (even old/unsolved cases) should be completely indexed and digitized for easy and immediate cross reference capabilities.

Why are we even discussing this in 2015? Seriously, how long has computer technology been available? There is no question that all these factors contribute to a low clearance rate. We can't expect cops to close cases if they are not provided the means to do so. If there's one thing I've learned while researching the murder of Janette Roberson it's that there are multiple systemic breakdowns that need to be addressed in Michigan, and probably nationwide. In this day and age of technology, there really is no excuse for record keeping so horrendous that the public is charged fees like $55 dollars an hour for an ungodly amount of hours because someone's having to rifle through mold-dappled boxes in a closet somewhere to find information. Neither is there any excuse for evidence not being processed in a timely, efficient manner. There's another side to this that I think bears mentioning, and I didn't even consider it until I got this email from change.org with a header that read: *This email contains graphic information that may be upsetting.*

Jeni –

In 1995, I found myself on a journey I would never wish on another human being. I learned that the man whom I had identified in court as my rapist and was sent to prison – the man whose face, breath and evilness I had dreamt about for 11 years – was innocent.

Through post-conviction DNA testing, Ronald Cotton, the man I had hated and prayed for to die, walked out of prison an innocent man. The man who I believed stole everything from me had unfairly lost 4000 days, eleven Christmases, eleven birthdays, and relationships with loved ones.

The DNA tests also found the man who had actually raped me, Bobby Poole. Without the DNA testing an innocent man would still be in prison and a guilty man would be free. Now, the future of the law that allows for this type of DNA testing is uncertain – Congress must reauthorize it by passing the Justice for All Act. I started a petition asking Congress to protect victims and the innocent by reauthorizing the Justice for All Act, which allows for post-conviction DNA testing. Click here to sign it. I had identified Ronald out of a lineup using a police sketch that was based on my own description of the assailant. I was 100% certain I had chosen the right guy – but that's just how fragile memory can be. And it's why we need post-conviction DNA testing.

Bobby Poole, the man who really raped me, went on to rape five other women. In prison, he bragged about how Ronald was serving time for his crime. It wasn't until Ronald heard about post-conviction DNA testing that he called his lawyers and urged them to get the DNA in his case tested. After Ronald was freed, I spoke with Poole's last victim. She told me what happened to her and it pained me to know that it could have prevented if Ronald had not been locked up for something he had never done.

> The Justice for All Act, which is up for reauthorization by Congress, allows men like Ronald to obtain post-conviction DNA testing that can lead to their freedom and to the conviction of the guilty. Without access to such testing, innocent men and women will remain in prison, real perpetrators will remain free, and new victims will have to experience the same horrors and indignities that I did. Please sign my petition asking Congress to reauthorize the Justice for All Act, which allows for post-conviction DNA testing.
>
> -Jennifer Thompson

Yes, I signed the petition. Of course I did. My point here is to illustrate how often the wrong thing happens because the right things aren't done as far as DNA testing, as far as common sense legislation and actual law enforcement. Sometimes balls get dropped. Innocent people go to jail. Guilty people remain free. I want everyone reading this to pay more attention to how the system around you works. Next time a crime is committed, it might be you on the receiving end, and you'll want a system that works the best it can. You'll want justice, and you'll want to live in a country where the system itself is set up to accomplish that.

You won't want people traipsing around crime scenes, destroying evidence; you *will* want evidence to be tested accurately and in a timely manner. You won't want a family member's suffering to be further exacerbated by a system that can't fix what has been broken. You *will want justice*, and you will deserve at least that.

Now... do you want to get *really* mad? No, seriously. Like pissed off to the point that you feel the need to call your local Congressman? *The Detroit Free Press* ran an article written by Tresa Baldas in October of 2011 about the murder of a teenager from Detroit.

> "Laura Wilson, a shy teenager from the Herman Gardens housing project on Detroit's west side, walked to a nearby convenience store to buy a carton of Oleo and two bottles of Pepsi for her mother. She had pleaded to go alone. Nine days later, her body was found in some bushes

> just blocks away from home. She'd been raped and beaten. Her head was smashed in with a brick. Nearly four decades later, her family still has no answers. Short of a confession, it's likely they'll never know who killed the 16-year-old because all of the evidence was destroyed or lost."
>
> "Her bloodstained clothing was ordered destroyed in 1977; the Pepsi bottle followed in 1978. A brick and a chunk of concrete marked with blood and hair strands were destroyed in 1984. The fingernail scrapings and rape evidence -- swabs taken during the autopsy -- are nowhere to be found. Her story illustrates what legal experts say is a pervasive problem nationwide -- the mishandling of criminal evidence largely because of a lack of uniform standards for retaining evidence."

Take a minute. Go ahead. I'll wait. When I read that, I needed one, too. Basically what it says is that even if you've somehow jumped every hurdle, even if the cops thought, "That's our guy!" in some cases, they wouldn't be able to put him away because there wouldn't be anything to take into court. No fancy DNA that juries these days want in order to send someone away for life.

Jurors take their jobs seriously. They've seen *Criminal Minds* and *Law & Order: SVU* so don't try and pull any crap on them. They know there's supposed to be DNA evidence, prints, hairs, fibers, yards of area blasted with Luminol—you get what I'm saying. God forbid police decide they know who the bad guy is, but they can't get anywhere close to a courtroom because someone decided it was time to make more space in the storage unit.

How about we decide that on ANY unsolved homicide case, if you get rid of related evidence while the case is still open, you go to jail? How about if you "loose" or "throw away" or "destroy" evidence on a case that is open, you get latrine duty for the rest of your days in some maximum security prison? How about we do whatever we need to do to make sure killers don't get to keep walking around eating Taco Bell and watching shitty reality TV after slaughtering someone? From the same Detroit Free Press Article:

> "A federal law requires biological evidence be preserved in a murder case where there's been a conviction, should the defendant wish to pursue an appeal. And 33 states, including Michigan, have similar laws. But when it comes to preserving evidence in unsolved cases, that's up to police departments."
>
> Joe Latta, executive director of the International Association for Property and Evidence, who has helped train Detroit police on evidence-handling methods, said it's not unusual for large police departments to be cluttered and unorganized, making finding items extremely difficult.
>
> "Think of Costco. They're that size," he said of evidence rooms. "And if you're looking for something that's the size of an iPhone or the tag came off or it's underneath something..."

You know what? I don't *want* to think of Costco. That explanation, while it *is* an explanation, is completely and utterly unacceptable. When did we become so apathetic that a mere plausible explanation takes the place of what is just and right and okay? Because it's not okay, none of it—not if it's *your* son or daughter or niece or sister or grandma, and it shouldn't be okay for anyone else. At what point do we say *I don't want to hear your excuses and explanations, I WANT YOU TO FIX IT.*

Fix it!

Make it right. Make it fair. Make it just.

Make it *work*. Make the system work.

Fix it, please.

Somebody.

[redacted]

JD-110 (Rev. 8-79) FILE COPY

MICHIGAN DEPARTMENT OF STATE POLICE	Original Date	Complaint No.
☐ Supplementary Complaint Report	January 19, 1983	62-113-83
☒ Additional Complaint Page No. 4	Date of Supplementary Report	File Class 0900-1

NATURE OF COMPLAINT:

Prosecutor JAMES TALASKE reports a Homicide at the Reed City Gamble Store.

INVESTIGATION CON'T;

The original call was given as a possible heart attack and

Officer FINKBEINER advised that another store employee, ANGIE TILLIE found the victim after she was missed for some time.

It was learned thru investigation that in addition to the Police Officers on the scene, Ambulance employees, and ANGIE TILLIE who found the victim, that the following people had entered the immediate area of where the victim was found at least once and some more than one time: JOHN ENGELS, Store Manager; DAVID ENGELS, Store Owner; THOMAS HAWKINS, a store patron; Dr. EARL WILLIAMS, MEdical Examiner; and Chief PHILLIP RATHBUN of the Reed City Police Department.

Identification of the victim was made by co-worker ANGIE TILLIE who found the body and also P.O. LARRY FINKBEINER who personally knew the victim.

Next of Kin, MARIAN FISHER, who is the Reed City Clerk and mother of the victim was notified by the Reed City Police. Mrs. FISHER and JAMES NORDSTROM, City Manager of Reed City notified the victim's husband, ALVIN ROBERSON, at their residence.

Short interviews were held with the person, employees and patrons, who were still at the Store: DAVID ENGELS, JOHN ENGELS, FLOSSIE EARNEST, ANGIE TILLIE, THOMAS HAWKING, ELKE JOHNSON, with the information from these interviews being carried further in this report. These persons were then released to clear the scene.

The original Gamble Store is located at 114 W. Upton Ave. which is in the main business block of the City of Reed City, just to the west of U.S.131 was seperated from adjacent buildings by brick/block walls however after the present owner purchased the business in 1980 the building to the east, 112 W. Upton Ave. was also purchased and in the wall seperating these buildings, doorways were installed both on the main(street level) floor and the basement to give access between them.

Reporting Officer	Reviewer
D/Sgt George D Pratt	JK

State of Michigan STANDARD CRIME REPORT

01
UD-101 (1-81)

FORM	VENUE COUNTY / CITY/TWP	DOMESTIC	PRIMARY FILE CLASS	ATTEMPT	LOCAL A	REPORTING JURIS NO.	INCIDENT NUMBER	ORIGINAL YEAR
1	8360	☒	0900	☒		281	173	83

STATUS	DATE REPORTED MO. DA. YR.	TIME OCCURRED DAY / NIGHT / UNK.	SEQUENTIAL FILE CLASS	TOOL OR WEAPON CODE 1 / CODE 2	VALUE OF PROPERTY DAMAGED (DOLLARS)
7	11983	☒ ☒ ☒	00		

SCENE: STREET OR HWY ☒ GAS STAT. ☒ CONV. STORE ☒ BANK ☒ INDUST. MANUF. ☒ STOR-AGE ☒ OTHER COMM. ☒ PUBLIC BLDG. ☒ SINGLE RES. ☒ OTHER RESID. ☒ ABANDONED STRUCT. ☒

ARSON: STRUCT. ☒ MOTOR VEHICLE ☒ OTHER MOBILE ☒ OTHER PROPERTY ☒

LARC. ONLY: PICK POCKET ☒ PURSE SNATCH ☒ SHOP LIFT ☒ FROM BLDG ☒ MV PARTS ☒ FROM MV ☒ BICY ☒ FROM COIN MACH ☒ OTHER ☒

STOLEN VEHICLE: LOCAL ☒ OTHER ☒ TYPE: AUTO ☒ BUS/TRUCK ☒ OTHER ☒ RECOVERED VEHICLE: LOCAL ☒ OTHER ☒

SUBJECT NUMBER	VICTIM PRIM. / SEC.	ARREST	SUSP.	DATE OF BIRTH MO. DA. YR.	RACE	SEX	INJ.	VOR.	COUNT	ARREST CHARGE	ARREST DISPOSITION
1	☒ ☒	☒	☒	102556	1	2					
	☒ ☒	☒	☒								

ITEM NUMBER	STLN.	RCOV.	RPOJ.	VALUE (IN DOLLARS)	CLASS	ITEM NUMBER	STLN.	RCOV.	RPOJ.	VALUE (IN DOLLARS)	CLASS
	☒	☒	☒				☒	☒	☒		

SEX: 1. MALE 2. FEMALE 7. BUSINESS 8. UNKNOWN

RACE: 1. WHITE 2. HISPANIC 3. BLACK 4. INDIAN 5. CHINESE 6. JAPANESE 8. ALL OTHER 9. UNKNOWN

ASSIST. JURIS NO.: 67 RELATED INCIDENT NUMBER: 70 YEAR: 83

TIME RECEIVED: 10:48 AM ☒ PM ☒

LOCATION OF INCIDENT: 114 Upton St. Reed City Mich

COMPLAINT/VICTIM NAME: Sheriff Neidham

ADDRESS: Reed City Mich.

TELEPHONE:

NATURE OF INCIDENT: Homicide of a Female [redacted] Gamble Store

INFORMATION

This Dept, was contacted at 10:48PM by Sheriff Neidham asking if we could furnish An evidence Tech, to help LAREN THORNSON of C.L. 10 in the prosseeing of the scene of the homicide.

At 10:50PM Sgt, Lund contacted me at home advosing me to come into work right away to go to Reed City with Sgt, Bailey.

At 11:00PM I arrived at the C.P.D. and was advised by Sgt, Lund that Sgt, Bailey would be picking me up. At 11:18PM we left this Dept. in route to Reed City.

VICTIM

JANNETTE ROBERSON--DOB--10-25-55, [redacted]

When we arrived at Reed City we went to the back door of 114 Upton St. which was the back of the Gambles store. We were meet there by a City Officer of Reed City. He let us in and advised that Laren was [redacted] and showed us how to get there.

Once [redacted] we meet with Laren, He advised that [redacted]

PAGE: 1 INVESTIGATED BY: Doornbos REVIEWED BY: REPORTED BY:

WORK

PROPERTY CLASS: 1. CURRENCY, NOTES, ETC. 2. JEWELRY AND PRECIOUS METALS 3. MOTOR VEHICLES 4. TELEVISIONS, RADIOS, CAMERAS, ETC. 5. CLOTHING AND FURS 6. OFFICE EQUIPMENT 7. HOUSEHOLD GOODS 8. CONSUMABLE GOODS 9. FIREARMS 10. OTHER WEAPONS 11. LIVESTOCK 12. ALL OTHER 14. FARM MACHINERY 14. FARM REPAIR EQUIPMENT 15. HEAVY CONSTRUCTION EQUIPMENT 16. CONSTRUCTION SUPPLIES OR TOOLS

12345 FOLLOW SAMPLES 67890

DO NOT WRITE IN THE SHADED AREA

Incident Number

File Class

[redacted]

Cadillac Police Department	Original Date	Complaint No.
	1-19-83	173-83
Additional Complaint Page No. ______	Date of Supplementary Report	File Class
		0900

PEOPLE WE FOUND AT THE SCENE WHEN WE GOT TO 114 UPTON ST, REED CITY MICH,

At back door,	PATROLMAN FINKBINDER	REED CITY OFFICER
Basment store	DET, KINGBERY	OSCEOLA COUNTY SHERIFF DEPT,
	DEPT, TERRY OYSTER	OSCEOLA COUNTY SHERIFF DEPT,
	PATROLMAN JOHN LUSHA	REED CITY OFFICER
	CHIEF RATHBUN	REED CITY CHIEF
	DET, GEORGE PRATT	MICH STATE POLICE REED CITY,
	LAREN THORSON	EVIDENCE TECH C.L.-10

Reporting Officer	Reviewer
DOORNBOS	

FULFILLMENT SERVICE

WEXFORD COUNTY SHERIFF ORIGINAL COMPLAINT REPORT	Entered in LEIN ☐	County: Wexford	Complaint No.: 0189-83
		Township:	File Class: 9900-8
Department: Wexford County Sheriff Department		City or Village: Reed City, Michigan	Original Date: 01-19-83

Complainant: Reed City Police Dept. & Northern Counties Evidence	Home Phone:	Business Phone: 258-8686
Address: Reed City, Michigan	Time Received: 10;50PM	Time Answered: 11:47PM

Received By: Bailey	Investigated By: Bailey

☐ UNFOUNDED ☐ CLOSED BY ARREST ☐ SERVICE RENDERED ☐ OTHER ☐ ARREST UNDER 18

Nature of Complaint: (ASSIST WITH MURDER INVESTIGATION)

VICTIM: Janette Gale Roberson of 5960 West LeRoy Road, Leroy Michigan. Opp's Number R- [redacted] DOB. 10-25-55, [redacted] (Not at the scene when this officer arrived there.)

LOCATION: Gambles Store Reed City Michigan 114 Upton Street [redacted]

OFFICERS AT THE SCENE: [redacted] door of Gambles Larry Finkbinder Reed City Police Department, George Pratt M.S.P. Detective Reed City, Detectives Southworth and Kingbarry Osceola Co. Sheriff's Department, Deputy Terry Oyster, Osceola County Sheriff Department, City Patrolman John Lucha, Chief Phillip Rathbun Reed City, Laron Thorson Northern Counties Evidence Service, City Patrolman Marvin Doornbos Cadillac City Police Dep[t] and Sgt D.A.Bailey

Compl; At the scene these officers Doornbos and Bailey was taken [redacted] of the Gambles Store [redacted] by Patrolman Larry Finkbinder, and we talked to Laron Thorson of Northern Counties Evidence [redacted]

EVIDENCE: [redacted]

Reporting Officer: Sgt David A. Bailey	Reviewer:

[redacted]

ADDITIONAL COMPLAINT REPORT

MPLAINT NO.	2. FILE CLASS	3. DATE, ORIGINAL	4. TIME	5. DATE OF SUPP. REPORT
26-83	900-1	1-19-83	4:00PM	

MPLAINANT'S NAME: Osceola Sheriffs Dept.
7. NATURE OF COMPLAINT: Homicide

EPORTING OFFICER(S): Ptl. Michel J. Primeau/Larry Finkbeiner

ORM USED AS CONTINUATION SHEET FOR CURRENT REPORT PAGE 2 ☐ FORM USED FOR SUPPLEMENTARY REPORT

TEM
IO.

[redacted]

CTIM: Janette Gail Roberson/DOB-10-25-55/ [redacted]
ite/Female. (See Pathology report for further physical discription.)

JURY TO VICTIM: Undersigned officers observed [redacted]
or further injuries see Pathology report). [redacted]

SPITAL INVOLVED: The above victim was transported to Blodgett Hospital located
Grand Rapids, Mi. Transportation for the victim was done by Osceola EMS.
e attendents were Gary McGee, and Tom Stanfield. Ptl. Michel J. Primeau of
e Reed City Police Department also went with the victim to the hospital.
tendents at the crime scene was Gary McGee, Tom Stanfield and Pam McDonald.
rival at the scene for the above was 4:04PM on 1-19-83. Victim was on Telemetry
Reed City Hospital, Dr. White at 4:13PM 1-19-83 [redacted]
gns. NOTE: Medical Examiner Dr. Earl Williams arrived at the scene about 5:00PM
1-19-83 and also confirmed the above referance victim.
e victim was enroute to Blodgett Hospital at 9:00PM on this date and did
rive at 10:21PM. Victim was [redacted] and turned over to [redacted] at 10:39PM this date.
See attached EMS report).

IDENCE: The crime scene was turned over to Jim Southworth of the Osceola
eriffs Department. Northern Counties Evidence Crime lab was notified and
d arrive at the scene under the direction of Laron Thorson. All evidence
llected was done by the above. (See Northern Counties Crime Lab report).

OTOS: Taken of the crime scene was conducted by Laron Thorson of Northern
ounties Crime lab. Detective George Pratt of MSP #62 also took photos of
e crime scene.

☐ UNFOUNDED ☐ CLOSED BY ARREST ☐ ARREST UNDER 17 ☐ OTHER
☐ SERVICE RENDERED ☐

REPORTING OFFICERS SIGNATURE Ptl Primeau & Ptl. Finkbeiner

COMPLAINT NO. 26-83 FILE CLASS 900

ADDITIONAL COMPLAINT REPORT

MPLAINT NO.	2. FILE CLASS	3. DATE, ORIGINAL	4. TIME	5. DATE OF SUPP. REPORT
5-83	900-1	1-19-83	4:00PM	

MPLAINANT'S NAME: ceola Sheriffs Department

7. NATURE OF COMPLAINT: Homicide

REPORTING OFFICER(S): tl. Michel J. Primeau/Larry Finkbeiner

FORM USED AS CONTINUATION SHEET FOR CURRENT REPORT PAGE 3

☐ FORM USED FOR SUPPLEMENTARY REPORT

ITEM NO.

NVESTIGATION: The above R/Os recieved a call from Osceola Sheriffs Department a radio dispatch that someone was inside the Gambles store in Reed City [redacted] After recieving this message the undersigned officers responded [redacted] the scene arriving at 4:04PM this reporting date. Upon arriving at the scene O observed the Osceola EMS vehicle also arriving at the scene. Undersigned ficers along with the EMS attendents entered the building (Gambles) thru the uth door or what is called the front entrence. Ptl. Finkbeiner was first to ter EMS crew was secound and Ptl. Primeau was last to enter. [redacted] First to enter this room was Ptl. Larry nkbeiner secound to enter was EMS crew. Ptl Finkbeiner after entering this om did observe [redacted]. Ptl. Finkbeiner turned EMS crew and stated "check her to see if she is alive". At this time EMS crew d enter the room and did examine the victim. At this time Detective Southworth the Osceola Sheriffs Department arrived and Ptl Finkbeiner stated to him re you an evidence technition?" Det. Southworth replyied "Yes I am"and Ptl. nkbeiner than stated "I would like you to take over this scene". Det. Southwort ah stated "secure the building do not let anyone leave or come into this buildi l. Finkbeiner than left the room where the victim was at allowing Ptl. Primeau enter the room. Ptl. Primeau after observing the victim did also leave this om where the victim was. [redacted] This was done immedeatly. [redacted] A short time ter Det. George Pratt arrived at the scene and was givin accese to the building also talked with [redacted] At about 5:30PM this date the Northern Counties Crime Lab. d arrive to investigate the crime scene. From 4:04PM to about 8:00PM this date e undersigned offers did maintain building secururity white crime lab conduct earch for evidence. At about 8:00PM Ptl. Primeau & Det. Southworth went to [redacted]. Det. Southworth arted to [redacted] to accompany the EMS crew with e victim to be taken to Blodgett Hospital in Grand Rapids, Mi. At about :00PM Gary McGee, Tom Stanfield and the undersigned officer left for Grand apids enroute to Blodgett Hosp. We arrived at the hospital at 10:21PM and id turn the victim over to [redacted] of he Hospital. [redacted] he undersigned offcer and the above EMS crew returned back to the crime scene. fter arriving back undersigned officer continued security of the building Gambles)until going off duty at 2:15AM 1-20-83.

COMPLAINT NO. ____ FILE CLASS ____

☐ UNFOUNDED ☐ CLOSED BY ARREST ☐ ARREST UNDER 17 ☐ OTHER
☐ SERVICE RENDERED

REPORTING OFFICERS SIGNATURE Ptl. [signature]

[redacted]

ADDITIONAL COMPLAINT REPORT

OMPLAINT NO.	2. FILE CLASS	3. DATE, ORIGINAL	4. TIME	5. DATE OF SUPP. REPORT
26-83	900-1	1-19-83	4:00PM	1-24-83

OMPLAINANT'S NAME: Oseeola Sheriffs Dept. Reed City

7. NATURE OF COMPLAINT: Homicide

REPORTING OFFICER(S): Ptl. Michel J. Primeau/Larry Finkbeiner

FORM USED AS CONTINUATION SHEET FOR CURRENT REPORT PAGE 4

☒ FORM USED FOR SUPPLEMENTARY REPORT

ITEM NO. FURTHER INVESTIGATION:

On 1-20-83 at 7:30AM this R/O was enroute to Grand Rapids, Mi to the Blodgett Hospital with Crime Lab Techrition Laron Thorson(Northern Counties Crime Lab). After arriving at the hosptial [redacted] . This R/O did stand-by at the labratory with the above and did observe Laron Thorson (Crime Lab) and both of the above doctors examine the victim for evidence to collect. After Crime Lab Tech. had completed his investigation relative to the victim R/O did leave with Crime Lab Technition (Laron Thorson) enroute to Reed City Police Department.

After arriving back in Reed City R/O went directly to the scene of the crime with Crime Lab Technition(Laron Thorson) for further investigation.

DISPOSITION: Open pending further investigation!!

ASISTING AGENCYS: Osceola Sheriffs Department
Michigan State Police Reed City, Mi.
Northern Counties Crime Lab.

☐ UNFOUNDED ☐ CLOSED BY ARREST ☐ ARREST UNDER 17 ☐ OTHER
☐ SERVICE RENDERED ☐

REPORTING OFFICERS SIGNATURE

COMPLAINT NO. ______ FILE CLASS ______

OSCEOLA COUNTY SHERIFF DEPARTMENT
ORIGINAL COMPLAINT REPORT

	County: Osceola	Complaint No. OC70-83
	Township:	File Class: 9900-8
	City/Village: Reed City	Original Date: 1-19-83

Complainant	Home phone	Bus. phone
Officer Larry Finkbiener		832-2245

Address	Time Received	Time dispatched	Time arrived
ReedCity Police Dept.	4:04PM		

Received by:	Investigated by	Time cleared
D/Sgt James Southworth	D/Sgt J. Southworth	

NATURE OF COMPLAINT:	Open	Closed
Assist Reed City Police Dept. on Homicide	☐	☐

Incident Location: Gambles Store 114 W. Upton, Reed City, Mich.

REPORT

On Jan 19, 1983, the undersigned had just left the Osceola Co. sheriff Dept, and was headed East on Upton St. It was 4:00PM. As I approached the Gambles store, I observed the Reed City ambulance service, and the Reed City Police Dept going into the Gambles store.

The undersigned pulled up acrossed the street from the store, and went inside to assist in whatever was going on. As I entered the store, I observed

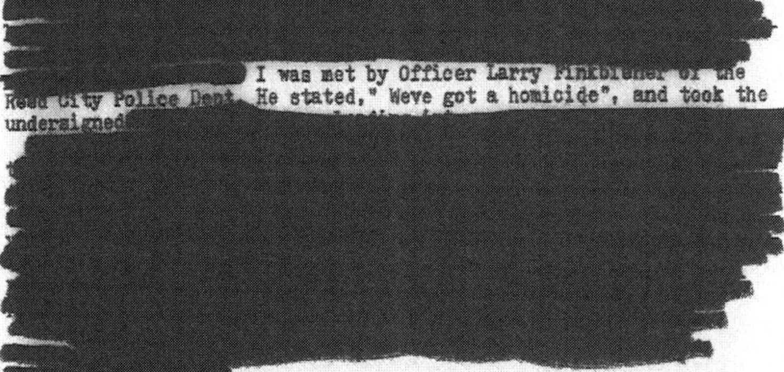

I was met by Officer Larry Finkbiener of the Reed City Police Dept. He stated," Weve got a homicide", and took the undersigned

At that time Officer Finkbiener stated to the undersigned, "You are an evidence technician, I want you to take over the scene." At that time the undersigned removed everybody away from the body, except EMS personell checking the body. Both doors to the store were then locked, so no one else could enter, The undersigned then went outside to the patrol unit and radioed the Sheriffs Dept to Notify Sheriff Needham, Chief Rathbun, and also to contact Deputy Tom Kingsbury, who had also been working as a detective for the past 3 weeks.

Compl. #

File Class

OC-2 Pg. 1

[redacted]

ADDITIONAL PAGE

Comp.# OC 70-83
Date 1-19-83

The dispatch was also advised to contact Northern Counties Evidence, and advise them we needed them at this location. Prosecutor James Talaske was also notified. On my way back acrossed the street towards the Gambles store, Sheriff Needham arrived, and went into the store with the undersigned.

When Prosecutor Talaske arrived, he advised that he had also contacted D/Sgt George Pratt of the Michigan State Police in Reed City to assist in the investigation. After a few minutes, D/Sgt Pratt arrived at the scene, and was taken downstairs to the Pet shop to view the murder scene, by the undersigned.

After viewing the scene, Officers then

The undersigned talked with

First Responders

RCPD and the Osceola County Sheriff's Dept. remain in these locations today. The MSP post closed to public traffic October, 2011.

In 1983 there were three separate law enforcement entities stationed in Reed City within blocks of one another, as well as the Gambles store on Upton Avenue where Janette Roberson was murdered. Reed City's Michigan State Police Post was 0.7 of a mile from Gambles, the Reed City Police Department was 0.5 of a mile, and the Osceola County Sheriff's Department was 0.2 of a mile; two blocks. Someone could literally sprint from the Sheriff's department to Gambles in under a minute if they were in mediocre health and inclined to do so. Three different law enforcement entities within a mile of the location of the crime scene, which is why they all converged, according to police reports, on top of one another.

As I researched this case, one of the most common public perceptions I encountered was that the first responding officers compromised the scene. I am not one to assume ill of law enforcement strictly on the basis of what someone else says. I like to read things and research things and see things with my own eyes—like, oh, I don't know, New York cops on video killing an unarmed man for selling untaxed cigarettes.

Generally speaking, cops have a tough, often shitty job, one the average citizen would do well to not take for granted. It's all fun and games to poke fun at the *po-po* until such time as you actually need them. So it was with skepticism and a grudging sense of irritation that I listened to numerous stories about corruption; tale after tale of Reed City citizens bemoaning speed traps, or how only "certain names" in town got certain municipal jobs. How special treatment is afforded to some, while others are *blah, blah, blah*... You've heard all the stories, I'm sure. If you live in a small town, came from a small town, or have read anything about small town life, it's practically a cliché. This isn't anything new. It wasn't far into my research, though, that I ran across a couple inconsistencies specific to this case. The first involved the Reed City Chief of Police at the time of the murder.

Phillip Rathbun passed away on November 27, 2013 at 78 years of age. According to his obituary, he was born April 19, 1935 in Lansing to Yale Rathbun and Alma Stickney, was raised in Lansing, and married in 1952. He worked as a pageboy for Michigan's Governor Gerhard Mennen "Soapy" Williams as a young man, and eventually joined the Army, serving in the 82nd Airborne Division. In 1963 he moved with his wife to the Reed City area where they raised five daughters. At one time, he worked as a butcher at the local A&P. He and his wife founded and operated the first ambulance service in Osceola County. Rathbun wore many hats in the community over the years, including chief of police, city manager, city councilman, mayor pro-tem and volunteer firefighter. He was police chief for 22 years, seven of those serving double-duty as police chief *and* city manager. Phillip Rathbun was dubbed "Mr. Reed City" and most people I spoke to had good things to say about him.

From a Cadillac News article written by Matt Seward that ran on January 19, 2010, the 27th anniversary of Janette Roberson's death:

> "Every time I go past the gravestone, I look it," Rathbun said. "I've even done some maintenance on it. One of the trees on it died, and I cleaned it off. I trimmed some other trees. It (the murder) is still on my mind; it's not forgotten, if you will."
>
> Rathbun was the Reed City Police Chief at the time of Janette's murder. He was out of town when it happened, but it took place while he was in charge of the police department.
>
> "That's one thing from my career that sticks out No. 1 in my mind," Rathbun said. "Not that I don't have other concerns, but it bothers me. It has been on my mind and always will until it is solved."
>
> Rathbun, who retired from the police force in 1998, admits that a lot of details have been blurred by time, but some things still stand out.
>
> "There was some kind of hostility, in my opinion," Rathbun said. "It was not just passion. Someone was mad at her."
>
> When asked if he believes the killer would be found, Rathbun didn't hesitate. "Yep," he said. "Something will drop out of the woodwork.
>
> "It is something neither one of us (Rathbun and Pratt) has dropped out of our thinking. I know (Pratt) has not closed the case on it."

INVESTIGATION:

The Undersigned was notified at the Post of the Homicide by the complainant at and arrival at the scene was Upon arrival after being admitted to the secured Gamble Store by a (rear door), Reed City Police Officers LARRY FINKBEINER, MICHAEL PRIMEAU and THEODORE FLATZ were reconized along with Sheriff DAVID NEEDHAM, Undersheriff THOMAS DETTLOFF, D/Sgt. JAMES SOUTHWORTH and Deputies TERRY OYSTER and THOMAS KINGSBURY of the Osceola County Sheriff's Department. Also present were Osceola County Emergency Service employees GARY mcGHEE, THOMAS STANFIELD and PAMELA McDONALD.

From P.O. FINKBEINER it was learned that P.O. PRIMEAU and himself were the first to arrive at the scene being dispatched by the Osceola County Sheriff's Department According to him D/Sgt. SOUTHWORTH, Deputy OYSTER, Deputy KINGSBURY and the Ambulance crew arrived immediately after them. The building was already secured at that time with TERRY KOOIKER giving admitance at the front(street)entrance.

Reporting Officer	Reviewer
D/Sgt George D. Pratt	

Chief Rathbun was not noted in the Michigan State Police report as having been among the law enforcement officers present when Detective Pratt arrived, yet on page four of the report, he is listed as one of the people who "it was learned through investigation" had "entered the immediate area of where the victim was found at least once and some more than one time."

Because the Reed City report—signed by officers Finkbeiner and Primeau—does not mention their boss's presence, it's unclear when he arrived and left that first time. In the Osceola County report, Det. Sgt. James Southworth writes that he contacted Chief Rathbun, though it is not stated where he was contacted, or the time he was contacted.

According to the Wexford County and Cadillac Police reports, Chief Rathbun returned at some point in the evening, because he was noted on both reports as being there, and both departments arrived much later in the evening to assist with evidence collection.

From P.O. FINKBEINER it was learned that P.O. PRIMEAU and himself were the first to arrive at the scene being dispatched by the Osceola County Sheriff's Department According to him D/Sgt. SOUTHWORTH, Deputy OYSTER, Deputy KINGSBURY and the Ambulance crew arrived immediately after them. The building was already secured at that time with TERRY KOOIKER giving admitance at the front(street)entrance.

Reporting Officer D/Sgt George D. Pratt

Reviewer

I spoke with Gladys and Terry Kooiker on Oct. 6, 2014 at their home. They were at Gambles on the day of the murder because they needed something from the store, though neither could remember, three decades later, what that something was. It's no wonder. Could have been anything from a mouse trap to a sink stopper, but whatever the item, its memory would forever be overshadowed by the events that played out once they entered the store.

Both Kooikers worked for Reed City schools and they'd stopped that day on their way home. Based on what time school let out, they estimate being there between 3:30 and 3:45pm. Mrs. Kooiker said they had been inside Gambles maybe 5 minutes, just long enough to find what they needed, and were standing near the register in the center if the store. This tracks with the ME report, which states the body was found at approximately 3:50pm.

Mrs. Kooiker remembers overhearing someone say, "Well, her coat is here..."

It wouldn't have been more than a minute or two that Angie Tillie would run back up the stairs from the basement. They didn't remember Angie screaming, but Mrs. Kooiker described her as distraught. Mr. Kooiker didn't remember her saying anything, which would tend to corroborate Flossie Earnest's recollection of Angie putting her head down on the desk near the register and pointing to the basement pet store entrance, unable to speak.

Mrs. Kooiker said that it only occurred to her later that evening, once they got home, that she didn't remember anyone checking the store to see if the killer was inside with them. Mr. Kooiker remembered seeing Officer Finkbeiner walking down the aisle toward him from the front of the store, but he did not recall Officer Primeau arriving with Officer Finkbeiner. In fact, he said that he was not at the front door when Finkbeiner arrived, *"with the door already secured at the time"*—as written in the Michigan State Police Report—but was told *later* to watch the door, by Finkbeiner himself.

According to Mr. Kooiker: "I suspect if Primeau was with Finkbeiner, he wouldn't need me to watch the door, would he?" He was clear about one thing: he was not manning front door when the officers arrived. This recollection by Mr. Kooiker is corroborated by Gary McGhee, who was one of the EMT's on duty when the call came in. According to McGhee, the call came in as a heart attack in progress. The Michigan State Police report also notes this. It's the reason the call stands out in McGhee's mind, all these years later. According to his incident report, the dispatch came in at 4:06pm and EMTs Gary McGhee and Pam McDonald pulled up in front of Gambles at 4:08pm. As he was hurrying out of the ambulance, McGhee recalls, "Larry Finkbeiner was holding the glass front door to the store open and people were hurriedly exiting the building. It appeared as if Larry was "shooing" people out of the store. However, this did not seem unusual given the circumstances we thought we were responding to."

Heart attack. Remember, they still think they're responding to a heart attack in progress.

McGhee believes there were three or four people, but he cannot be sure of the exact number. "Not a crowd, but three or four people." He says he was later asked by state police if he could identify any of the folks Officer Finkbeiner allowed to leave the store since he was a local, but could not. He and his partner, Pam McDonald, were busy grabbing their gear, and if there was a heart attack occurring, clearing the area would tend to be an appropriate response. (Gary McGhee is the son of the man who was the Reed City State Post Commander at the time, also named Gary McGhee.)

Officer Finkbeiner was the only law enforcement officer McGee remembers seeing as they arrived at Gambles. He also recalls seeing Angie Tillie as they entered the store and she was "visibly upset." He and his partner were told nothing. No one spoke a word to them as they were led down to the basement by Officer Finkbeiner. They walked down the stairs behind him, "...stepped to the right a little, down an aisle" and through the pet department, where they followed along the far right wall to the back of the room. According to McGhee, Officer Finkbeiner pushed open a door at the rear of the room and just inside was a woman "...lying beneath a rack of animal cages that was elevated off the floor."

The birds were squawking like crazy, that's another thing he remembers, because it added to the surreal nature of the scene. While McGhee jumped into action, his partner froze in the doorway behind him. It took him a couple seconds to realize he wasn't being assisted. He looked up and saw Pam McDonald unable to move because she also expected to find a heart attack victim, not a gruesome murder scene. She was crying and shaking.

McGhee told me, "I feel bad about it now, but I screamed at her to go upstairs." It was clear to him she wasn't going to be able to help. He said the victim was not breathing when they found her and that her body was "cool, not cold" so he believed it had not just happened but had been a little while.

I said to Gary, "The report says, *Attendants at the scene: Gary McGhee, Tom Stanfield, and Pam McDonald. Reed City Hospital, Dr. White at 4:13. The victim was on telemetry.* What does that mean, telemetry?"

"People can only legally/officially be declared dead by a physician. As paramedics, we make an assessment of the patient including obtaining an electrocardiogram (ECG). We then call the hospital and speak with a physician. The physician then, based on our reported findings, "pronounces" the patient deceased. The medical examiner is then notified if indicated and may or may not come to the scene. In Osceola County at the time, I was a Medical Examiner Investigator, appointed by the Medical Examiner. As such, in certain types of deaths (i.e. auto accidents) where the cause of death is obvious, we were trained to perform certain examinations and tests, complete specific forms, and then submit them to the Medical Examiner without the Medical Examiner actually having to come to the death scene. However, because of the situation, I requested that the medical examiner (Dr. Williams) actually come to this scene. I remember that he was there before we left at 5:26pm which is consistent with the report."

"In this situation, as documented, I made my assessment at 4:10pm which included obtaining an ECG which depicted the total absence of any electrical heart activity. This time would have been recorded (printed) on the ECG tracing obtained at the time. I then called Reed City Hospital on the "bedside" telemetry (UHF) radio we used at the time, and spoke with Dr. Catherine White (D.O.)—who was the physician on duty at Reed City Hospital Emergency Department. This contact was made, as documented, from the victim's side in the basement at 4:13pm and the victim was "officially" pronounced deceased at that time. The actual time of death was obviously some time before that—but not too long, based on my findings. Dr. White never came to the scene."

Then he said, "Did the reports mention anything about the blood I stepped in?"

"*Huh*?" was all I could muster.

It was clear that McGhee was chagrined about it, even three decades later.

"Please remember, I have been involved in fire & EMS for over thirty six years. I am nearly fifty-four years old now. This incident occurred over thirty years ago, when I was relatively young (twenty-two) and a relatively inexperienced paramedic. What I did—or observed then—may not have been as good as it is now. I know my documentation was not nearly as thorough then as it is now. My memory of the incident is also limited. I received my paramedic degree in June 1981 and started at Osceola County EMS in October that same year, without any prior experience at the paramedic level. The blood spot/puddle was located outside the entrance to the back room through which I entered, maybe eight to ten feet. Definitely closer to the entrance to the back room than to the stairway. I admit that I did not see it when I was walking toward the doorway; I was not looking for anything like that since I thought I was responding to a heart attack victim. I did not see the blood until when I was leaving the room to go back upstairs. It was then that it became evident that the initial assault most likely occurred outside the room where she found and that she had been dragged or otherwise moved to where the body was located. The blood was still wet. I did not know for sure that I had stepped in it while walking toward the entrance to the back room but there was the possibility, since I walked right through the area where it was located."

"I remember telling Officer Mike Primeau when I got back upstairs that I might have stepped in the blood on my way into the room. He told me that they might need my boots then to match/rule out against any footprints that they might find during the investigation. In light of this, I called my fiancée and she brought me another pair to the store. She came to the front door of the store and handed them to me through the open door. She did not enter the store. I did not take my boots off until she arrived with the other pair. Admittedly, probably a mistake. I took my boots off and they were placed in a paper bag. I remember that it had to be a paper bag. I don't know for sure what happened to them thereafter. I left the store with my other boots on. I remember getting my boots back a few days later; they were at the EMS office when I returned to work one day."

I felt bad for the guy. He was obviously horrified it had occurred in the first place, but to my mind, he wasn't at fault. He was following directly behind a police officer.

"Officer Finkbeiner led you down there, right? Did he even *know* the blood was there? Did you see boxes blocking the aisles, or any reason why he would have led you directly through an area with obvious blood on the floor? Presumably there were other ways to get to the back of the store."

"I do not remember there being anything blocking our path to the back room. I did not see the blood on the floor until I was leaving the back room. It was only then that I suspected the initial assault may have occurred there, and also realized—to much embarrassment—that I may have walked through it on my way into the room."

When asked, McGhee was not sure if Officer Finkbeiner had been down to the basement before EMTs arrived, or if he was seeing the body for the first time with them. One has to wonder, though, how Officer Finkbeiner would have known exactly where to find the body if he was just going down there the first time with the EMTs and nobody exchanged any words. McGhee said there was no discussion as they walked from the front door where Finkbeiner had been "shooing people from the store" while he led them downstairs. Did Finkbeiner know they had a murder at this time? Presumably he would have heard the same dispatch from his patrol car radio that everyone else heard: Heart attack in progress.

When did Officer Finkbeiner become aware they were on a murder call and not a heart attack? His report states he arrived and entered with the EMTs. If that is true, how did he know exactly where the body was? Even if an employee had told him it was in the basement, how did he know where, *exactly*? Did one of the employees tell him before the EMTs pulled up, *before* he was shooing people out of the store? He led EMTs in a straight path directly to the back room and opened the door. The Reed City report states Officers Finkbeiner and Primeau arrived at 4:04pm. According to their report, the EMTs arrived at 4:08. That's four minutes of unaccounted for time. Did he spend it all shooing people out of the store, or did he go downstairs and view the body, alone or with others, prior to EMTs arriving? According to the Reed City report that Officers Primeau and Finkbeiner signed, *"Upon arriving at the scene PO observed the Osceola EMS vehicle also arriving at the scene. Undersigned officers, along with the EMS attendants entered the building (Gambles) thru the south door or what is called the front entrance."*

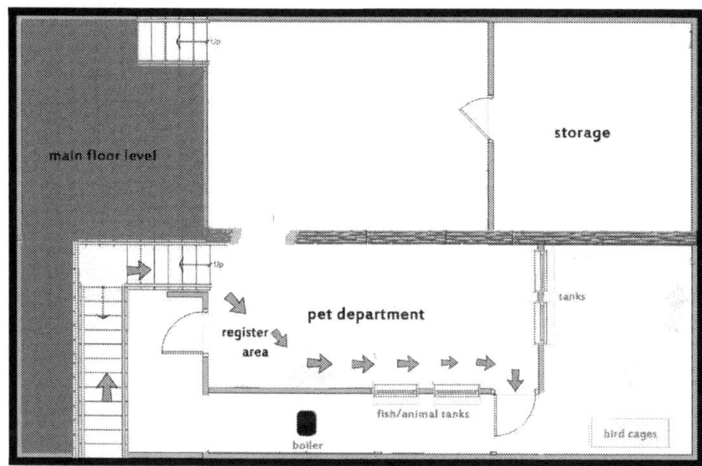

Path EMTs walked to back room, led by Officer Finkbeiner

Four minutes between the times the Reed City report says their officers arrived and when EMS states they arrived. Did he stand out on the sidewalk and shoo customers out for four whole minutes? The city report clearly states they all arrived at the same time.

Asked if he recalled any other law enforcement officer arriving, McGhee said, "I do remember Mike Primeau being in the basement where the body was located while we were still down there, but I am not sure when he arrived. He definitely came in after me. Osceola County's Jim Southworth was there, and I remember him being in the basement while I was assessing the victim. Once it was determined that the victim was deceased, I left the basement and went back upstairs where I remained until I was authorized to leave. I don't recall going back downstairs at any time until we went back to pick up the body for transport to Grand Rapids. Officer Mike Primeau accompanied Tom Stanfield, (the replacement for Pam McDonald) and me in the ambulance when we transported the body to Blodgett Hospital in Grand Rapids. This was to preserve the chain of evidence. He also returned to Reed City with us in the ambulance and we took him back to the Gambles store when we arrived back in Reed City. When we arrived at Blodgett, the receiving pathologist (or assistant) did a visual examination of the body with me, Tom, and Mike Primeau present. It was from that examination it was determined that there was an item with a particular shape that was used in the assault. We returned to the Gambles store to drop Officer Mike Primeau off and advised the investigators that were still present what to look for as a possible weapon. It was early morning, as documented, 1:00am."

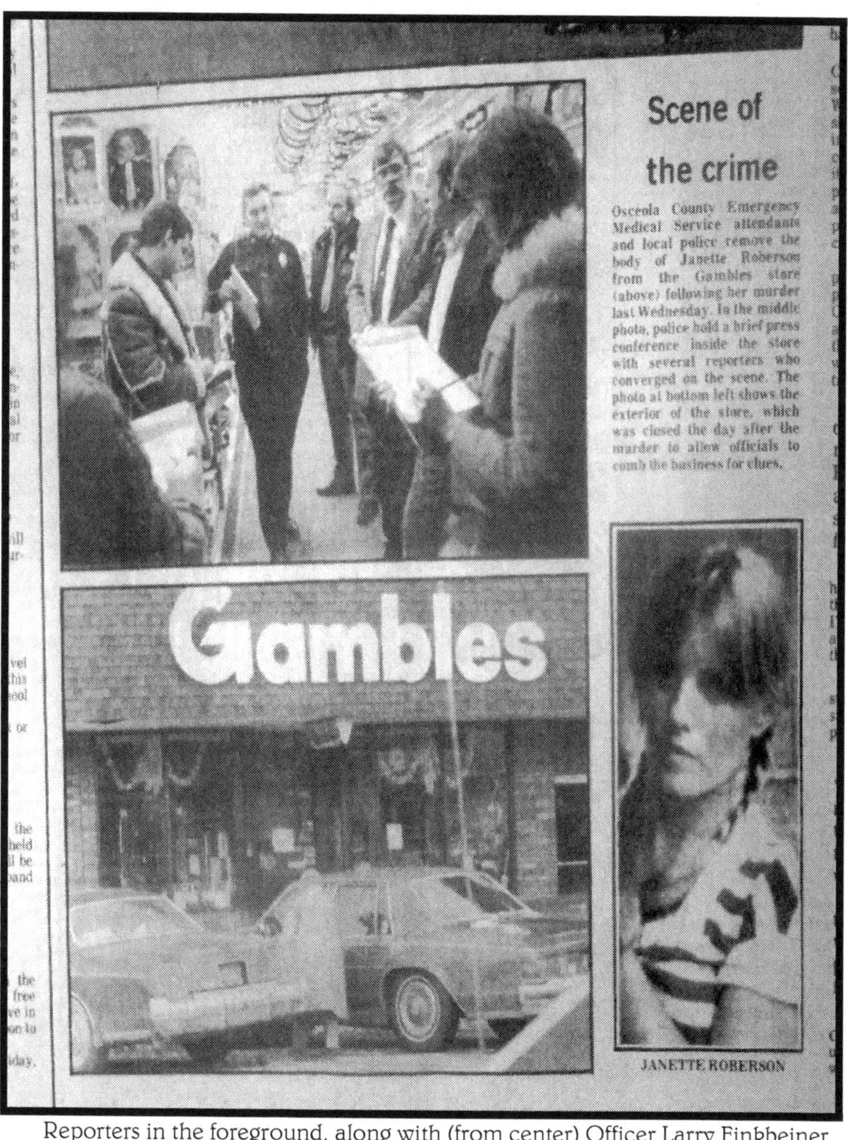

Scene of the crime

Osceola County Emergency Medical Service attendants and local police remove the body of Janette Roberson from the Gambles store (above) following her murder last Wednesday. In the middle photo, police hold a brief press conference inside the store with several reporters who converged on the scene. The photo at bottom left shows the exterior of the store, which was closed the day after the murder to allow officials to comb the business for clues.

JANETTE ROBERSON

Reporters in the foreground, along with (from center) Officer Larry Finkbeiner, Deputy Terry Oyster, and Det. Sgt. George Pratt.

DISPATCH

> "I worked at the sheriff's dept. at the time of that murder and I dispatched the officers, detectives, and ambulance there. The problem with solving that case is that the officers in charge of the investigation and the store owners let everybody and there brother down the basement before they decided to start an official investigation in other words they dropped the ball..." ~Raymond Haight

I ran across the above comment on a Facebook thread dedicated to the murder of Janette Roberson, so I contacted Mr. Haight to see if I could get his memory of the event. Raymond Haight said he had just come in to work about 3:45 to the Osceola County Sheriff's Department. His shift was from 4:00 to 12:00pm. Not more than 3 minutes after his butt was in the chair, according to him, the call came in from Gambles.

"It was David Engels and he said there was a murder in the basement at Gambles."

Haight says he turned to the two deputies standing in the sheriff's department at the time and told them what they had. To his recollection, the deputies present were Terry Oyster and Tom Kingsbury. Their shift change was the same time as the dispatchers, so that's why they both happened to be standing there at the time, according to Haight.

"They weren't even out the door and I was on the line dispatching EMS. Then I contacted the State Police post. They were the ones that called the Reed City officers." Back then, Haight said—and it was confirmed by Gary McGhee—the Reed City MSP post dispatched the city police.

He said dispatches would have gone out to all cars, but not the EMS, as they were on a different frequency. So anyone manning a patrol car in the area would have heard the dispatch. This, however, contradicts the Finkbeiner/Primeau report which states they were notified by Osceola County Dispatch. I asked Mr. Haight again and he was very clear. He said he did not dispatch the city police. He called the State Police Post, and it was they who were to contact RCPD officers.

It was Haight's understanding that when the first officers arrived on scene, the doors were not secured and the owner was "...letting people to go in and out, and down into the basement." That seems to corroborate the MSP report, based on how many people had been listed as being in the vicinity of the body. Surely all of those folks weren't allowed near the body *after* Officers Primeau and Finkbeiner arrived?

When asked if any related calls came in about the scene that day, Haight said the sheriff's department got word about ten or fifteen minutes after the initial call that there was a possible suspect on a bus leaving Reed City—someone described as having run out the back door of Gambles in an army coat toward where the bus picked up, down by the Osceola Inn, which was on Upton Avenue, about a block from Gambles.

I told Mr. Haight that the Michigan State Police, Reed City, and Osceola reports all said the call came in as a heart attack, and that Gary McGhee remembered it vividly as a heart attack because that was what he thought he was responding to until the moment he saw Janette's brutalized body. Haight assured me that the call did not come in as a heart attack, and repeated that the call he took was from a person saying they were David Engels calling to say there had been a murder in the Gambles basement.

Could more than one call have come in, I wondered, aloud? I asked Haight if 9-1-1 was in use then, and he said no. So I asked if a citizen needed the police, who would they call? He said they would call the sheriff's office directly, or the state post, and then he rattled off a number: 832-2211.

Haight was silent for a few seconds, and then said, "You know what could have happened? It didn't *come in* as a heart attack, but maybe we dispatched it that way because of the scanners. See, you wouldn't want to call in a murder, because too many other people would hear it because of the scanners." He said he thinks that's what may have happened. The call came in as a murder, but he dispatched it as a heart attack.

"But that would have been done at the order of Sheriff Needham," Haight said. "He would be the only one to give that order." It is of note, though, that Haight did not have independent recollection of that occurring. This was just supposition.

"So Needham must have been there at the time the call came in, then?" I asked. Haight said he was always around. His residence was attached to the jail.

Another thing Haight remembered was the birds. He had two parakeets at the time. On his way to work that day, around 3:30 or so, he considered stopping into Gambles to get some birdseed because he was out. But when he got downtown he remembered he was in uniform.

"I didn't wanna go buying birdseed for a parakeet in uniform." So he didn't go. All these years later, he wondered aloud, "What if I had? Maybe I'd have seen something."

In all likelihood, at that time the only thing he would have seen was that the pet department clerk was missing. Nobody I spoke to could find Janette from noon on.

But Raymond Haight's is not the only *What if?* story I heard in relation to this case.

On the day of the murder, Roger Soper picked up his then mother-in-law from Meadowview Apartments, the same apartments where Janette and her family lived. Soper's mother-in-law and her son were friendly with Janette. Soper and his wife worked at the hospital in Reed City, different shifts. He worked 3:00 to 11:00pm, his wife worked the 8:00 to 4:00 or 9:00 to 5:00 shift, so his mother-in-law would watch the kids for a couple hours until his wife got home.

Earlier in the week they'd discussed stopping by Gambles because his mother-in-law said Janette wanted her to come look at a parrot she wanted to sell her. The mother-in-law even asked Mr. Soper to pick her up a few minutes early that day. But as often happens when routine overrides best laid plans, they both forgot on the day they'd planned to go.

When they arrived at his house where he would deposit her for babysitting duty before heading off to work, Soper remembered. "Oh, we forgot to stop at Gambles about the bird." Mother-in-law assured him they could go another day. Based on his schedule, he said they would have been in the pet store around 2:30. They never made it.

He heard about the murder around 4:30 that day in the cafeteria at the hospital. He said it was all over the hospital pretty fast. Little did he know that his forgotten trip to look at a bird, along with a familial connection to someone related to the case, would years later bring the Michigan State Police to his door.

January 19, 1983

NATURE OF COMPLAINT: Prosecutor James Talaske reports a homicide at the Reed City Gambles store – Osceola County, Michigan.

LOCATION: 112-114 West Upton Ave., Reed City, MI

TIME: The offense occurred between [**REDACTED**] this date, Wednesday, January 19, 1983.

OWNER: The owner of the Gambles store is David Engels.

VICTIM: Janette Gail Roberson.

SCENE: The victim was an employee of the Gambles store in the pet shop, which is located in the basement of the original Gambles store, 114 W. Upton Av.

Osceola County Prosecutor James Talaske, the complainant in this matter, was contacted at the scene and he advised that it was his request that the Undersigned (Det. Sgt. George Pratt, Michigan State Police) handle the investigation.

AGENCIES INVOLVED: Reed City Police Department, Osceola County Sheriff's Department and Michigan State Police.

One of my first questions was this: *Who called the county prosecutor, and why*? Was that standard operating procedure in 1983? The report notes that Detective Sgt. George Pratt was notified at the Reed City MSP Post of the homicide by James Talaske at [**REDACTED**] and his arrival at the scene was [**REDACTED**].

Question number two: What possible reason would Michigan State Police have for redacting the arrival time of their assigned Detective? I put this question in writing, multiple times in separate FOIA requests, and was repeatedly turned down. The last request I made in that regard was a request for that piece of information alone, Detective Pratt's notification time and his subsequent arrival time on scene. I even noted the page they could find the information on. The request was flatly denied and the exceptions they invoked were as follows:

1. It would interfere with law enforcement proceedings.
2. Deprive a person of the right to a fair trial or impartial administrative adjudication
3. Constitute an unwarranted invasion of personal privacy.

Let me break down my responses to those points:

1. No it absolutely would not.
2. No it absolutely would not.
3. No it absolutely is not.

But I learned pretty quickly that not all public information is created equal. If an entity doesn't want to hand it over, for whatever reason, there are a great many ways they can get around it. Once I learned that I would have an opportunity to speak to Detective Pratt, I jotted that one down on my ever-growing list of questions.

Detective Pratt writes that, "Upon arrival, after being admitted to the secured Gambles store by the rear door, Reed City Police Officers Larry Finkbeiner, Michael Primeau and Theodore Platz were recognized, along with Sheriff David Needham, Undersheriff Thomas Dettloff, Det. Sgt. James Southworth, and Deputies Terry Oyster and Thomas Kingsbury of the Osceola County Sheriff's Department. Also present were Osceola County Emergency Service employees Gary McGhee, Thomas Stanfield and Pamela McDonald."

According to the MSP report, a Reed City hospital employee, who was listed as having been in the vicinity of the body at some point, followed the EMTs into the store because she was a nurse and "It was felt that she possibly could be of assistance." The report states that she was "just passing by the store at the time," although Gary McGhee does not recall her assisting at all, and since he knew her quite well, believes he would have. When asked about her presence, McGhee noted, "I vaguely remember her being in the store. She may have come downstairs, but I do not remember her ever being allowed in the back room where the body was. She may have peeked in but I would not have let her become involved if she was in the room. She was a nurse at the hospital. Paramedics were a relatively new phenomenon at the time, especially in Northern Michigan. Many nurses, this woman included, were opposed to paramedics performing ECG's, starting IV's, giving medications, and other advanced procedures we are trained to perform in the pre-hospital setting. She was not a big supporter of the EMS system in Osceola County."

Officer Finkbeiner advised Detective Pratt that a store employee, Angie Tillie, "found the victim after she was missed for some time."

From the initial MSP report:

"It was learned thru investigation that in addition to the police officers on the scene, ambulance employees, [the nurse who happened by], and Angie Tillie, who found the victim, <u>the following people had entered the immediate area of where the victim was found, at least once, and some more than one time:</u> John Engels, Store Manager; David Engels, Store Owner; Thomas Hawkins, a store patron; Dr. Earl Williams, Medical Examiner, and Chief Phillip Rathbun of the Reed City Police Department."

The Reed City PD report does not mention Reed City Police Chief Phillip Rathbun's presence at the scene, or when he arrived, unless that information is included in the redacted portions, in which case I would be curious as to why that would be.

"Identification of the victim was made by co-worker Angie Tillie, who found the body, and also Officer Finkbeiner, who personally knew the victim. Next of kin, who is the Reed City City Clerk (and Treasurer) and mother of the victim was notified by the Reed City Police. Mrs. Fisher and James Nordstrom, City Manager, notified the victim's husband, Alvin Roberson, at their residence."

Detective Southworth appears to have been sent on a number of tasks, including canvassing local businesses and interviewing Janette's husband. At the time of the murder, Ronald Goold owned The Buckboard Bar, having purchased it from Ivan Youngs and his family prior. He eventually sold it back to Ivan months after the murder. The bar itself is directly next door to the Gambles store on the side that had recently been expanded into. I spoke to him briefly and he was kind enough to get me in touch with his daughter, Carrie

Bevard, who was working at The Buckboard on the day of the murder. She recalls Detective Southworth hurrying into the bar that day with a couple other officers.

"There really aren't any front windows on the building. I remember they came in suddenly and were emptying trash cans, going through the bathrooms... They didn't say what they were doing at first, but I did have to unlock the basement door for them. We knew there was something going on, but did not know what."

On the day of the murder business was slow, only a few regulars in the bar. Carrie said it was sometime after lunchtime. "They told me there had been a murder next store and they needed to check my basement. I unlocked the basement door—it was padlocked—but I didn't go down with them."

Carrie said she rarely went down to the basement to begin with and then only to get extra mops or buckets. "It was creepy." She was aware of a door on the front of the basement wall below where the front door at street level would be, beneath the sidewalk, and from what the detective told her, that doorway opened into a passage that accessed the entire block below the sidewalk. These access points were once used for coal deliveries. Carrie said she believed some businesses had their doors blocked, so she did not know how far the killer could have gotten around below ground at the time, but according to police there was a question, at least at that time, if the killer could have been moving around down there, underground. She said police didn't make her close the bar while they searched, but would not let any new customers inside. She was told by one of the officers that Janette had left for lunch and was murdered shortly after returning. Because Carrie went into the pet store occasionally, she knew who Janette was, but didn't know her personally.

Carrie and the regulars in the bar were questioned in a group, asked things like: "Anyone strange or acting strange come in or out? Anyone go in the bathroom for a long time? Did anyone see anything? Had anyone been in the pet store that day? Did they see anything unusual? Did anyone know Janette? Had they seen her that day?"

Carrie added, "The thinking was that the person had maybe come in there and used the bathroom to clean up. I thought the whole theory of someone coming in there in the middle of the afternoon was ridiculous, since during the day it was usually regulars, and anyone different would surely have been noticed, especially if they had suddenly popped out of the basement."

Carrie said police were there for twenty or thirty minutes, but didn't appear to find anything and didn't take anything out as evidence. She said she was really scared knowing there was a killer on the loose, and in the days to follow she would get regular escorts by one of the Reed City Officers—Finkbeiner or Lucha, usually—to and from her car when she opened and closed the bar.

Of his interaction with Alvin Roberson on this date, the Michigan State Police report notes: "To determine that the husband of the victim, Alvin Roberson, had been notified of her demise, D/Sgt. Southworth went to the Roberson residence. Alvin Lee Roberson was interviewed at his home. He was advised of his Constitutional rights, which he advised that he understood and waived. It was learned that he is employed by Kysor Unitest in Marion, Michigan, working the first shift, 7am to 3:30pm but that he is laid off for this week, 1-17 thru 1-21. He advised that he and his wife had been married for eleven years, being the first marriage for both. They have two children, Kelvin (8) and Jennifer (9). They moved to Michigan from [**REDACTED**] on 8-12-80. Prior to coming to Michigan they both had been employed at Costal Auto Parts."

What follows are blank pages. Whatever information Alvin Roberson supplied to investigators on the day his wife was murdered remains unavailable to the public, as does almost every word of every witness statement included in the Janette Roberson murder investigation file the Michigan State Police has conducted, to date.

Back at Gambles, before they were allowed to leave, short interviews were held with the employees and patrons who were still at the store, among whom were David Engels, John Engels, Flossie Earnest, Angie Tillie, Thomas Hawkins, Elke Johnson and David Sandlin.

As of this writing, Thomas Hawkins is incarcerated in the Saginaw Correctional Facility on multiple counts of Criminal Sexual Conduct, with an earliest release date of 2030. One has to assume that since he had to provide fingerprints at some point in that process, they've been compared to those at the Roberson murder scene and he's been ruled out. Or, you don't have to assume anything of the kind, rather, feel free to entertain the possibility that perhaps he did kill Janette, then cleaned up somehow and stood around the store waiting for her body to be found, then waited a little more for cops to arrive, and a little bit more after that to be interviewed, before he decided to go home.

I'm gonna go ahead and assume he's not our guy.

On the day Janette Roberson was murdered, Hawkins may have visited Gambles twice—once to bring Karl Johnson to the store, and once to drive his wife, Elke, later in the day, at least according to Karl Johnson, former husband of Elke Johnson:

"Our muffler was broken on our car, so I think Tom Hawkins drove me down to the store so I could sell our baby gerbils to Janette. It must have been between ten and eleven. I waited in the basement [pet department] for about fifteen minutes and then I went back upstairs and asked the manager when Janette would be back. He informed me that her husband had been there a couple of times and she might have gone home with him. I did not ask further questions. Tom drove me home and Elke took the gerbils again later, but she called me from the store and said Janette had been murdered and that she would be questioned by the police. The police never asked me anything until we were in Germany. I had told "Dan"* about Janette's murder and they were interested in his response when I told him, but I did not remember anything unusual."

*("Dan" is a pseudonym.)

Elke does not recall Hawkins driving her to the store that day, but admits her memory of details is bad, some three decades later. To his recollection, her ex-husband Karl believes Thomas Hawkins drove Elke because their car was not in service on that day. Karl said, "I believe it was the store manager I spoke to. I talked to him a few weeks later and he told me he was convinced her husband did it. He said it was unusual for [the husband] to come into the store as often as he did that day. He was convinced Janette's husband killed her."

Hawkins, as well as "Dan" lived in the same apartment complex as Janette Roberson. They would both be questioned by Michigan State Police in the months and years following the murder.

"I think "Dan" was fascinated with Janette," Karl said. "He spent as much time as he could with her, and she was very patient with him. In my opinion, he was in love with her."

When asked about the gerbils, why he would be bringing them back to the store to Janette, Karl clarified. "We bought the gerbils from [Janette] and she told me to bring the babies in to sell them back to her. She said they sell good so she would buy them back."

When asked about Janette's relationship with Hawkins, Karl said, "Elke was friends with Janette. I do not think Tom [Hawkins] knew her, and if he did, it was casual. Elke spent time with Janette and we were in her home a few times. We had aquariums and gerbils so we went to Gambles when we needed food or accessories."

When my assistant spoke to her the first time, Elke Johnson maintained she was the one who found Janette and alerted an employee, presumably Angie Tillie. When I spoke to her on the phone, weeks later, she said she'd been thinking about it and it's possible she first saw Janette *after* she went up to get an employee that last time, Angie Tillie, and may have seen the body over Angie's shoulder. This many years later, she couldn't be sure, and she started doubting her own memory, but her first instinct was that she found the body and alerted Angie Tillie. According to her, she was up and down those stairs looking for someone to help her a few times and nobody seemed to know where Janette was.

Elke said she went back to Gambles with the gerbils that day sometime around 2pm. She went downstairs. No Janette. She waited in the pet department for what she says was about twenty minutes. Nothing. She went back upstairs to ask where Janette was and a female employee said she was at lunch. According to Elke, this process was repeated three or four times. She'd go back downstairs to the pet department, wait fifteen or twenty more minutes, then go upstairs and ask if Janette had returned. The employee kept saying she was at lunch. Elke thought, 'That's a *long* lunch.' She felt like she'd waited a really long time.

"After the last inquiry upstairs, I thought perhaps Janette just got too busy with birds and did not check to see if a customer was outside. So I pressed against the door to peek in and called her name. I saw Janette on the floor. Her hair was red with blood, her face beaten in, and there was a pool of blood around her head on the floor."

Elke hurried upstairs to inform the woman she'd already spoke to several times. "I don't remember what I said to her. I assume I told her I found Janette on the floor. It's all really a blur after that."

She did remember them locking the doors and keeping everyone there at some point. When pressed on times, Elke said it felt like she was at Gambles for around an hour waiting for Janette, between going up and downstairs each time.

"All I remember is being very angry that someone could do such a thing to someone as nice as she was."

According to the ME report, Janette was found at approximately 3:50pm by a fellow employee and she was last seen alive at approximately 1:25pm. EMT Gary McGhee remembers her being "cool, not cold" and according to him, it likely had not just happened. This would tend to corroborate Elke's memory of events, given it is noted in the MSP report that she was at the store when the body was found, and felt she'd been there at least an hour. Even if she got there closer to three o'clock and was up and down those stairs for about an hour, the killer had probably come and gone by the time she arrived because she saw and heard nothing out of the ordinary while she was down in the pet department.

Still, Elke remains haunted by the possibility that the killer was in the back room of the pet department, having just murdered her friend when she arrived, and that he somehow snuck out of the basement, possibly via the back stairway in the expanded-into area, during one of the times she went upstairs to ask after Janette. According to Elke's recollection, she walked around the pet store and looked at the aquariums during the period of time she spent in the basement. Since they were installed within the walls between the pet department and back room, if there was someone moving around back there while she was looking at the fish, there's a chance she'd have seen them. But she saw nothing out of the ordinary.

If the killer had already come and gone by the time Elke arrived at Gambles—and presuming she arrived sometime nearer to three o'clock and spent the next fifty minutes, or so, going up and down from the pet department to the main store upstairs before the body was discovered—it would indicate the attack occurred sometime between 1:25, the last time Janette was seen according to the ME report, and around 3pm, when Elke arrived. I should note that I have never found anyone who saw Janette around the time of 1:25. None of the customers I spoke to who were there that afternoon around that time saw her. Just Gene Johnson around 11:30. Perhaps the 1:25 time was the last time *another employee* said they saw her. What is clear is that at some point, *none* of the employees could say where Janette was when asked.

It didn't occur to Elke until much later how eerily quiet the birds were while she was down in the pet department, given they normally made a lot of noise. To her, it felt like they were too quiet.

The other employee noted on the MSP report as one of the "employees and patrons who were still at the store" and participated in a "short interview" that day was David Sandlin. According to his wife, David Sandlin (now deceased) was hired to work at Gambles mainly on truck days. Sometime shortly after the murder, to her recollection, the police came and took his clothes to be tested. Mr. Sandlin told his wife absolutely nothing about the day, other than Janette had been murdered. He had been in the military, his wife said, and had protected her from all of that. It stood to reason he was doing the same regarding Janette's death. It was something upsetting and he didn't like to upset her. He was protective, she said.

When contacted in prison regarding his memory of events, Thomas Hawkins—another of the store patrons who participated in a "short interview" that day, and was also noted to have been in the vicinity of the body—wasn't inclined to talk. He sent the following letter. It's clear he's not exactly chummy with police. Given where he is and why, it's no wonder.

Jim
Im very sorry to inform you that I cannot be of any help to you on this. The Reed City State Police post should have done things different. Detective George Pratt and Detective Jim Southworth were to interested in harrasing inocent people rather than getting on there jobs and finding the man I discribbed to them comming out of Gambles that day. Reed City State Police Post has not changed at all over the years. They still do not do there jobs. If they did, you wouldnt have had to write me in prison. Again, I am sorry I cannot be of any help on this matter.

Sincerely Yours
[illegible]

P.S. Do not worrie about the stamped envelope thing, its not a big deal.

January 19, 1983 was a long night for the police. According to the Cadillac PD report, Sheriff Needham of the Osceola County Sheriff's office contacted them at 10:48pm to request assistance in processing the scene. At 10:50pm, Sgt. Lund of Cadillac called Officer Doornbos at home and by 11:00pm he was at the station in Cadillac. Along with Sgt. Bailey of Cadillac, Doornbos left at 11:18pm en route to Reed City. Cadillac is roughly thirty minutes from Reed City, so they'd have arrived sometime just prior to midnight and they were quick to note who was present when they got to the Gambles store. From their report:

When they arrived at 114 Upton, Reed City, they found Patrolman Finkbeiner (RCPD) at the back door. At that time, these are the people they noted as having been in the basement: Deputies Kingsbury and Oyster – Osceola County Sheriff's Dept.; Patrolman John Lucha – Reed City officer; Chief Rathbun – Reed City Police Chief; Detective George Pratt – Michigan State Police, Reed City; Laren Thorson – Evidence Tech.

From the Cadillac PD report: "When we arrived at Reed City we went to the back door of [**REDACTED**] which was the back of the Gambles store. We were met there by a city officer of Reed City. He let us in and advised that [**REDACTED**] was in the basement and showed us how to get there. Once in the basement we met with Laren. He advised that he had worked his way down the steps and to the cabinet with the cash register on it. He asked if we would start in the middle of the room and work the aquariums there and work our way back."

The area referred to is the pet store itself, which had to be thoroughly scoured for evidence, in addition to the back room where Janette was found. Just the latent print lifting alone must have been an overwhelming job. Anywhere the public moves in and out of with regularity could have hundreds, if not thousands of prints. Based on a supplemental Cadillac Police Department report I was able to obtain, the technicians who were called to assist Laren Thorson lifted a number of prints from the pet department, as well as found and turned over an object of possible evidentiary value before finally leaving the secured building at 4:01am.

The Crime

"The partially clad body of a 27 year old woman was found slain in the basement of the Gambles store in Reed City." According to Michigan State Police Detective Sgt. George Pratt, "We have no motive and no prime suspect. It was a violent type cause of death."

The article in *The Pioneer* newspaper the day after the murder, January 20th, went on to say that Janette had been a store employee for a little over six months and was working downstairs in the pet department when she was murdered. Robbery was not a motive according to "officials who were interrogating subjects who had been in and out of the store."

"One subject, who had been in the store and was known to be leaving town was stopped and taken off a bus in Big Rapids for questioning. However, the subject is not in custody and is not believed to be connected with the murder, authorities said."

The Michigan State Police report states, "On January 20, 1983 officers working on the homicide from all agencies met in the Reed City Police Department with an agreement reached for this location to be utilized as the investigation center. News releases were made for information to be called to the State Police Post in Reed City. As the tips began to filter in, they were assigned to officers of the investigating agencies for follow-up. The Gambles store, which had been secured by the undersigned [Det. Pratt], was re-checked again for anything overlooked the previous day."

On Friday the 21st, two days after the murder, police began interviewing witnesses. They had done brief interviews with the employees and store patrons still in the Gambles store on the day of the murder, but it was not until Friday that these same witnesses were questioned at length.

According to the Michigan State Police report, Angie Tillie, Bonnie Engels, and John Engels were all questioned on Friday by Detective Pratt, along with Hiram Thompson – a salesman who'd stopped into the store that day. Detective Southworth (along with Det. Sgt. John Waber from the Rockford MSP Post) interviewed David Sandlin and a woman by the name of Patricia Knapp, who lived in the same apartment complex as Janette.

That same day, *The Pioneer* ran an article and Janette's obituary. The article was titled **$2,000 Offered for Conviction**. "In the aftermath of Wednesday's brutal slaying, no suspects have been taken into custody as of late Thursday afternoon." The same article says that according to the autopsy report, as noted by Osceola County prosecutor James Talaske, "Mrs. Roberson died from a blow to the head with an instrument or instruments unknown."

At that time Prosecutor Talaske would not comment on whether Janette Roberson had been sexually assaulted, but went on to say, "Anyone who may have seen or heard something that was unusual in or around the Gambles store between 1 and 4pm is urged to contact the Michigan State Police Post in Reed City."

From Detective George Pratt: "We are looking for an individual who made a purchase of fish food, strainer, siphon and a thermometer who may have seen something that would be helpful in the investigation. I urge this individual to call us at any time at the state police post." Detective Pratt went on to say the store had a receipt detailing the purchases and he stressed that the person who made them was not a suspect, but that they may have information.

The article mentioned that the Reed City Chamber of Commerce, area merchants and several citizens had raised $2,000 reward money for the "person or persons who supply a clue or clues which lead to the arrest and conviction of the murderer."

Talaske made a final plea: "Again, if anyone may have seen someone trying to get rid of something, or maybe even [saw] someone who had blood on their clothing—which I'm assuming would have been somewhat obvious—please call the state police post at 832-2221." He added, "It just kind of shocks your sense of security when this sort of thing happens in a nice, small town such as Reed City."

Obituary:

> REED CITY — Mrs. Janette Roberson, 27, of Meadowview Apartments, Reed City died Wednesday January 19th. She was born October 25, 1955 in Detroit. She was married in Georgia to Alvin Roberson who survives. Also surviving are one daughter, Jennifer (9) and one son, Kelvin (8); her parents, Marion Fisher of LeRoy and Ralph Fisher of Traverse City; her grandmother Ethel Clark of LeRoy; two sisters, Mrs. Anthony (Marlene) Boone of South Carolina and Mrs. Donald (Lana) Mason of Hamburg, Michigan, and one brother, Kelvin Fisher of LeRoy.
>
> She came to Reed City 2 ½ years ago from Georgia and had worked as a clerk at the Gambles store. She was a member of the Kingdom Hall of Jehovah's witnesses. Services will be 3pm Sunday at McDowell Funeral Home. Burial will be in Woodland Cemetery.

On Saturday the 22nd *The Pioneer* didn't have much to add to what they'd already reported in previous days. "Police said Roberson died from a blow to the head from a heavy blunt object," was a slight variation on their earlier description of "object or objects unknown." It was noted that "Police are looking for two women who purchased fish equipment and may have witnessed the crime." They went on to add the women were not suspects "...but [police] feel they may have important information concerning the bizarre death."

Clearly those specific customers were being sought because there was a possibility they may have crossed paths with the killer—at least in the minds of law enforcement at the time.

Prosecutor Talaske went on to describe the basement as "...comprised of half pet supplies and half storage area." He said Janette had been described by fellow employees as a woman who was easy to get along with and that "...there had been no reported problems in the store during the past few weeks." He concluded by noting that police were checking into the possibility of someone hiding in the basement before the attack but said, "There is no evidence to suggest it."

The only person listed in the Michigan State Police report as having been interviewed that Saturday the 22nd was Theodore Platz. Platz was an officer with the Reed City Police Department who had assaulted two Michigan State Police troopers and a resident at The Buckboard Bar (next door to Gambles) a month before the murder. In the MSP report regarding Janette Roberson's murder it says, *"Theodore Platz was interviewed on January 22, 1983 regarding his attendance at the Gambles store on January 19, 1983."*

Earlier in the report, Detective Pratt noted: "Northern Counties Evidence Service had been requested to do the scene prior to the Undersigned's arrival with Director Laren Thorson coming to the scene being assisted by Evidence Technicians Sgt. Marvin Doornbos of the Cadillac Police Department, Sgt. David Bailey of the Wexford County Sheriff's Department, PO Theodore Platz of the Reed City Police Department and D/Sgt. James Southworth of the Osceola County Sheriff's Department along with the Undersigned in processing the crime scene."

It is unclear when Officer Platz arrived, or who called him, although former Osceola County Prosecutor James Talaske told me Platz was present when he arrived at the scene. According to Northern County Evidence Service technician Laren Thorson, "I wasn't sure of his role at the scene." No other law enforcement officers or medical personnel are listed as having been fingerprinted or formally interviewed. When I spoke to EMT Gary McGhee, he told me that he and the other technicians were not printed. In fact, at that time, he believed they didn't even wear gloves to crime scenes. He had a specific recollection of cleaning his hands with alcohol pads from his kit that day because they were instructed not to use the sink in the store.

According to the incident report regarding the assault at The Buckboard Bar involving Officer Platz, weeks prior to the murder, Michigan State Troopers Lisle and Norman were at the Reed City Post when the barmaid phoned. Trooper Lisle took the call and she asked who was on duty for Reed City PD.

> "Sgt. Horchner attempted to raise a Reed City PD car but obtained no reply. Suddenly the complainant was heard to yell over the phone, "Hey, Hey!" Trooper Lisle then indicated that he was still on the phone and the complainant asked that a patrol unit be sent as Ted Platz was in the bar drunk and beating on one of the patrons and she wanted him to leave. Troopers Lisle and Norman responded and Sgt. Horchner stated that he would get a hold of the Reed City Police Chief and ascertain if anyone from Reed City PD was working and advise them of the incident. While en route, radio traffic from the Post advised that no one was working for Reed City PD and that the Reed City Chief was not going to respond and advised that he wanted our department to handle the incident."

(**NOTE**: Notice the MSP State Post is dispatching this call, as Gary McGhee and Osceola County dispatcher Raymond Haight described was the norm.)

While the troopers tried to contact Police Chief Rathbun multiple times, they were eventually told by him that he was not coming to the scene and they were instructed to "Do what they must do." Rathbun held a party that night which Officer Platz had attended, according to an interview he did with *The Osceola Herald* newspaper in March following his firing. There were multiple witnesses to the incident at The Buckboard. According to the barmaid, Platz came into the bar around 12:30am, she served him one drink, and it was obvious he was already inebriated. He sat down next to a couple that he knew—a husband and wife—and began a conversation. At some point he referred to the female as a "broad," to which the husband took exception. He told Platz not to make comments about his wife and a brief argument ensued, which then settled back into a conversation shortly thereafter. "Moments later," according to the witness report of the barmaid, she heard the husband say, "One of these times you are going to be without your uniform."

Platz unzipped his jacket and said, "I don't have it on now!"

The barmaid's statement continued to describe what occurred: "[The husband] then asked Platz if he wanted to go out back and discuss the matter, and the two men got up and left the bar and walked into the restroom together. It was at this time that [*the barmaid*] phoned the State Police requesting officers. [*The barmaid*] states after hanging up the phone she heard loud voices and loud thumping noise coming from the men's restroom. At this point a young man also seated at the bar got up and said to the barmaid, "I am sorry all this is happening. I'll be right back." [*The young man*] went into the restroom and the barmaid heard loud voices again and it sounded like the walls were going to come down. "I [*the barmaid*] went to the men's restroom door and opened it and found Platz holding [*the young man*] against the wall by the neck and yelling, 'I don't need any motherf----- kid telling me what to do,' then Platz DROVE [*the young man*] to the floor hard!" At that time I went back to the bar and the State Police officers came through the front door. Platz, coming from the restroom towards the bar, saw the State Police officers and stated, "What is the State Police doing in my City!" Tpr. Norman asked me to tell Ted Platz to leave and I did. At this time, Platz was telling the other officer that he was not going to leave. The officers spoke with Platz asking him to leave, then Platz grabbed the officers and he was taken from the bar."

The young man—listed as a 28 year old bar patron—also gave a statement. "Mr. Platz came into the bar and called [REDACTED's] wife a broad. At this time they started to argue. After a short time they went into the bathroom. We in the bar could still hear them arguing so I went into the bathroom to quiet them down. I told them that all I wanted was a quiet drink and Platz told me to get out. I said that we were being bothered by the noise and then Platz shoved me against the wall. He then shoved me into the urinal and punched me in the (left) eye. He then left the bathroom and went back to the bar area. At this time the State Police arrived. Mr. Platz was arrested and transported to jail. Prior to being transported to jail, Platz was giving the State Police a hard time as to if he was leaving the bar or not. The barmaid had already told Mr. Platz that he was supposed to leave. Mr. Platz at this time pulled away from one of the officers and told him that he would leave when the barmaid told him to, which she had already done. Mr. Platz then argued with the State Police for a few minutes. After this argument Mr. Platz pushed away from the State Police, the officers had to use force to restrain Mr. Platz as he grabbed both officers and they had to handcuff him for transportation."

When the young man was asked by Tpr. Norman who or what started the confrontation, he said, "Mr. Platz grabbed both officers by their coats and started pushing them backwards."

The husband—who wasn't all that happy with Mr. Platz calling his wife a broad—also gave a statement. "At about 12:05am Officer Ted Platz came into the Buckboard bar in Reed City. I have known Ted for a long time and always been able to talk to him. This time was different. He called my wife a broad. I was mad because he said that. He started to talk about things that happened a few years ago. My wife moved because she didn't want to hear him. I asked him if he would talk to me in the restroom. We went into the restroom and Ted Platz and I started discussing things, probably loud, and Mr. [*young man*] came in the restroom and started yelling at Ted. Ted yelled at him and hit him in the face, and hit him in the face again. He (Ted) turned him around and hit him again. We then went out of the restroom and the bartender asked everyone to leave. There were two State Police officers telling Ted to come along with them. He (Ted) said "No way," not until the bartender tells him to leave, so then he antagonized the State Police until they had to use force and take him to the floor, when glass and bottles and chairs were broken in the bar."

When the husband was asked by Tpr. Norman who or what started the confrontation he said "Ted Platz wouldn't leave, I did not see who started the pushing first."

86106127 ~~86~~727

UD-110 (Rev. 8-79) FILE COPY

MICHIGAN DEPARTMENT OF STATE POLICE	Original Date	Complaint No.
☐ Supplementary Complaint Report	December 21, 1982	62-2282-82
☒ Additional Complaint Page No. 3	Date of Supplementary Report	File Class 1300-2

INVESTIGATION OF AN ASSUALT AND ASSUALT ON POLICE OFFICERS

ARRIVAL AT SCENE:

Officers arrived at the Buckboard Bar and upon entering found Victim#1, ██████ sitting with his back towards the door, on the South end of the Bar. The complainant, ██████, was behind the bar on the south end. Mr. ██████ was just sitting down to the bar towards the north end and about in the middle. ██████ was seated at the bar in the stool next to where Mr ████ was just sitting down and to the south. And the suspect, THEODORE EARL PLATZ, was walking towards the south end of the bar from the area of the rest-rooms and as officers were viewed by the suspect he stopped just behind the now seated ████.

TPR LISLE moved to where Mr ████ was sitting and inquired as to what was happending. At this time Mr. SMITH advised that everything was alright now and it didn't matter.

TPR NORMAN approached the complainant and was inquiring as to what had occurred.

The suspect yelled at officers, "NORMAN & LISLE; "WHAT THE HELL IS THE STATE POLICE DOING IN MY CITY". TPR LISLE responded by telling him they had been asked to come to the bar as there was no one working for Reed City PD. The suspect then yelled,"OH HELL, I'M TIRED OF YOU TWO WORKING IN MY CITY." "YOU WANT TO KNOW WHAT HAPPENED? I TELL YOU WHAT HAPPENED, I HIT THAT SON OF A BITCH." And pointed to Mr.████ And further added, " I HIT HIM RIGHT IN THE HEAD, NO YOUNG PUNK IS GOING TO TELL ME WHAT TO DO!"

Tpr LISLE then inquired of Mr. ████ if he had been hit and he replied, "YES". And Tpr LISLE asked if Mr. PLATZ had been the one who struck him and he again replied, "YES." Tpr LISLE then asked if he was alright or if he was hurt and he replied that he was "OK".

TPR NORMAN ascertained from the complainant that an assualt had occurred and the suspect had committed the assualt and that she wanted him to leave. Tpr NORMAN then requested the complainant to inform the suspect to leave and she turned to the suspect and advised him that she wanted him to leave. The suspect made no movements to leave and continued to yell obscenities at Mr. ████ and both officers.

ATTEMPTS TO PERSUADE THE SUSPECT TO LEAVE:

The suspect while still yelling obscenities moved towards the south end of the bar and stopped. Officers then moved to the suspect and informed him that he had to leave. The suspect, yelled; I'M NOT LEAVING BECAUSE THE STATE POLICE SAY I HAVE TO LEAVE AND I HIT THAT SON OF A BITCH(pointing again to Mr. ████), ARREST ME, GO AHEAD ARREST ME! Tpr LISLE advised the suspect that the complainant wanted him to leave. And he replied, I'M NOT GOING TO LEAVE, AND THE STATE POLICE CAN'T MAKE ME, I'LL ONLY LEAVE IF SHE SAY'S I HAVE TOO and pointed to the Complainant. At this time Tpr LISLE asked the complainant to again tell Mr PLATZ he had to leave. The complainant looked at the suspect and then the suspect asked, "DO YOU WANT ME TO LEAVE". And the complainant replied,"YES, TED, I THINK IT IS FOR THE BEST".

The suspect then replied, "OK, I'M LEAVING BUT ONLY BECAUSE SHE WANTS ME TOO AND NOT BECAUSE YOU TWO SAY I HAVE TO, FUCK THE STATE POLICE! The suspect then started to move towards the South doorway past the officers. But the suspect then stopped and turned around and walked back up to the officers and yelled, "YOU TWO CAN'T GO AROUND PUSHING PEOPLE AROUND, AND YOU, NORMAN, I DON'T CARE IF YOU WERE SHOT BEFORE, IT DOESN'T GIVE YOU THE RIGHT TO PUSH PEOPLE EITHER." Tpr NORMAN then informed the suspect again that he would have to leave and if he didn't then we would have to escort him out. The suspect became visible upset then,

Reporting Officer	Reviewer
TPRS LISLE & NORMAN [signature]	[signature]

[redacted]

0 0 6 1 0 6 1 2 2 7 8 2 5 7 2 8

UD-110 (Rev. 8-79) FILE COPY

MICHIGAN DEPARTMENT OF STATE POLICE	Original Date	Complaint No.
☐ Supplementary Complaint Report	December 21, 1982	62-2282-82
XX Additional Complaint Page No. #3	Date of Supplementary Report	File Class 1300-2

INVESTIGATION OF AN ASSUALT AND ASSUALT ON POLICE OFFICERS

ASSUALT ON TPRS LISLE & NORMAN:

Upon hearing Tpr NORMAN's statement that if he didn't leave that officers would have to escort him out of the bar. The suspect became visibly upset. And yelled, "YOU TWO THINK YOU CAN MAKE ME LEAVE" and then repeated the same statement. Officers made no reply and the suspect raised both of his hands and pointed a finger of each hand towards the officers and yelled,"YOU TWO CANT MAKE ME LEAVE " and gestured with the pointing finger of each hand towards the officers. Suddenly the suspect reached and moved towards the officers and grabbed the front of each officers jacket and drove with his body and hands the officers back. The officers were forced backwards and into two tables and several chairs. The suspect continued to push forcifully the officers backwards. The action casued the tables to be overturned as well as the chairs and caused empty bottles on the tables to be broken.

SUSPECT SUBDUED:

TPR LISLE was able to free himself from the grasp of the suspect and gained a submissive hold on the suspect's right arm and applied leverage. This action coupled with the driving action of the suspect caused the officers to slam to the floor along with the suspect. The suspect having hit the floor forcifully layed some what passively and Tpr LISLE maintained the enought pressure to insure he would remain passive until Tpr NORMAN cuffed the suspect.

Also Tpr NORMAN had also gained a leverage hold on the suspect's left arm which also contributed to the suspect being quickly subdued and which aided officers in preventing any further injuries to be sustained by the officers.

SUSPECT'S INJURIES:

The suspect sustained a contusion to the forehead caused when both the officers and the suspect slammed to the floor. Also the suspect had a small amount of blood just below the nose which also occurred upon impact with the floor. These were the extent of the injuries sustained by the suspect while in the custody of Tprs LISLE & NORMAN.

OFFICER'S INJURIES:

TPR NORMAN sustained an abrasion to the knuckle of the little finger of the right hand and contusion and abrasions to the front of the shin of the right leg.

TPR LISLE sustained a slightly wrench left elbow and contusion to the back of the left calf muscle of leg.

THREAT STATEMENTS:

After the suspect had been subdued and was being led by Tpr LISLE out of the bar the suspect yelled; "NORMAN, YOU'RE DEAD, I'M GOING TO KILL YOU." "YOU MOTHER FUCKING SON OF A BITCHING NIGGER."

At the Osceola Co Jail the suspect continued to say that he was going to kill that nigger son of a bitch and that he will never see the daylight again. These statements were repeated over and over by the suspect.

Reporting Officer	Reviewer
TPRS LISLE & NORMAN [signature]	[signature]

0 6 1 0 6 1 2 3 2 7 7 2 9

UD-110 (Rev. 8-79) FILE COPY

MICHIGAN DEPARTMENT OF STATE POLICE	Original Date	Complaint No.
☐ Supplementary Complaint Report	December 21, 1982	62-2282-82
☒ Additional Complaint Page No. 14	Date of Supplementary Report	File Class 1300-2

INVESTIGATION OF AN ASSUALT AND ASSUALT ON POLICE OFFICERS

OTHER STATEMENTS OF THE SUSPECT:

The suspect while being handcuffed by Tpr NORMAN and held submissively by TPR LISLE stated twice, " I'M SORRY LISLE".

And just as the suspect and Tpr LISLE started throught the door going out the suspect stated," 16 YEARS I'VE BEEN A POLICE OFFICER AND I ONLY HAVE ONE MORE YEAR BEFORE RETIREMENT." AND NOW THAT'S GONE.

REQUEST FOR ASSISTANCE:

Just prior to officers attempts to persuade the suspect to leave the Buckboard Bar, Tpr LISLE used his Portable radio to contact the post for the Reed City PD Chief to come to the scene as the suspect was very intoxicated and it was felt that the suspect would not be cooperative with officers and it was their intentions to avoid violence with the off-duty Reed City Police Officer.

After the assualt by the suspect on the officers and the subsequent arrest of the suspect; TPR LISLE again contacted the post via portable radio and advised the post of the assualt and arrest of the suspect. Tpr LISLE again asked if the Reed City Police Chief was enroute to the scene. The Post advised that the Chief was not coming to the scene and for the officers to do what they must do, in the words of the Chief.

The Post advised that seeing the Chief would not come for backup he had at the suggestion of the Reed City PD Chief called for an Osceola Co Sherrif Department Unit for backup.

SUSPECT TRANSPORTED TO OSCEOLA COUNTY:

As Tpr LISLE and the suspect were exiting the bar, Officer DAVIS of the Osceola County Sherrif's Department arrived. The suspect was placed into the County Patrol Unit with the prisoner cage due to the suspect's still violent condition. The suspect was then transported to the Osceola County Jail.

OSCEOLA COUNTY PROSECUTOR:

The Osceola County Prosecutor was contacted by TX and the incident was reported and afterwards the Prosecutor advised that he would meet with the Officers and issue aWarrant for Assualt on a Police Officer. Officers will seek a two count warrant & another for assualt.

BOND:

Tpr LISLE contacted the magistrate for the 77th District Court in Reed City, J. WAKEMAN, and she placed a $5,000 Cash bond on the suspect or $50,000 C/S.

COPIES:

Prepaired for the prosecutors office by undersign were of the complaint,criminal history and the driving record of the suspect THEODORE PLATZ.

Reporting Officer	Reviewer
TPRS. LISLE & NORMAN	

On December 29th, less than a month before Janette Roberson's murder, *The Pioneer* ran a short couple paragraphs on the assault.

RC officer pleads innocent to assault

By JUDY ZAJEC
Special to the Pioneer

REED CITY — A Reed City police officer has pleaded innocent to charges of assaulting a man and two state police troopers while off-duty at the Buckboard Bar on Upton Avenue Dec. 21.

Theodore Earl Platz, 42, of Reed City, was released on personal recognizance and $1,000 bond on the two charges. He demanded examination and waived the 12-day rule in 77th District Court.

Platz is charged with assaulting Robert A. Smith at the Reed City bar. Troopers Gary L. Lisle and Harry E. Norman Jr. investigated that complaint. Platz allegedly assaulted the officers when they arrived on the scene.

Reed City Police Chief Phillip Rathbun said his department did not reply to the call as there was not an officer on duty at that time. It was a routine "off-time" for the city department.

Platz is on sick leave at this time. He called in saying he had a broken hand, Rathbun said.

According to Chief Phillip Rathbun in the February 22nd 1983 edition of *The Pioneer*, "Effective February 18, 1983, Theodore Platz was notified of his termination of employment with the city."

According to City Manager James Nordstrom, "Under the union contact, an officer can use vacation and sick time and still collect a paycheck while incapacitated."

What is unclear—at least from the Michigan State Police report of Janette Roberson's murder—is whether Theodore Platz was technically suspended at the time he was assisting in processing the crime scene. One can only imagine what a jury would think when tasked to evaluate evidence collected at a crime scene where there are already significant issues like people inadvertently walking through blood and witnesses allowed to leave the scene before being questioned, but then add to that the presence of an officer who'd assaulted two state troopers and a resident a month prior.

On Sept 12, 1983 Theodore Platz pled guilty to Attempted Resisting, Obstructing or Assaulting a Police officer in Osceola Circuit court before Judge Lawrence C. Root.

Apparently, Osceola County is extremely forgiving. Mr. Platz went on to become the head of the probation department for Osceola County.

Proposal B

The assault at The Buckboard Bar in December of 1982 may have been a reflection of what was going on between law enforcement entities at the time of the murder. As I earlier noted, there were three different law enforcement entities located in Reed City in 1983, and it doesn't appear they were always interested in playing nice.

A Michigan State Police Department Amendment (Proposal B) was on the November 1982 ballot in Michigan as an initiated constitutional amendment and was heartily defeated. (Yes votes: 720,915; No votes: 2,111,802)

According to *Ballotpedia*, "Proposal B would have created a Michigan Department of State Police; provided for its personnel; prescribed its duties; and required minimum staffing."

An initiated constitutional amendment is an amendment to a state's constitution that comes about through the initiative process. Of the twenty-four states that have some degree of direct democracy, eighteen of them have a provision for initiated constitutional amendments. In several of these states, including Illinois, Massachusetts and Mississippi, the requirements for placing a proposed amendment on the ballot through an initiative process are so prohibitively difficult that the process has rarely if ever been used.

In this case, the voters were clear by an almost 75 percent margin. It is harder to determine, however, if that high margin was due to voters understanding what the proposal was about, or if police in general get such a bad rap, that anything they asked for would have been summarily declined at the ballot box. Depending on which law enforcement entity you asked at the time, you were likely to get a different answer as to what Proposal B even was. What surrounded it, though, was a great deal of contention.

On October 28, 1982, the Osceola County Herald ran an advertisement titled WHO THINKS PROPOSAL B IS BAD FOR MICHIGAN? Among the names on the list, along with their smiling faces, were both the Democratic and Republican candidates for Governor that year. You can't get both parties to agree on almost anything, but apparently in 1982, neither party wanted anything to do with Prop B if they were up for election. Even the director of the Michigan Department of State Police said *no thanks*.

Locally, it was Reed City Police Chief Phillip Rathbun and Osceola County Sheriff David Needham vs. the State Troopers. Dueling pieces ran together in the same edition of The Osceola County Herald.

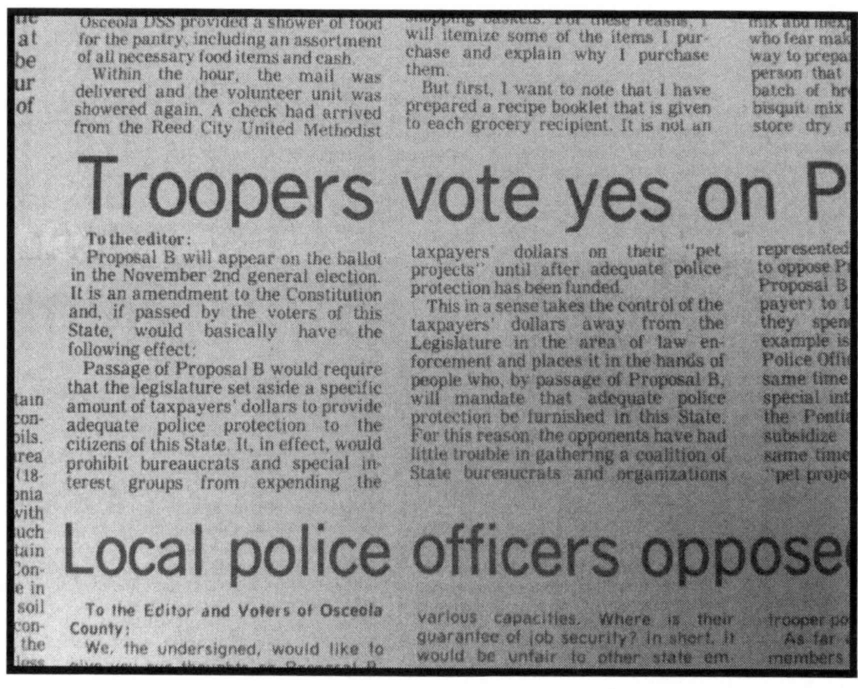
Osceola DSS provided a shower of food for the pantry, including an assortment of all necessary food items and cash.

Within the hour, the mail was delivered and the volunteer unit was showered again. A check had arrived from the Reed City United Methodist

will itemize some of the items I purchase and explain why I purchase them.

But first, I want to note that I have prepared a recipe booklet that is given to each grocery recipient. It is not an

Troopers vote yes on P

To the editor:

Proposal B will appear on the ballot in the November 2nd general election. It is an amendment to the Constitution and, if passed by the voters of this State, would basically have the following effect:

Passage of Proposal B would require that the legislature set aside a specific amount of taxpayers' dollars to provide adequate police protection to the citizens of this State. It, in effect, would prohibit bureaucrats and special interest groups from expending the taxpayers' dollars on their "pet projects" until after adequate police protection has been funded.

This in a sense takes the control of the taxpayers' dollars away from the Legislature in the area of law enforcement and places it in the hands of people who, by passage of Proposal B, will mandate that adequate police protection be furnished in this State. For this reason, the opponents have had little trouble in gathering a coalition of State bureaucrats and organizations

Local police officers oppose

To the Editor and Voters of Osceola County:

We, the undersigned, would like to

various capacities. Where is their guarantee of job security? In short, it would be unfair to other state em-

According to the city and county cops, it went a little deeper than the "**Keep Troopers on the Job**" bumper stickers that were all over town would have you believe. They alleged that the state troopers wanted to be placed under the state constitution. From the October 28th Herald Article titled **Local police officers opposed to Proposal B**:

> "First of all, they (the Troopers Association) would have the Dept. of State Police be the only department out of twenty as part of the constitution and guaranteed their jobs. How about the nineteen other departments which are equally as important to the operation of the state? We're sure they have equally as many, if not more, dedicated people who are serving the citizens of this state in their various capacities. Economically speaking, why guarantee a segment of public employees immunity to the checks and balances of good business?"

The State Troopers countered with this:

> "The opponents of Proposal B do not want you (the taxpayer) to tie their hands as to where they spend your tax dollars. An example is that in 1981 some 80 State Police officers were laid off and at the same time the Legislature, because of special interest pressures, had given the Pontiac Silverdome $800,000 to subsidize its purchase. Concern for where your hard earned tax dollars are being spent has been a long standing problem in Michigan. Now is *your chance to tell the legislature of this state where you want your tax dollar spent."*

Politics at its finest, to be sure. After Prop B was defeated in November of 1982, the Troopers again took to the press to air their thoughts. They were not happy campers. (*Figure 1*)

Even Theodore Platz—weeks after his termination from the Reed City Police Department—had something to say about Prop B within the context of his firing.

"It's not a secret that I had complained to the state police post in Reed City as well as my chief on the increased activities of two state police troopers, namely the troopers that arrested me," revealed Platz. "Also, I'm an officer who quite vocally opposed the Proposal B issue... much to the displeasure of several troopers. I should also note that after the proposal failed, some of the troopers held grudges against me."

One has to wonder if this sort of animosity between law enforcement officers played any part in the Janette Roberson murder investigation.

[redacted]

letters

Trooper comments on defeat of Proposal B

To the editor:

Elections have come and gone, and I, for one, am glad its over. It was entirely the worst mud-slinging campaign that I have ever heard. We are disappointed with the defeat of Proposal B. We will accept that as the voice of the people because that was their decision and that is the way the election process should work.

Perhaps the defeat of the proposal was our own fault, due to lack of good publicity. If that were the only reason we humbly accept the defeat and apologize for not giving the people the proper publicity. Our problem was we ran out of money.

We feel, however that our lack of supportive information was not the real reason for the failure. The real credit should go to the Michigan Sheriff's Association, the Michigan Association of Chiefs of Police, the Michigan Deputy Sheriffs Association, and the Police Officers Association of Michigan who collectively and with a lot of others garnered outside help got their heads together and put out some of the best propaganda that was in this election campaign. Their publicity, without exception to any single statement, was totally comprised of false statements, misleading statements or complete fallacies, which in turn misled the people, or confused them to the point that people voted no because they didn't know what to believe.

Those statements were a total surprise and a disappointment also. I still can believe that our local officials, people that we work with every day, would lower themselves to the level of mud-slinging politicians and personally endorse such material.

It was stated that we were sacrificing our integrity. I can't understand how. We simply put an issue on the ballot for the vote of the people. We told no lies, we printed no fallacies and we gve you, the people, no misleading statements. I think it would be rather foolish for us to even attempt a ballot issue on lies and fallacies. If anyone sacrificed their integrity, in my book, it was the mudslingers of the campaign, and I am sorry for them that they felt they had to put themselves in thuh position.

The literature said Michigan would become a "Police State" with the passage of the proposal. We asked only for an additional 114 men which would have put us up to the authorized enlisted strength that we had two years ago. Was it a police state then? They also said that Proposal B would threaten the future of neighborhood police and sheriff departments. Were they threatened two years ago? No, in fact the sheriff departments were "beefed" up with the secondary road patrols, House bill 416! They said it would write the Troopers and Sergeants union contract into the constitution. That is a flat out lie. There was no wording in the language of the proposal that said anything about our contract or our collective bargaining being a part of the constititutional amendment, and to say otherwise is lying.

I could go on and on but I'm not going to. In closing, I want to emphatically state that we had no intention of deceiving anyone. We are not a bunch of deceitful liars trying to "rip off the public" as was implicated. We are appalled by the malicious and vicious attack upon us by the aformentioned associations.

We hope that at least some of the people will have recognized the propaganda for what it truly was — political mudslinging. The people can rest assured that we still continue to do our job as we have always. We are a proud bunch of people and we have sworn to do the job for which we were hired. Nothing as changed because of the failure of proposal B.

There, I have said what I wanted to say. I feel there is a possibility of a response to this letter from someone wanting to defend their actions and I guess that is their prerogative. In any case, I feel the issue is dead, I have said all I am going to say and I will not respond to any more attacks.

Thank you for listening
Richard King
Michigan State
Police Troopers Association
Reed City
Post Representative

Figure 1

JANUARY

...FOUR DAYS AFTER THE MURDER

According to the Michigan State Police Report: "On Sunday January 23, 1983 the funeral of Janette Roberson at the McDowell Funeral Home, 138 West Slosson St., Reed City, MI was covered. Due to the weather and time of year, there was no interment."

In an email exchange, a friend of Janette's named Sharon mentioned an incident that she allegedly witnessed at the funeral:

> I worked briefly with Janette at Nartron in Reed City back in 1980 or 81. We worked on the same line. We weren't close friends by any means, but we were friendly acquaintances. She was such a kind person and I remember telling her she looked like Cheryl Ladd...she found that funny. She told me about sweet potato pie and I'd never heard of it, so she brought it to a potluck one day and I raved to her about how delicious it was. She was so happy about that! I took guitar lessons from [the same man Janette did, Ray Truman]. Janette is the one who told me about him because I had shared with Janette that I was interested in learning guitar and she gave me his name and told me she'd started taking lessons from him. He was the grandfather of one of the girls who worked at Nartron. Anyway, I began taking lessons from him. I took lessons for a year or two from him, can't really remember now. The summer before Janette's murder she was so excited because she and I were working on the same difficult song and she had practiced and practiced and finally mastered it! I on the other hand didn't practice as much and told her

> I still didn't have it down. The guitar teacher had told me how beautifully Janette played the song. He seemed proud of her. I believe his name was Ray Truman or Roy Truman. I think he was in his 70s at the time and couldn't walk well. After Janette's funeral, which he told me he attended, he shared with me that he'd told her husband [Alvin] after the funeral that Janette still owed money on the guitar she was buying from him. I remember he told me that her husband looked really oddly at him. I thought it was very odd/stupid of him to say something like that to a family member at the funeral! I didn't go back for any more lessons after that. The last time I saw Janette was when I stopped at the Dairy Depot in Reed City for ice cream. She was there with her two little kids and her mom getting cones. I was so happy to see her and asked what she was up to (she'd left Nartron a couple months prior to this). She said she had gotten a job at the pet store in the basement of Gamble's hardware and that she loved it. I told her how envious I was (we were all trying to find a job other than Nartron!) and that it sounded like a dream job and how lucky she was to have gotten out of Nartron. That struck me as so ironic. Later I remember her smiling/laughing and saying it was good to see me and then getting in the car. That was the last time I saw her.

Although the bit about Janette still owing Mr. Truman money for the guitar may have been mentioned at a highly inappropriate time, it was likely true. In a letter written by Janette to her father, Ralph Fisher, she mentions the guitar lessons.

Transcript of Janette's letter—pages 7 thru 10:

> I haven't done anything this morning. Got a guitar lesson after Mama leaves after lunch so I'd better go over that.
>
> Okay, that's over and done with. At least I did practice this week. The piece I'm learning is my 59th lesson and it's called *Say it with Music* adapted from Tchaikovsky's 5th 2nd movement.

Bud (the maintenance man) is clearing the snow out of the courtyard outside the kitchen window. He cleared most of it with his truck. Now he's going back over it with a miniature snowplow deal. It looks like a lawnmower tractor with a cab on top and a cute little snow plow in front. It looks so funny. I am sleepy. I'm going to bed early tonight. (That's what I always say.) I know I'm going to yawn all the way through my lesson and Mr. Truman will think that I think he's boring. Oh well.

Guitar lesson wasn't bad. Mr. Truman wants me to study Hawaiian guitar when I'm through with flat top. Did I tell you my guitar broke? It just sort of started to fold up. The neck came loose from the body and the bridge came unglued. Mr. Truman couldn't keep it in tune so I couldn't play it.

I felt pretty bad when he showed me where it was breaking, 'cause you can't play a broken guitar. He drove me over to Clare to look at some new ones and he bought one for me and told me I could pay him back $5.00 a week. It's a concert size like my other one, but has an adjustable neck. I even got a case with it. It's not a fancy name – not a Gibson or Fender. They had a Fender electric guitar, but they said they had to have $525.00 for it. They said it was a $900.00 guitar. That's not including the amplifier or case.

Did I tell you I have a little bluegill? A lady came down to the pet store with it and wanted to feed the turtle. The turtle couldn't catch it, and the boss said I had to get it out of the store because it was illegal for pet stores to have them. So I took him home and set up a 10 gallon tank for him. I haven't seen him eat yet, and I've had him about a week. I'm feeding him dried shrimp pellets, dried mosquito larvae, and dried flies. I started feeding him frozen beef heart, but he didn't eat it and it smelled up the tank. I know he'd like some worms but I can't find any. He's only 3 inches long. In the spring I'm going to turn him loose.

Well, I gave away three male gerbils and got that little black and white one from Tiffany. Everyone here is fine. Alvin is laid off from work for a week but we are doing

> good. I made a little extra last week because I worked an extra day and that helped. I really like my job. The boss is a little hard to like sometimes. I think she forgets that I haven't been in this business as long as she has.
>
> Oh well, the customers are nice, too. The ladies that work upstairs sometimes ask me to come up and have coffee with them in the morning. Well I guess, Daddy, that I'd better close this and stick it in the mailbox so you will get it before next year, so I'll talk to you later, okay? Love, Nette.

On January 25th *The Pioneer* described Janette's funeral.

"A somber throng of around 200 mourners paid their final respects to Mrs. Roberson at funeral services Sunday at McDowell Funeral Home in Reed City."

The article said police were still searching for the two women who purchased fish equipment on the day of the murder "...and may have witnessed the bizarre crime." Osceola County Prosecutor James Talaske went on to say the time of death occurred sometime between 2 and 3pm. "We are urging anyone who may have seen someone giving Mrs. Roberson a hard time or bothering her in any way prior to her death to call the state police post in Reed City." He added, "Someone may have even overheard something between Janette and her assailant that would be extremely beneficial to us."

The reward money had gone up to $2,700 and anyone wishing to donate was urged to contact Talaske at his office. Meanwhile, police were still busy interviewing witnesses. Detective Pratt interviewed Elke Johnson—Janette's friend who'd been in the store trying to bring back baby gerbils.

Thomas Hawkins—a customer in the store when the body was found, who is currently incarcerated—was interviewed on January 26th by Detective Pratt regarding his observations while in the store on the day of the murder.

Hiram Thompson—the salesman Detective Pratt had spoken to previously—was again questioned, this time by Det. Sgt. Eugene Ambs of the MSP Post #21.

Also on the 26th, Bonnie Engels—store owner David Engels' wife—contacted the police regarding possible evidence found at the scene. Four items were turned over by her to be used in analysis and for comparison purposes.

The opening paragraph of the *Osceola County Herald* on January 27th, 1983 reads as follows: "A Michigan State Police sketch artist will be in Reed City Wednesday, and will attempt to sketch several people who were seen in the Gambles store last week at the approximate time of Janette Roberson's death."

"This is a real baffler to say the least," from Prosecutor James Talaske. "We're checking out approximately 200 different tips at the present time, although nothing yet is concrete. The people the artist will sketch are not considered suspects, but may have valuable information concerning the murder." Talaske added, "The police are doing just a great job in this investigation, and have handled it in a very professional manner. State Police Detective George Pratt has investigated several murders in the past, and has considerable knowledge in this kind of work." His final plea, "Again, if anyone may have seen someone with Janette prior to the crime that may have been harassing her, or even just hanging around her a lot, please call the state police. We are seeking absolutely any source of information that could ultimately help us in solving this most unusual case."

On the 27th *The Pioneer* spoke with locals about the "grizzly murder." Colin Hayward—Chamber of Commerce Secretary—said, "The tragedy of Wednesday afternoon showed the worst in one individual, but the best in the community has surfaced and it's been heartwarming with pledges of support for the arrest and conviction of the perpetrator of this heinous crime. I would like to compliment the Reed City State Police post, the Osceola County Sheriff's Department, and the Reed City Police on the professional manner in which they have handled this tragedy."

Jim Nordstrom—City Manager—was equally complimentary of law enforcement. "The basic honest truth of the matter is that it's a tragedy. I think that the reward fund is reflected in the strength of our small city. I'm pleased with the cooperation between law enforcement agencies, as they have been working just great together in this investigation."

The local merchants, however, were more concerned about safety. John Lazzati—owner of Terra Pines Gift Shop in Reed City—had this to say: "I think that all of us are acting more cautiously than we have in the past. Perhaps it's the kind of caution we should have acted in all along. We're being more realistic since the murder, and realize this sort of unfortunate incident can happen in Reed City."

Winnie Snyder, Manager of Mutual Savings: "We have changed our store hours on Friday night, as we're closing now at 5:30. We had given thought for several months prior to the murder to closing earlier, but now in light of the murder we have changed our closing time. The murder was the final contributing factor to our early closing. It's just unbelievable and very tragic that something like this could take place in Reed City. I am very sorry for the family of the victim involved."

Reverend Richard Krugler of Trinity Lutheran Church said, "I think, like everyone else, I'm shocked. It brings us to the reality that evil exists in the world. Our prayers are with the family."

Also on the 27th Alvin Roberson was re-interviewed at length by Detective Pratt in the presence of his court appointed attorney, David Porteous. On January 31st Detective Pratt contacted the store owner, David Engels, about obtaining the names of the truck drivers who delivered supplies on the day of the murder. Three names and their contact information were turned over. The final paragraphs in the first supplemental report attached to the Michigan State Police report—dated Feb 1, 1983 but pertaining to the work done in January—read as follows:

REMARKS: Investigators in this matter have worked on a daily basis following up tips that have been turned in to the police regarding possible suspects and/or composite lookalikes. Several consultations have been held with other criminal investigators and others regarding this case. As of this writing, no strong suspects have been identified in this case.

COMPLAINT STATUS: Open.

FEBRUARY

On February 1st, 1983, *The Pioneer* released composite sketches.

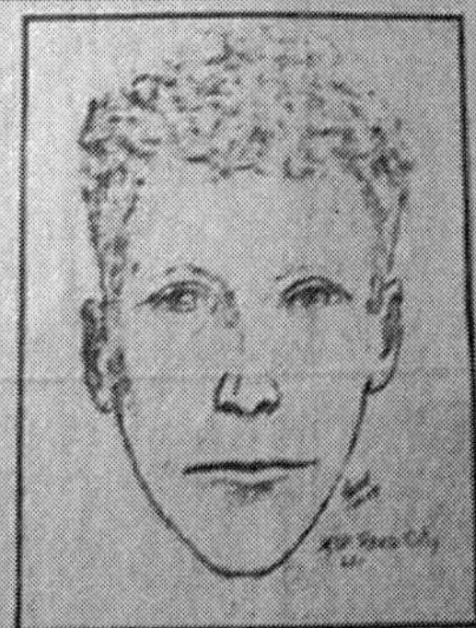

May have information about murder

Police release artist's sketches

REED CITY — Police officers investigating the Jan. 19 slaying of Janette Gale Roberson in the pet shop of the Gamble's department store in Reed City are requesting the assistance of the public in identifying a white male who may have a clue in connection with the grisly murder.

The man, approximately 20 to 30 years of age, about 5-foot-8 to 5-foot-9 in height, has light to blondish brown hair, weighs about 170 pounds and was possibly wearing a blue jacket.

Three sketches of the person, described by three different witnesses have been reproduced (see accompanying sketches). The person is believed to have been in the Gamble's store shortly before the estimated time Mrs. Roberson was murdered — between 2 and 3 p.m.

Det. Sgt. George D. Pratt of the Reed City state police post and Det. Sgt. James E. Southworth of the Osceola County Sheriff Department have emphasized that while officers are interested in talking with this person, he is not considered a suspect. Officers hope that he may have seen or heard something that may be of assistance to them.

Anyone knowing a person matching the description or one of the sketches is urged to contact the Michigan State Police at [illegible] at once.

Local groups, business persons and individuals have pledged [illegible] in reward money for information leading to the arrest and conviction of the perpetrator. Anyone else with any other information regarding the murder is also asked to please call the state police.

Flossie Earnest says she was one of the people who was questioned about this witness and gave a description. According to her, she was describing someone who frequented the pet store and had been in earlier that day on the day of the murder.

Police Still Searching for Murderer was splashed across the front page of the *Osceola County Herald* on February 3rd 1983, along with the sketches of the witness (or witnesses) they were looking for, a shot of the body being removed from the Gambles store, a picture of Janette herself, and a notable shot of an impromptu press conference held inside the Gambles store. In addition, there was a letter written to the killer by Janette's mother, Marion Fisher.

> To the murderer of Janette Roberson:
>
> Janette was a wonderful person—not only to her family and friends but to every person she ever came in contact with. She tried to help all creatures when they needed help—humans, birds, fish, plants, and animals alike. Her heart went out to everybody and everything. She is one of God's children. Yes, she had a heart, a heart as big as the universe itself. I love her, everybody loved her—except one person—you.
>
> Maybe you didn't know her, and then again maybe you did. But nevertheless, from the moment you committed the greatest sin against God and his children you were condemned to hell—a hell that will follow you every moment of your days... a hell that will increase in velocity until it will not let you live any longer on this earth. Our great God in heaven is the only one that will ever be able to help you now. Maybe, just maybe, he will find it in his heart to forgive you of your great sin and have mercy on your soul. Janette's soul is with her god. Her human body is lying in a coffin, and her husband and children are mourning for her just as I am. It will be hard for them to begin their lives again without their mother and wife. With God's help they will do it. However, there is still a shadow hanging over them—you, Janette's murderer.
>
> **My plea to you is to confess your sin and ask for God's mercy.**
>
> By our great God, I appeal to any person who was in the Gambles store on that fatal day or anyone having any information, no matter how small it may seem to you, to come forward. Your little bit of information will help put the puzzle together. Please get in touch with the state police, sheriff's department, or the Reed City police immediately, and may God bless you.
>
> Marion Fisher - Janette's Mother

On February 3, 1983, The Pioneer ran an article titled **Osceola Commissioners OK $2,000 for Reward Fund**. They approved a donation toward the reward money "for information leading to the arrest and conviction of the murder of Janette Roberson." This brought the total reward to $7,000. Prosecutor Talaske said in this article that the donations had ranged from five dollars to the $1,300 check donated by Norm Rautiola earlier in the week. Mr. Rautiola owned (and still owns) Nartron, where Janette had worked previous to the pet department at Gambles. Osceola County Prosecutor James Talaske said the donation would be a small price to pay if the reward worked.

"This thing is really hanging over our town. It effects everyone... more people are buying guns. It's the little things that are happening that change the feeling of the whole community."

On February 1st tip #200 was received from the Grand Haven MSP Post about a subject who "is not working and has a violent temper." A request was made to contact the subject to determine if he looked like the composites, as well as his whereabouts on January 19th 1983, especially from 1:00pm to 4:00pm.

That same day—regarding tip #185—information was received about another subject who apparently looked like the composite sketches and was in Reed City on the day of the murder. This subject was said to have possibly been at the unemployment office and Gambles. It was requested that the Paw Paw MSP Post contact the subject to determine more information about his whereabouts during the 1:00 to 4:00pm timeframe.

"In the event that it is learned either subject was in the Gambles store in Reed City on January 19, 1983, it is requested that it be determined who was with them, what may have been purchased, where it was paid for (location of cash register) and what the amount was, including what was used to pay for it. Also a complete clothing description of them or anyone with them, and anyone they might have seen. If possible obtain a Polaroid photograph of anyone that was in the store."

Between February 1st and 3rd multiple interviews were done by Detective Pratt. He interviewed Ralph Fisher (Janette's father) and

Christopher Casavettes – a patron of the store that day who (according to his son, Chris) had been there earlier that morning to make a purchase. David Sandlin was also re-interviewed, and a court order was obtained for clothing items that his wife mentioned the police had come and taken.

Marion Fisher, Janette's mother, was interviewed at length at this time. Based on her recollection of who showed up at Janette's apartment the night of the murder, "Dan" is interviewed by Detective Pratt. He lived at the same apartment complex as the Robersons and according to multiple witnesses I spoke to, appeared to have a "crush" on Janette.

Also during this time period, the Georgia Bureau of Investigation was contacted about obtaining any information they could on Alvin Roberson, who had lived in Georgia with Janette prior to them moving to Reed City. They would later contact Detective Pratt on February 16th to advise that they were "...unable to obtain any information of any problems with or between Mr. and Mrs. Roberson."

On February 10th, 1983 the *Osceola County Herald* ran an article titled **Murdered Clerk Had Received Calls**. According to the story, Osceola County officials had discovered a "new development" the previous week—that Janette had "allegedly received obscene telephone calls, and had received two calls in which an individual hung up the phone without speaking the day before she was murdered."

Osceola County Prosecutor James Talaske said, "It's my understanding that the phone rang twice and the person on the other end hung up without saying anything. The calls could have been made in result of someone dialing the wrong number," he clarified, but stated that a friend of Janette's had told him she'd previously received obscene phone calls. The article went on to say the reward money was now up to $7,100 and that law enforcement officials had received thirty separate tips concerning the sketch of the possible witness or suspect.

This article also mentioned the editor of the *Herald*, David Casterline, and Reed City Chamber of Commerce secretary Colin

Hayward had seen a man fitting the sketch description in the newspaper office just days earlier. The man apparently purchased a newspaper and was "acting nervous," according to the men, before abruptly leaving. The State Police were called and the incident reported. Hayward and Casterline said the man was driving an older-model green pickup, but they weren't able to get the license plate.

In *The Pioneer* on February 12th 1983, a small four paragraph blurb was run in the left column of the front page titled **Police Seeking Customer**. Investigators working on the Janette Roberson murder were looking for the person that had contact with Janette in front of a pet store in Big Rapids on January 11th, and again on the 12th at Gambles where she was seen giving a man two brown and one black gerbil in front of the store. The man in the green truck was mentioned in this article as well. Officials had apparently questioned him, but he was not taken into custody and, according to the article, was not considered a suspect. The man who'd purchased a newspaper may not have been acting nervous, so much as the news editor and Chamber of Commerce secretary may have been letting current events get the better of their imaginations. It's easy to do in a small town when the big story is murder, yet there appears to be no viable suspect. Everyone starts playing investigator.

Police Still Seeking Murder Suspect was the title of the February 17th 1983 article in *The Osceola County Herald.* "Nearly a month after the heinous crime, police still have no suspects and they're hunting feverishly for the murderer."

Excellent use of adverbs to heighten the tension!

The article goes on to give more details on the man in the green truck. "In a related incident, police officials found a man who had been sought for questioning for over a week. The man fitting the composite sketch drawing, which was released several weeks ago, was spotted in the Osceola County Herald office Feb. 2nd. The man entered the office, purchased a newspaper, and then sped off in a green older-model pickup truck. Police searched for a week for the truck and its driver before someone anonymously tipped them off last Thursday morning on who the driver of the truck was. Investigators questioned the man however he was released shortly after and was not taken into police custody. Police say they do not consider the man a suspect in the murder."

Thanks for clearing that up, *again*, Osceola County Herald. Old news—even slightly more detailed old news—is better than no news at all, I guess.

In the article, Detective Pratt said the tip numbers were up. "We've had over 300 tips thus far and they're still coming in. Over 100 tips have come in concerning the sketch of the possible witness to the crime. We're following up all tips, but thus far we don't have anything to go on. We're working hard in trying to solve this crime."

The article finished by saying that investigators were using a special computer terminal to help them store leads. Detective Pratt called it "a very helpful device in aiding officials in their continuing investigation."

Technology for the win! I feel I should jump in here and say that the current status of the Janette Roberson case file does not suggest all of the items (or any) have been entered into the computer system used now for crime reports. Remember that almost 6 thousand dollar fee Michigan State Police wanted to charge me?

> Good morning Jeni!
>
> We haven't talked in a while so I wanted to touch base. Renee has been working with the Detectives at the post to be able to get a good faith estimate for you. It looks like she has compiled an estimate for you and that will be mailed today. I wanted to give you a breakdown before you received it. There is an estimated 5000 pages. As I stated before we estimate 1 minute per page to review/redact exempt material, so Renee has estimated the 84 hours for that plus the time to copy that which is (probably more) estimated at 2 hours. We are looking at an estimate total of **$5,999.25**. Minus the credit of the other 2 payments which was $170.52.
>
> Jessina Beckner, Supervisor
> Freedom of Information Unit
> Michigan State Police
>
> **"A PROUD tradition of SERVICE through EXCELLENCE, INTEGRITY, and COURTESY"**

What this was for, essentially, is everything *after* the beginning of 1986 done on the Janette Roberson investigation, which is what we'd already received.

(NOTE: Snarky recreation alert→) Once I'd gone through what they sent me I was like, "Dude, where's the rest?" Jessina Beckner, the head of the department was all like, "*Dude*, that last chick didn't check everywhere. There's more stuff at the local police post. Do you want it?" I was all, "Dude, *yes*!" Then she was all, "No prob! You and your assistant cancel your outstanding requests, we'll meld them together, and I'll apply your money to that. I really, really, really want to help you!"

Weeks later we got the letter above. "Dude, *my bad*. There's LOTS more stuff, but if you want it we need, like, a whole lot more money because it's in boxes and not on the computer."

Now you're up to speed on the bullshit, gentle reader. Welcome aboard! (Please take small children and the elderly by the hand.)

According to MSP inspector Cam Henke, when I spoke to him in August of 2014, at that time the Janette Roberson murder investigation file was not indexed for cross-reference or digitized. That's the startling reality. Cases go cold, files get stuffed in boxes, boxes get shoved into dusty spaces, and thirty years later you're emailed an invoice saying it'll take around eighty-four hours to pull out the information you're looking for—*Oh!* and it'll set you back about 6 grand. Or, you know, you can give up and stop asking for the information.

To me, it would be more honest to say, "Sorry, we don't want you to have this" or "Are you sure you want us to take the time and charge you the money to go through those boxes? In all likelihood, we'll do the work and not send you much of anything anyway." That's really nasty in my book. One has to wonder if that's what the Michigan State Police are counting on... people giving up.

Should it be that hard to access public information? Should it be that costly? Should taxpayers foot the bill for abysmal record keeping? Should this vein in my forehead be throbbing? All questions for another day, and we'll get there, don't you worry.

Back to February, 1983...

Near the end of February, known inked impressions, (or information concerning inked impressions) were forwarded to the Grayling Crime Laboratory with a request they be compared against the latent lifts obtained in the Gambles store on the date of the murder. The names listed on the fingerprint request included all of the Gambles employees previously interviewed, (David, Bonnie, and John Engels) as well as Ralph Fisher (Janette's father), Theodore Platz (Reed City PD), Christopher Casavettes (customer), and George Wilson (AKA Injun George – a local indigent man), and three other names (males) that turned up nowhere else in the report.

Lab information was slowly filtering back in to the Michigan State Police this month and on February 16th Detective Pratt met with the Investigative Resources Team and a psychologist out of Lansing about the case. The team had previously travelled to Reed City and reviewed the crime scene. This group would meet again, along with Dr. Steven Cohle MD, Forensic Pathologist, and another member of the Pathology Department at Blodgett Memorial Medical Center. A total of three meetings took place in which the case was reviewed "...in an attempt to determine avenues of pursuit and an insight into a possible potential killer."

On February 22nd 1983, George Wilson, aka "Injun George," was interviewed by Detective Pratt. His name came up a great deal when I spoke with Reed City residents regarding this case. I found that for the most part, people generally pointed a finger in his direction because he was a local eccentric who collected bottles and cans and was generally odd enough to make people uncomfortable. A common knee-jerk reaction is to assume the local weirdo is the bad guy. In this case, it doesn't appear so.

According to the MSP report, on February 23rd 1983 David Engels, the owner of the Gambles store, contacted Detective Pratt with a concern that someone may have had keys to the Gambles store. "The concern arises due to two incidents where the alarm to the store was triggered, and on both occasions nothing was found amiss. These alarm calls were answered by the Reed City Police Department."

On February 28th a supplemental report regarding tip #185 was forwarded to Detective Pratt from the Paw Paw Post. Subject Jonathan Thorne was interviewed by MSP State Troopers Bruder and Paul about having been in Reed City on the day of the murder. They learned that Mr. Thorne had recently moved to that area from Stanwood. Under REMARKS, the report notes that he was co-operative with officers, did not volunteer or anticipate questions, said he had nothing to hide, and that he didn't do it. It appears the information gleaned was adequate to rule the subject out, because when Detective Pratt was contacted, he advised no further assistance was needed, and by April 1983 the status of the supplemental report was changed to CLOSED.

On February 28, 1983 a list of items was obtained from Reed City Police Chief Phillip Rathbun, who'd gotten them directly from Marion Fisher, Janette's mother. These items were to be forwarded to a woman by the name of Trixie Shepherd. This is the last item on the supplemental dated March 1, 1983, which covered February's work done by Michigan State Police.

The final notations on the page are as follows:

TIPS RECEIVED: As of this writing three hundred twenty (320) tips related to the murder investigation have been received and are being followed up on. None of the information received as of this writing has provided a good investigative lead as to the murderer.

COMPLAINT STATUS: Open.

[redacted]

Michigan Department of State Police

UD-1 (Rev 1-79)

PROPERTY REPORT, RECEIPT, AND REQUEST FOR LABORATORY ANALYSIS ORIGINAL COPY

[X] Property Report 1 [ ] Request for Analysis 2 [X] Property Receipt 3	District, Division, Post, Section, or Unit 4: Reed City Post # 62
Confiscated 7 [ ] Recovered 8 [X] Other 9	County 10: Osceola
M.S.P. Lab No. 5	Complaint No. 6: 62-113-83
File Class 11	0900-1
Official Receipt No. 13	Original Date of Complaint 14: 1-19-83
Nature of Complaint 12	Murder of JANETTE ROBERSON
From Whom and Where Obtained 15	Obtained from Chief PHILLIP RATHBUN, Reed City P.D. at the Post
Date Property Received 16	2-28-83

Item Number 17	DESCRIPTION OF PROPERTY 18	Estimated Value of Each Item Listed 19
#9.	One City of Reed City 4"X91/2" white colored mailing envelope containing:	
	One (1)	
		nil
		nil
	One (1)	nil
	One (1)	nil
	One (1)	
	One (1)	nil

Total Value of This Page Only 22: NIL

D/Sgt. George D. Pratt

Type Name: D/Sgt. GEORGE D. PRATT

Owner 23: MARIAN FISHER

Address of Owner 24: R 1, Leroy Rd., Leroy, Mi.

Victim 26: JANETTE GALE ROBERSON, W/F, dob 10-25-55

X

D/Sgt. George D. Pratt

Date: 2-28-83

RELEASE OF PROPERTY

D/Sgt. George D. Pratt 3-3-83 2:PM

Signature of Person Receiving Property: T.C. Shepherd

Type Name of Person Receiving Property: T. C. SHEPHERD

Address: 1487 Cohoctah Rd., Box 307, Cohoctah, Mi.

DESTRUCTION OF PROPERTY

Date and Time Destroyed 43

How Destroyed 44

Destroyed By (Signature) 45

Witnessed By (Signature) 46

Complaint No. 62-113-83

File Class 0900-1

Trixie Shepherd is a psychic. Well, she *was* three decades ago, before she had the stroke. I don't even know if she'd call herself a psychic. It's just a gift she had, along with her sister. They could see things. Things the rest of us can't see, apparently. There are notations about Trixie Shepherd in the MSP report, including two property receipts signed by her. The first was when she received personal items of Janette's, the second when she turned the items back over to police.

Trixie's stroke happened seven years ago, she told me when I first spoke with her on October 15, 2014 in the afternoon. At the end of the conversation, we set up another meeting for October 21st at noon. After having chatted for about thirty minutes about Janette's murder, then about her memory and stroke, Trixie said, "I'm glad you're coming because I have some other things to talk about."

My lower forty clenched, ominously. "Well that makes me nervous!"

I don't want to know those kinds of things about myself or loved ones. Not that I believe in psychics, but I don't ***not*** believe in them, either. I don't presume to know everything about the Universe. There are far too few things I can say with absolute certainty, and whether there is or isn't such a thing as psychic ability is decidedly not one of them.

Trixie chuckled lightly and told me that she wasn't psychic anymore, not since the stroke. I asked if that disappointed her and she said no because it often made her sick, knowing all those things.

So I asked her to tell me how she came to be involved with the Janette Roberson investigation. Because she had a speech issue, I let her talk and didn't interrupt until she was finished. I knew I'd be able to follow up when we met in person. In halting breaths she told me her sister had called to tell her about the murder in the Gambles store. She lived out of town, so the next time she was in Reed City she went to the police station and told them she needed something Janette wore, something personal so she could do a reading. At some point she received a necklace she was told was Janette's, but she didn't get much off it, so she told them she needed other items.

The Michigan State Police property report receipt shows five items were turned over to Chief Rathbun from Marion Fisher, Janette's mother, and forwarded to Trixie. To the best of her recollection, all of her readings happened about one month after the murder. Trixie said she met with police a total of three different times. During the next two visits, they went to the Gambles basement pet department, and drove to where Janette lived.

The first trip was to the Gambles store. Her sister accompanied her, along with Detective Pratt, according to Trixie. She said as soon as they walked down the stairs into the basement, her sister's stomach started to hurt and she said she thought something had happened to Janette's stomach. Trixie told me she believes Janette was choked unconscious before most of the other injuries occurred, and the killer carried her to where her body was eventually found.

"There was a man in the back room, he moved a board and then he was lying in sand. I saw him put a cigarette out in that sand." This is one of the visions she described on the phone.

She said when they first went downstairs to the pet department there was a tarp hanging in the doorway between the pet department and what she thought might be another room. She asked to go through it and when she did, saw the second set of stairs. She told them she "saw" the killer going up those stairs, but there were boxes stacked upstairs in front of the stair entrance on the day Janette was murdered.

"That's why nobody saw him," she told me.

She said once they left Gambles that day, they went to the police station and she was shown some pictures. She looked at the first picture and said: "That man will be lucky if he lives a month." She said they told her he was lucky. The pictures had been taken about a month before, she explained. She said he was an older man, thin faced, and his eyes were set back in his head a bit. He looked sick and drawn.

"I didn't see the heart attack, but I thought it might be his heart." She told me she believed he died not long afterward.

When shown the next picture, she said, "He's worried about his wife."

The next picture, this time a woman: "She's pregnant and the cord is wrapped around the baby's neck. They need to watch out for her when she delivers."

Another picture. "That man is a cop killer. He's going to kill a cop one of these days." Trixie says the police told her he tried, but was now locked up.

She said the police showed her two other pictures, but she couldn't remember who they were or what they looked like.

Trixie said on her next trip, police took her to Janette's house. She couldn't remember now if it was a house or apartment because since the stroke, some things were fuzzy. She said they never went in and she didn't even know which one was Janette's, but she told the detective, "There's a horse by the window."

She said one of the police went up to the window and when he came back to the car, told her there was a horse statue there that he could see through the window.

After hearing all that, I wasn't sure what to expect when I met Trixie in person the following week. I pulled into the Assisted Living Facility and she was the first thing I saw when I entered the foyer. It was mail time and she was sitting in her wheelchair at the double doors watching the mail lady put envelopes into all the silver boxes.

"I thought you might be waiting for me," I told her as I walked up. "Trixie, right?

She smiled. "I'm waiting for my mail."

Touché, psychic lady. Touché.

I waited with her, noting the table full of elder folk watching us, probably wondering who I was and what I was doing there. It was a small facility, and now that I've been there on a few more occasions to see other people, I can tell you that the tenants are all up in eachother's *shiz*. Picture the Golden Girls, but there's a dozen of them and they have their own apartments plus a common area from which they fritter away the hours. They are, in a word, delightful.

Once the mail lady was finished and locked all of the boxes, Trixie slowly rolled into the vestibule and opened her box with the key, removing her mail. She did the same with another key, and then rolled back into the foyer and across the room, handing another older woman her key and mail. She waved to me over her shoulder and then slowly made her way down a long corridor, using her feet to move the wheelchair rather than rolling it by the wheels with her hands. Her apartment was at the very end of a long hallway lined with doors on both sides, most of which had signs that read:

NO SMOKING: OXYGEN IN USE.

It was a tiny living space—kitchen to the right as soon as you walk in, overlooking the living area, and a small hallway off to the right where I assume the bedroom and bath were. We never left the living room. She took her time getting into her chair, which was one of those orthopedic jobs that could, at the touch of a button, rise up and a bit forward, making it easier for a person to back into before they used that same button to lower it to a fully seated position. I sat down in the chair next to her and pulled out my pencil. I didn't even have my notebook out before she'd foraged in the pile of paperwork beside her and pulled out a piece of notebook paper.

"I drew this for you."

I'm sure my eyes became the size of saucers as I looked at it, mainly because her drawing—over three decades after the murder—was probably more accurate than the one I came up with the day after visiting the basement for the first time.

I've since been down to the basement of what is now Reed City Hardware a few times. Once, the owner—Gary Smith—chastised me for leaving the lights on the time before. He's okay. A bit gruff, but he's been very accommodating. Last time we spoke, he suggested I bring him some Dr. Pepper for his troubles. I think that's the time I asked if I could bring a psychic in with me at some point. That never happened, but I probably still owe him a case or two of soda.

Nothing in Trixie's story changed the second time we spoke, but she did elaborate a bit, and with the help of the diagram, said she'd remembered a little more. She said she had talked to her sister since we spoke, who had requested I not use her name.

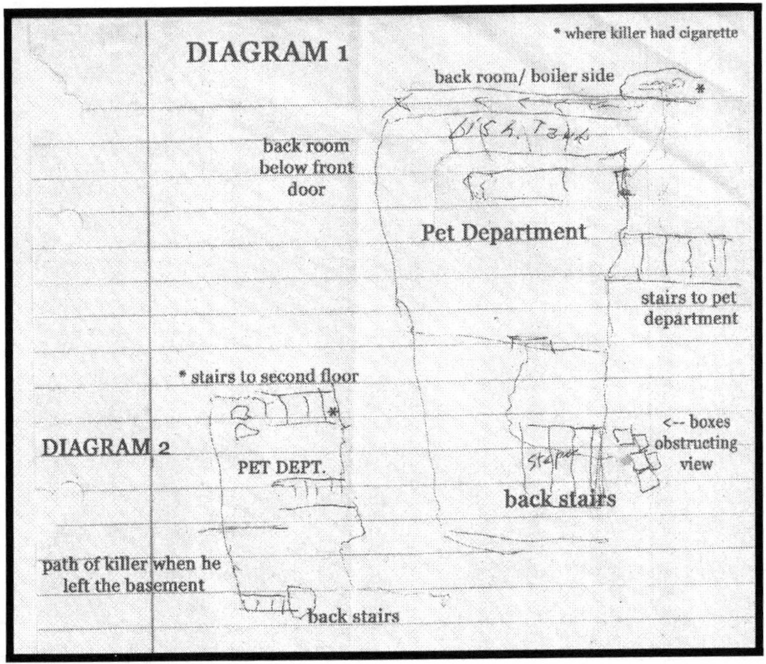

"Just call her *The Sister*," Trixie said, looking sheepish. I laughed and told her it wasn't a problem. I spoke to a number of people who didn't want their names mentioned in connection with this case.

The first thing Trixie wanted to tell me is the other thing she'd "seen" in relation to Janette. She didn't believe she'd shared it with police. It was regarding a man in Janette's life. She saw him in a gray suit. She said Janette was thinking about him while it was happening, and wanted him to know what was happening to her. Trixie described her own near death experience to me, and then told me that while she was unconscious, Janette was still aware and "floating" above herself, watching. This is when she said Janette thought about the man in the suit, and it occurred during the time she was "passing over."

Trixie went over her recollections regarding the pictures again. She said the man with the heart problem who died was a "kind person." Nothing about him bothered her. The other man, the one who was worried about his wife, he was thin—not as thin as the man with the heart problem and sunken eyes, but of thin build. He had dark hair. She believed the female she was shown in the picture was his wife, and she was pregnant. She repeated that the cord had been wrapped around the baby's neck, but the baby had been born okay. The man she'd told police was a cop killer had light hair, Trixie said, and he gave her a "terrible feeling." She was scared of him.

Trixie again discussed being taken to Janette's residence and not getting out of the car, but telling the officer there was a horse. She said the officer went to check and came back to the car, telling her there was a horse statue just inside the window. She said she spoke to Detective Pratt for quite a while and told him the two people that concerned her. Again, because this is an ongoing investigation, I feel it would be irresponsible to name potential suspects, but mostly because this is a *psychic* we're talking about, for God's sake, not an eyewitness.

I have no way of knowing if the pictures I showed Trixie were any of the same ones police did, though I think it is likely a few of them were. I also believe a couple were new to her, and a few that I think may have been shown to her by police, I did not ask about, simply because by the time I met with Trixie, I believed they had been ruled out.

Of the six pictures I brought, two made her uncomfortable. She pointed to one said, "I think he's hiding something." And that was it. A bit later, mid-conversation, she motioned for the pictures again, went through them, pulled out the same two and stared at them, shaking her head. "These two. Something with these two."

Watching her, looking at her eyes, it was like watching someone try to grasp an object that was just out of their reach.

She again went over what she'd experienced when she went to Gambles pet department with the police. She told me she had descended the stairs into the pet department and pointed to where the tarp hung, after her sister complained about her stomach.

"Can I get through here?" Trixie said they pulled the tarp back and let her into the storage area where the back stairs were. That is where she "saw" the killer go up the stairs that had been obstructed by boxes at the first floor level. "I can see it..." she said, quietly, then told me about the killer having a cigarette in what she described as the corner of that back room which makes a backwards "L" shape that runs along the side and back of the pet department. Back in the crook of that "L" is the area where she said he'd "moved a board aside" and smoked a cigarette, then put it out in the sandy area and waited for Janette to come down. According to Trixie, he grabbed her somewhere in that narrow area of the back room, put a hand over Janette's mouth, and grabbed her by the neck, choking her. When she was passed out, he carried her down the narrow walkway, laid her down, and proceeded to do the "...things he did."

Trixie paused and shuddered. "It was terrible."

There seemed to be gaps in the action she was telling me, meaning she couldn't see everything as it had happened in real time. It was at this point that something occurred to me.

"Trixie, you don't see the killer, do you? I mean, you can't describe him."

"No."

"What do you see, then?" I asked.

"I see what he's doing."

I stifled a gasp and my stomach flopped.

"You mean you see it from a first person perspective? You see what *he's seeing*?"

"Yes," she nodded, her eyes still closed.

I swallowed hard as Trixie described how when he was finished with the "terrible things," he went back up that narrow hallway, out through the pet department to the adjoining storage space, and up the back set of cement stairs. She said he waited until it was all clear and then went out, not far, to the left and up another stairway to what Trixie thought looked like an office.

"How does he feel, Trixie? Can you tell?" She'd been concentrating so hard with her eyes closed, moving and pointing with her hands in different directions as she spoke.

"Really mad. Upset."

"What else do you see?" I asked, wondering just how much of her "gift" she'd lost to the stroke. It looked to me like it wasn't all gone.

"Clothes. Gloves. He's putting them in a bag."

"Paper or plastic?" I asked. I had to choke down the urge to laugh. Not really a laugh. It was more like a choked gasp. How many times have I heard that at the grocery store? Paper or plastic?

"Paper, I think. I'm not sure."

"Where did the gloves come from?" I asked. "When did he put them on?"

"After he had the cigarette. In the sandy place. They're dark-colored. Gray, I think. Like work gloves."

And for the second time, something occurred to me. "So he was wearing them during the attack?"

Trixie nodded. "Yes, I think so."

"Can you see any weapons, Trixie?" I knew none of this was of any evidentiary value, but it was riveting, nonetheless. I just asked questions like I would if she was describing something she was *really* seeing, because to her it seemed like she was.

Trixie closed her eyes and paused. "A knife, I think. A jackknife." There was a pause and then she opened her eyes. "No gun or anything like that." Then she said it again. "He did horrible things."

I nodded. There wasn't anything I could say to that. Whoever it was did do horrible things to Janette Roberson. Things for which he had yet to pay. Justice was still waiting, and if it was anything like me, Justice was becoming pretty damn impatient.

"I don't think she ever regained consciousness." She said it like she was trying to console herself, and it's the only thing Trixie told me that I choose to believe, without question. Janette's injuries—numerous and brutal—were not quickly sustained.

The only way I can see this through is to believe, unfailingly, that Janette Roberson never regained consciousness at any point during her attack.

The alternative is unfathomable.

Viola, Venus & Jan

Trixie wasn't the only psychic I learned had become at least peripherally associated with this case. I was told by a few locals that a woman named Viola Rehkopf—a well-known and liked member of the community—told numerous people that she believed a prominent businessman had murdered Janette. In fact, I heard that from more people than I can even number.

Terry Hall (a friend of Janette and her brother) spoke to Viola right after the murder. She told him that she didn't usually involve herself in active police matters, but thought this case was so horrible, she made an exception. She said the person who did it was a prominent Reed City businessman, and that eventually the guilt would eat him up and he'd surrender and confess. I had also been told Viola received an anonymous call telling her she should stop working with police on the Roberson case, if she knew what was good for her.

Viola M. Rehkopf died at the age of 101 on Easter Sunday, April 11, 2004. She passed away at home surrounded by her family after a brief illness. She was born January 11, 1903 in Evart to Floyd and Edna Stevens, and according to her obituary, spent most of her life in the Reed City/Evart area. Also noted in her obituary, as written by one of her daughters:

> "Mother has been called the one woman lost and found. I don't run across many people who haven't heard of her. Even past age 100 she was getting phone calls from people who had lost things (dog, checkbook, important papers, rings, etc.) frequently. She could describe in detail where the missing item was which usually helped in the recovery. I remember the police asking her help in finding missing persons. I was surprised to learn that more than 20 years ago, Mom helped the family of a local woman locate the wreck of her husband's airplane and recover his body...

> everyone was looking in the wrong direction and they would never have had closure on his death if not for Mom."

I spoke with Blanche Erickson, Viola's daughter, on November 20, 2014 after having left my number in a private message with a family member. When the phone rang days later, I wasn't expecting it.

"Hello?"

"Hello, is Jeni Decker there? This is Blanche Erickson calling. Viola's daughter."

Viola... Viola? Oh! Viola! My inner monologue's memory is really bad.

"Oh my goodness! This is so great," my outer monologue blathered, as it is wont to do when the body attached to it is scurrying across the room, away from the loud television, grabbing a pen and paper before heading for quieter ground. "This is so great!" I think I repeated it again. "I make all these contacts over the computer, and then I'm never sure when people will call back, so it's always a gift when someone does. How are you?" I finally found the presence of mind to ask.

"Blessed. Every day." That was Blanche's immediate response. I immediately liked her.

I went on to explain who I was, that I was working on the book, and that I'd heard from quite a few people that her mother, Viola, had some connection with the case. Basically Blanche told me the same thing Terry and a few others had—that Viola believed a prominent Reed City businessman had committed the murder. Blanche clarified that it wasn't someone Viola knew personally, and they would've had to show her pictures of the person in order to identify them. To Blanche's knowledge, her mother had never told anyone who this businessman was. I asked her about the anonymous phone call, which she confirmed, and then added a detail. She said there was an incident around the time of the call, she wasn't sure before or after, where a black car pulled into Viola's driveway at 3am one morning and remained parked there for about an hour. But she and her sister SaraLee couldn't come to agreement as to whether that car incident happened around the time of the Lintemuth case, or Janette's case. Both had been local unsolved crimes from the 1980s.

About halfway through the conversation, Blanche offhandedly said, "I was in there that day around noon and—"

"Wait… Gambles? *The day of the murder*?" I asked, my voice shooting up two octaves. Yes, I cut her off. I do that when I get excited.

"Well, yes…" She sounded like she assumed I already knew that.

That's another thing I got, repeatedly, when I spoke with people. Everyone knew their personal involvement in the Janette Roberson investigation intimately, so once I told them I had the Michigan State Police report, they assumed I knew everything they knew. That's where everyone would be wrong.

Because I only had part of the report, I found no record of a great many of the people I spoke to in the report itself. It is possible that city or county police did a lot of the tangential interviews, since most of those folks didn't remember speaking to Detective Pratt when I asked them. When, where, and *if* those reports ever made their way to the Michigan State Police file is still a question, even when I spoke to the Inspector in charge of the cold cases. During one of our conversations, he told me he'd have to check whether they had all of the other entities' reports. This did not inspire confidence, given my interaction with the Osceola County Sheriff's Department.

I had filed an appeal of the Reed City Police Department's denial of my request for their first responders report. I won that by appearing in front of the city council and pleading my case, while enduring the curmudgeonly city manager's tone which suggested he didn't like the fact that I was there asking for the documents in the first place. Mind you, these documents had never before been released, and there were plenty of people interested in what the city and county officers did in those early minutes before Detective Pratt arrived on scene. *So interested*, I'm not sure why the local press never thought to request copies of the reports themselves. Maybe it never occurred to them.

A few days after my appearance at city council, I received an email from the Reed City city attorney:

> "...in the interest of full disclosure, the Osceola County Sheriff's Department delivered additional documents concerning this case to us after you filed your FOIA appeal. Most of its contents duplicate those of our rather small file—or are exempt under the FOIA. But if you wish to renew your request, the City is prepared to undergo the same review process regarding the newly-received documents."

I had requested the documents from Osceola County not once but *twice* and was told they did not have them, or they did not exist. When I asked when the Osceola County Sheriff's report had been turned over, and by whom, I was met with stony silence. I never did find out. When an entity flat out lies to you—not once, but *twice*—you tend to get a little twitchy, and maybe not so trusting. Which is why, to this day, I'll need more than anyone's word about documents when we're talking municipal government. I'd love to be the trusting doe I once was, but sneaky humans have forever ruined me in that regard.

Anyway... back to Blanche.

"You were at Gambles the day of the murder?" I said, with a great deal of incredulity.

"Well yes..."

Way to bury the lead, Blanche!

"Okay." I clenched my pen more tightly in anticipation. "Tell me about that."

Blanche said she had goldfish back then, and that day she'd gone to the Gambles pet department around noon looking for a product called "Ick." It was something she said was supposed to keep the tank from getting yucky. She went down there but found no salesperson in the pet department. She looked around for a couple short minutes, but nobody came. When I asked her how long, Blanche estimated she was down there maybe five minutes, then went upstairs and told one of the female clerks, "It'd be nice if there was someone downstairs to ring people up."

From this time (noon-ish) forward, every customer I located who'd been in the pet department said the same thing. They went down and there was no Janette.

Blanche never got her "Ick." Her sister SaraLee Rehkopf told me that right after the murder, Blanche said she'd gotten a very cold, uneasy feeling when she was down there, and that's why she left so fast. Blanche said there were no other customers when she went downstairs. She remembered a blue tarp hanging in that doorway area between the two basements, and thought expansion was going on at the time. She said she was tempted to look behind the tarp, but her mother always told her *if it's not your business, keep your nose out.* Blanche said that to this day, she's glad she kept her nose to herself, in case the killer was back there at the time, waiting.

NOTE: A quick Google search tells me that *Ich* is a protozoan disease (parasite) that is often called 'white spot disease.' The scientific name for the disease is ichthyophthiriasis and it is widespread in all freshwater fish, but more common in aquarium fish, possibly due to the closer contact and stress involved with aquarium species. There's your Bill Nye the Science Guy moment for the day. You're welcome.

After I spoke with her, Blanche passed along my contact info to her former sister-in-law Jan Palumbo. "I think Jan was one of the last people down there before they found her."

My incredulity meter hit a high note for the second time in our conversation. "Oh yeah?"

"What's her last name now?" I heard Blanche ask her husband, who she told me was shaking his head at her.

I laughed. "Ha! My husband shakes his head at me all the time."

We chuckled then she started mumbling, "*P*, I think. It starts with a *P*. I'll tell you what. Let me make some calls and I'll find out. I'll have her call you."

I thanked Blanche profusely and hung up thinking, *Wow, you know what? People are good.* Kindness of strangers, and all that jazz.

It was maybe an hour later when Jan called. "Is Jeni there?"

"That's me!" I said. "I'm Jeni."

"This is Jan."

Another gift of a return call, followed by a repeated explanation of what I was working on, and then Jan Palumbo told me her story. She and her sister-in-law, Venus Aris, were in Gambles that day for quite a long time. See, Jan had just bought a fifty gallon tank and they needed supplies. To her recollection, she and Venus left her house around 1:30 that day. Jan and Venus appear to be the two women who bought fish supplies that the newspaper articles had repeatedly put out calls for.

"Somewhere between 1:30 and 2:00 we got there."

They had two kids with them, and when they descended the stairs into the basement pet department, there was no clerk. The two women spent a great deal of time watching the fish swimming around in the tanks, walking around the department, and setting aside items they would need. At some point it occurred to Jan that they'd been there an awfully long time, but no salesclerk had ever appeared. She also remembered the blue tarp and admitted to peeking behind it.

"We were there a *really* long time. I got bored," Jan said, almost embarrassed.

"Hey, I would've peeked too. Don't feel bad," I told her. "Do you remember what it looked like on the other side of the tarp?"

"Just a big empty space. I think there were some boxes, but a big room about the size of the pet department. Not much in there that I can think of. I think the floor may have even been dirt. Maybe not. Maybe it was cement. Just looked like a basement with no windows to me."

"How long do you think you guys were there at the store?" I asked.

"It seemed like a *long* time. Almost two hours, I think. Seems like we left Gambles a little before four o'clock. It was weird. We'd been there forever when I went upstairs and left Venus down in the pet shop. I found a woman and asked if anyone was working downstairs. The woman told me Janette should be down there and she looked at me sort of quizzically, like confused."

Jan said she told the woman there was nobody down there, so the woman came downstairs with her to look. Jan didn't remember any customers coming down and browsing in the pet department while she and Venus and the kids were down there waiting, but she had a faint recollection of a male coming down at some point and he said, "There's nobody down here?" Jan said no, and he went back upstairs.

Jan said when she finally went up to find someone and the woman employee walked back downstairs with her, it seemed like suddenly there were a bunch of customers who'd followed them down into the pet department. I asked Jan if she thought they might have been employees and she said she didn't think so. She believed they were customers and it felt like they had all come down at the same time. She said she remembered thinking maybe work had just let out or something because it was late in the afternoon.

"So, did you end up buying the fish stuff?" I asked.

"You know, I can't remember. I didn't get rung up at the register upstairs, so if I did, it would have been downstairs, but I can't remember now. It was so weird. I just remember leaving, and a group of customers being down there when we left. But I can't imagine I'd have left without the stuff after being there so long."

"Were there customers upstairs, too, when you were leaving?" I asked.

"I remember seeing people—nobody I knew personally, just customers."

"Is there anyone you remember seeing at all?"

"Just one man standing at the register. I remember thinking it was weird. He was holding a lunchbox."

"Are you sure he was a customer?"

"I think so," she said. "He was standing at that register just outside the entrance to the pet department."

"What kind of lunchbox?" I asked.

"Just the kind that men carried. You could put the thermos inside."

"Metal?" I asked. "Like a Coleman?"

"Yes, like that."

I asked Jan to describe the man with the lunchbox. She said dark hair, moustache, hair was a little long, to his ears. She remembered thinking he needed a haircut. She couldn't specifically recall descriptions of anyone else. She said he was the only one who stood out, but she doesn't know why. He just did.

Since the autopsy report states the body was found at 3:50, that would mean Jan and her sister-in-law Venus left fairly close to the discovery of Janette's body, if her timing wasn't off. Two hours seems like a long time to wait around with two kids for a clerk to come help you. She said they just took their time, the kids were looking at the fish and they remained well behaved so they were just browsing all of the tanks and supplies, trying to decide what fish she might get, and it ended up being a pretty long time.

"We never saw or heard anything weird while we were there," Jan said. She mentioned looking through the fish tanks into the back room, wondering if anyone was back there, but never saw any movement. It wasn't until days later that she learned about the murder. She saw a plea from police on the television news for two women who had been in Gambles in the afternoon with two kids to please contact them. Jan said she immediately called and gave the police her name, but she kept seeing the plea on the news airings, even after calling, so eventually she called again.

At some point, police came to her home and questioned her, though she wasn't sure which law enforcement entity they were with. She said their questions were around who they had seen in the store while they were there. Police wanted descriptions of as many people as she could remember.

Jan suggested I speak to Venus and she said she'd pass along my number. It occurred to me that if it kept up like this, they'd pass me right along, from person to person until I reached the killer, himself.

Two days later, Venus Aris returned my call, and she was as likeable and kind as Jan and Blanche had been. She had much of the same information to offer as her sister-in-law did, with a few more details thrown in. It was her two kids that had been with the women that day—Andy and Gary, both redheads. They were 3 ½ and 2 ½ years old at the time, and that day they were wearing matching coats made for them by a family member. The reason Venus remembered this is because she had a photo the police took when she went in, days after the murder, to give a statement. She had also seen the news plea for the two women who'd been in Gambles with two children on the day of the murder to please call police. It was the first Venus had heard of the murder, just as it had been with Jan. She said they didn't subscribe to the local papers back then.

When I asked Venus what time she thought they were in the store, she remembered that she had to be home to do chores by 4 or 4:30. On further questioning I learned that "chores" meant milking and taking care of cows, which they did at the same time every day, so she believes they left Gambles sometime just prior to four o'clock. To her recollection they went in the store sometime around two, and it was "dead." Venus didn't see any customers roaming around. She repeated that they were down in the pet shop a pretty long time and after they'd been there for quite a while, she said Jan went up to find a clerk to ring her up. She said Jan left her down there for about five or ten minutes, and the boys had followed her up so she was alone. She said she remembers it felt a little eerie. Silent. No music over a sound system. No customers but herself. Just quiet. She recalls seeing about two inches of "light" coming from above what would have been the right wall if you were facing the back of the pet department, and what looked to her like they might be cages on the other side, but she wasn't sure. She's not the inquisitive type like Jan, so she did not look behind the door or the tarp, and she can't believe if there was a door back there that Jan didn't open it and peek because Jan *is* the inquisitive type. I told her the walls and door may have been paneled in such a way that the door wasn't noticeable, to blend in with the wall rather than stand out.

She said she remembers a woman, "...small, at least 40, and I want to say she had glasses, but I'm not positive..." came down a little bit after Jan, and she believes that woman rung up her sister-in-law's items. She could picture the woman at the register by the bottom of the stairs, and she doesn't think they left without the purchases, but she doesn't recall standing there while Jan was being checked out, either. Venus thinks while Jan was paying, she headed upstairs, maybe even took the boys to the bathroom, and then they left. She doesn't remember any customers coming down at any time, even at the end when Jan remembers seeing them.

Venus clarified, "I never stand and wait for someone to be checked out. Since we'd been there a really long time, I think while Jan paid, I went upstairs, maybe to take the boys to the bathroom first, but then out to the car." To her recollection, they parked out front. She said as they left, the store still seemed pretty empty of customers, really quiet both upstairs and downstairs the whole time, from her perspective.

Venus said that thinking back, one thing was strange. When the woman clerk came down, she didn't recall her looking for Janette or calling out for her. She believes the woman just took care of Jan's purchases and they left, Venus exiting the pet department just before Jan.

She couldn't remember when it was, but sometime in the week following the murder she saw the news report on television, so she went to the Reed City MSP Post and they interviewed her and took a picture of the two boys. Not her, though. Just the boys.

"Just the boys, not you?" I asked, confused.

"Yep, just them."

I wondered aloud if they only took the boys' picture because their striking red hair and matching coats had stood out in the mind of another witness and they just needed it to confirm.

"Maybe. Now that you mention it, it is strange. I figured it was for security. Like the killer could have seen the boys or something. I don't know. It is weird, now that I think about it."

March of 1983 began with Detective Pratt contacting Det. Sgt. Eugene Ambs of the MSP Metro Post to have him interview Barbara Terrill, a friend of Janette's. She worked in sales at the Cadillac 9 & 10 News office at the time. I spoke with Barbara on Saturday October 18, 2014 in the afternoon. She called me after I'd left a note for a relative, trying to get in touch with her.

"My niece was very intrigued by your message," she said. Her voice was pleasant. Barbara said she was afraid she didn't have much information to share. Her connection with Janette was that they were both Jehovah's Witnesses and they'd drive to church together often when Janette lived in LeRoy with her mother. Barbara said the kids would come, too. Barbara also worked at Kaiser-Unitest with Alvin prior to moving to the job at 9 & 10 News in Cadillac. She said that while she didn't know him well, it appeared to her that he adored his wife.

Once Janette moved to the Meadowview Apartments in Reed City, they stopped going to church in Cadillac together, so the two women began meeting for lunch sometimes at Dairy Depot, though she couldn't recall if it was called Dairy Depot at the time or not. Barbara said the police questioned her about Janette and Alvin's relationship. She said they also asked if she knew anyone that didn't like Janette, or any enemies she may have had. Barbara told me she was at a loss because both Janette and Alvin seemed like very nice people. According to her, Alvin did not seem the type to hurt her and she knew of nobody that would.

"Janette was such a nice person. I couldn't understand it," Barbara said, and then recalled that in the couple months leading up to the murder, she hadn't seen Janette or Alvin at all.

March 3rd 1983 is the date the report says personal items of Janette's were forwarded to Trixie Shepherd. That same day, two search warrants authorized by Osceola County Prosecutor James Talaske were obtained from 77th District Court Judge George Vankula "...in regards to obtaining fingerprints of the victim's husband, Alvin Roberson." They were authorized to obtain blood, saliva, and hair samples "in sufficient quantities for comparison analysis." On that date, Detective Pratt also took two complete sets of finger and palm prints from Alvin Roberson at the Michigan State Police Post in Reed City.

March 7th 1983 a supplemental subject report was received from Det. Sgt. Carl Goeman regarding an interview done with a subject named Kris Mills based on a tip called in by a woman named Cindy Trowbridge. The order of events leading up to this was as follows:

—Friday February 4, 1983, Detective Pratt called Post #21 regarding a tip they had received. Detective Goeman contacted Ms. Trowbridge on February 7th and interviewed her regarding the information passed along by Detective Pratt. Only one line is left un-redacted from this interview:

"Contrary to what she had told Detective Pratt, she told me [Detective Goeman] that Mills' parents do own a cat." Below that it says Detective Pratt requested the officers interview Kris Mills.

—February 11th Detectives Goeman and Chapel drove to Bellaire to contact Kris Mills. The subject was not available.

—February 16th Detectives contacted Mills' boss concerning his employment on the date of the murder, as well as his route times. (Kris Mills drove a truck for Curtis Wire Products.)

After numerous attempts to locate the subject, on March 4th Kris Mills contacted Det. Sgt. Goeman and was interviewed that evening. Based on the detective's handwritten notes, it was determined that Mills had travelled through Reed City on a run on January 19, 1983. Where he ate lunch is scribbled next to the time period between 1:00 and 3:00pm, which is noted as the time he passed through Reed City. There is a sentence about Mills stating his parents had a cat, and he obtained scratches from the cat two days after the murder. A time of 6:00pm is given as Mills' arrival time back in Petoskey. The last page of this report has June 23, 1983 as the date this complaint was CLOSED with Post #21. There is a notation about the Reed City case still being open, and they were advised there were no suspects at that time.

More lab reports came back on March 14, 1983, and a copy of the Northern Counties Evidence Service Crime Scene report was received by the end of the month. Also, in the March Issue of the Michigan Law Enforcement Bulletin #402 dated March 13, 2013 the information concerning this homicide was published.

On March 24th 1983, it appears the leads had run dry. A short article in *The Pioneer* was titled **Police Asking for Help**. "Numerous persons from the surrounding area who were in the [Gambles] store that day have been contacted by police. *Those persons, and anyone not contacted,* have been urged to phone the State Police, the Osceola County Sheriff, or the Reed City Police." All three phone numbers were given. Michigan State Police had issued this press release on March 22, 1983 (two days earlier):

> "Investigating officers of the Reed City Police Department, Osceola County Sheriff's Department and Michigan State Police are requesting public cooperation in the Janette Roberson homicide investigation. On January 19, 1983, numerous persons of the surrounding area were in the Gambles store in Reed City. Hopefully all of you have been contacted regarding your visit there on that date. Officers are asking that anyone, whether you have been already contacted or not, please contact the Michigan State Police, Reed City, 832-2221, and provide the requested information as asked. Officers are particularly interested in what was purchased/cash register receipt, time of the day the visit was made, and who may have been with you and/or who you may have seen."

The above portion is underlined in the Michigan State Police report. Below the press release it states, *"This information was released to the area television, radio, and newspapers. Unfortunately it was not published in the newspapers as given, however the radio and local television did carry it properly.*

In the article, Detective Pratt said response to their pleas of help from the community had not been good. "We could sure use a few more (calls)," Pratt said. "A lot (of people) think they have nothing to contribute, but they may have something we really need."

I can almost feel his frustration. Perhaps people didn't think they had anything of value. Maybe they didn't want to get involved. Whatever the reason, law enforcement was at a loss. The last notation in the supplemental report of March 31, 1983 states that the employment records of Janette Roberson from Nartron Corporation were reviewed. They revealed that she was employed by Nartron from October 7, 1981 thru December 7, 1981, at which time she was laid off. She was called back to Nartron in August of 1982 but refused, as she was already employed at the Gambles store at that time.

"Investigation into this case continues with the tips that are received being followed up and whatever other information that comes in."

COMPLAINT STATUS: Open.

Let's take a moment to discuss the part media plays in helping to solve crimes. Recently, a four minute spot about the Janette Roberson murder aired on one of our local news affiliates and it left me feeling slightly chafed. Did I say chafed? I mean pissed. Later I found I wasn't the only one. When I griped about it to a local print reporter, I got this reply.

"It was upsetting to me, too, because I felt like it was packaged with the rest of their "spooky" stories running up to Halloween. Even if they didn't explicitly say so, it certainly seemed to be used that way when it was listed out along with all their other Halloween stuff. How disrespectful. There's a family who's still living that "murder mystery." If they wanted to do some kind of reminder, I think the timing needed to be considered a bit more."

I was so excited when I first learned, a few days before it aired, they'd be doing a story on Janette. One of the things you want when a case has gone cold is as much coverage as possible. Newspapers, television, regular local events highlighting the story— it all goes a long way toward helping find those folks out there who may have information, but haven't come forward, for whatever reason.

Transcript of what aired on Oct 30, 2014—

> A decades-old murder still haunts a small town in Osceola County. That's because whoever killed Janette Roberson back in 1983 is still a mystery. 9&10's Evan Dean sat down with Janette's family and the Reed City Police Chief. He has part one of our special series: Mysteries of Northern Michigan.

A young mother and wife. "I was told that she was always very friendly, always very nice... that she was a great mom." Janette Roberson was a true giver.

"Very giving with her time, with her energy. Always looking out for everyone else," explained Elena Cavender, Janette's niece.

Back in 1983, Janette lived in Reed City and worked in the pet department in the basement of the old Gambles store. Today, you'd recognize it as Reed City hardware.

"She loved animals. There's a picture of her with a horse, and how much she loved horses."

But pictures and stories are all Elena Cavender knows of her aunt. In the middle of the day on January 19, 1983 Janette's life was tragically cut short.

"She went to work, they found her body I think at around 4:00. An employee went down there and found her. And called police."

More than 30 years later, you can still see the animal cages from the store where Janette worked. It was here, in this back room where she was found brutally murdered.

Reed City Police Department Chief Chuck Davis said, "The victim received a number of injuries. This was a brutal murder."

"It's just hard for me to believe that somebody was able to do that to her," said Elena.

Multiple injuries, multiple murder weapons, an autopsy report too horrific to stomach and, suddenly, a murderer on the loose.

"When a homicide occurs, the first 48-72 hours are the most important and crucial," explained Chief Davis.

But in the days immediately following Janette's murder, police made no arrests.

"After that point, it's not hard for something to go cold."

A couple of weeks later, a development in the case. Detectives released three separate sketches. Three different witness descriptions of a man who police wanted to talk to.

"We couldn't call him a suspect. A person of interest maybe a suspect, but at this time, could only be a witness. They were looking for anybody that was in that store one day. They could have been someone who went down the staircase."

But nothing came of the sketches. The mystery man was never found.

And as investigators explored every avenue, the biggest question of all still lingered, why would someone do this?

Elena said, "No idea at all."

"My thought today, is that this was like a get even type thing," Chief Davis said. Far too brutal for a random attack or a robbery. "Somebody was pretty angry at this person."

So detectives looked into those closest to Janette, and discovered that she and her husband, Alvin, were getting a divorce.

"It's pretty well known that the husband, Janette's husband and her were not together at that point."

It was even discovered that Alvin Roberson was seeing another woman. Still, detectives at the time were eventually able to rule out Alvin and his then-girlfriend as suspects.

Meanwhile, in Reed City, bizarre rumors started to swirl.

Was there more to Janette Roberson than people knew?

"There's no indication she was doing anything outside the ordinary other than just a normal, hometown girl that was having some issues at home," Chief Davis said. "Could it have been somebody who had an infatuation with her? Yes. Is that a possibility, yes."

Months, years, decades passed, and still to this day, no arrests. No charges. Not even a suspect.

"There is no true suspect at this point."

Elena said, "There's no justice brought to the family. Plus, it's kinda scary for me. You don't know who's out there."

But the family isn't giving up hope.

Memorial walks, picnics, even a Facebook page and a website, all created in just the last couple of years to get "Justice for Janette."

"We try to talk to as many locals as we can at the time, see what they remember, see if they saw anything strange or weird."

"I think we have more hope than we did 10 years ago. With people calling and the activity," said Chief Davis.

Hope, for a break in the investigation. Maybe even a deathbed confession. Something to solve Janette's horrific murder, once and for all.

"I still think there's a 50-50 chance. I'm not gonna lean one way or another. Because I hope that we can put closure to this."

"I want justice. Whoever did this needs to pay for what they did to her. And to her family," Elena said.

Okay, here's my beef with this. The story aired more than three decades after the murder and Alvin Roberson had been *ruled out* as a suspect, according to the report itself. So why are we discussing the state of their marriage? While that information may have been relevant thirty years ago—before the husband had been ruled out—it certainly has no relevance today. (Just like the composite sketches, but you'll have to wait a little bit to learn about those. We'll get there, I promise.)

Looking at the husband is always important when the wife turns up dead. But once you rule him out, maybe don't waste precious seconds of a four minute TV spot on the salacious globs of irrelevant bullshit. Perhaps utilize the scant time you have to highlight areas where the public can help, rather than muck around in the TMZ-like gossip just to garner high viewership. That is, in a word, *disgusting.* Maybe I'm just being judgy, but I like my media to *not* resemble the National Enquirer. After viewing the report, I went to the Facebook page for the news organization that had aired the story and posted this comment:

> *"Perhaps what should be focused on - rather than the state of their marriage - which is [apparently] widely known, is that a first responder was seen "shooing people out of the Gambles store" when EMTs pulled up. State police may not have tracked them all down, and there is a good chance that officer let a killer walk right out of the store - or at the very least, a witness who may have seen or heard something important. The focus of that story being on the state of Janette's marriage, given the fact that Alvin Roberson has been RULED OUT as a suspect, shows a glaring callousness toward the victim. His wife was slaughtered in her place of business, yet he continues to be maligned - despite law enforcement noting he is not a suspect. What will it take for the press to look at how this crime scene was handled by police? The inconsistencies are right there in the reports if they care to gather them and question a few people. It is disheartening to see coverage around salacious parts of the story, while important aspects continue to be ignored. I encourage anyone who was in the store that day who may*

have left before being questioned to contact Michigan State Police."

Later that day I received a private message via Facebook from the reporter who'd done the story:

REPORTER: Jeni -- Thanks for the comment regarding the story on Janette's murder. I'd like to respond to some of your concerns. First -- it's been well-established that police are still trying to track down people who could've been in the store that day. That's why they released those sketches. I didn't cover that up, it was mentioned in the story.

Second -- In any murder case like this, the spouse of the victim is always looked into. It's protocol. It HAD to be mentioned. However I made certain to say that Alvin WAS ruled out. It was not the entire focus of the story, just briefly mentioned. Maybe 30 seconds out of a 4+ minute report.

Third -- We did obtain both the police report and the autopsy report. And I prepared my story, in part, according to what was there. You have to understand the danger in choosing sources for a story like this. There are endless rumors, and everyone has an different opinion... it would not be hard to find 5 people to interview, all with wide-ranging opinions on what happened... but that wouldn't be responsible on our part. We spoke with police and Janette's family, and I felt confident in that -- and in obtaining the facts. Hearsay is a dangerous game.

Fourth -- In any long-standing unsolved crime, people always question how the scene was handled by officers. It happens every time. Obviously the police chief defended the work that was done. The family is certainly frustrated, but they've been working with police and, for the most part, are appreciative of the work done by officers.

There are facts... and then there are opinions and rumors. And keep in mind -- even witness accounts aren't always accurate.

I appreciate your comment. Trust me, I did some digging. I was told that someone is trying to write a book on Janette's murder. I was also told that his/her work hasn't been well-received by police or Janette's family. I do not know if there's any truth to that, but I did not want to go that route -- the route of making enemies. I didn't want to disrespect Janette's family -- that's the last thing her loved ones deserve, after suffering through this. That was not my intention. More than 30 years later, that's not likely to help the investigation. My hope is that answers can be found without pinning people against each other.

Anyway, thank you for the interest. I hope you have a great day.

ME: First, to be clear, *I am writing the book*. That is how I have this information. I have spent a year so far collecting reports. It is how I know about Officer Finkbeiner allowing witnesses to leave the store, though you will find no record of that in the reports. I spoke with the EMT who responded to the scene, himself, who witnessed it. He was later questioned by MSP as to if he recognized any of the witnesses let go. He was also led, by the same officer, directly through a puddle/spot of blood in the crime scene... The first time I spoke with Chief Davis <u>he told me</u> the first responders handled the scene badly. This is well known by locals. I spoke to the man who dispatched the call as well. I also keep in touch with the MSP Inspector who is considering this case for his cold case team. He is aware I am working on the book, and we have been in recent contact. I understand that Janette's sister is unhappy about the book, though she was not when I was helping her get information. Only when I stopped sharing it because of how she was mishandling delicate info did she begin publicly stating her negative feelings. Just know that from day one, our *first email*, I was up front about the possibility of writing something. So, that's where we are. I thought you might want to have more details rather than bits of the information.

REPORTER: Jeni— Here lies the issue, from my perspective. You say one thing. The family says the other. Police tell me one thing. You say the other. Finkbeiner says one thing. The EMT says the other. (According to what you just wrote). So... who's right then? Who do you trust? My point is, the story can be entirely different depending on who you ask and who you interview. From my perspective, the police chief and Janette's family were the BEST people to interview. I built relationships with those people and felt confident airing what they told me. It corresponded with the report and autopsy that I obtained. With the facts. The story is about finding justice for Janette... I didn't want it to be different sources slinging mud at each other about whether or not someone made a mistake 30 years ago. Again, I do appreciate your interest in the story. I wish you the best of luck with your endeavors.

Let's autopsy that comment, shall we?

1. The sketches. He asserted that "First -- it's been well-established that police are still trying to track down people who could've been in the store that day. That's why they released those sketches. I didn't cover that up, it was mentioned in the story."

The sketches had nothing to do with the aforementioned three or four people the first responding officer shooed out of the store. Perhaps some of those folks are out there right now and have never been questioned. My thought is, if you want to do a responsible story on something like this, you specifically say, *"If you were in the store that day – if you left before police had a chance to speak to you about anything you might have seen, please contact, blah, blah, blah..."* It's pretty common sense stuff. Unfortunately it's not sexy, sexy ratings stuff. Also, the sketches probably aren't even relevant today, and he might have known that if he'd talked to Detective Pratt. But I guess he didn't.

2. "In any murder case like this, the spouse of the victim is always looked into. It's protocol. It HAD to be mentioned. However I made certain to say that Alvin WAS ruled out. It was not the entire focus of the story, just briefly mentioned. Maybe 30 seconds out of a 4+ minute report."

Yes, dear man. They *are* looked into, and wisely so. UNTIL THEY ARE RULED OUT AS SUSPECTS. You also slapped Alvin Roberson's picture up there and said the world *girlfriend* a couple times for good measure. Gentle reader, I'll let you be the judge and jury as to whether any of that was necessary.

3. We did obtain both the police report and the autopsy report. And I prepared my story, in part, according to what was there. You have to understand the danger in choosing sources for a story like this. There are endless rumors, and everyone has

> an different opinion... it would not be hard to find 5 people to interview, all with wide-ranging opinions on what happened... but that wouldn't be responsible on our part. We spoke with police and Janette's family, and I felt confident in that -- and in obtaining the facts. Hearsay is a dangerous game.

Notice the words "police report." *Singular.* There are numerous reports associated with this investigation, and it doesn't appear they used the Michigan State Police report in their story. You know—the law enforcement entity *assigned to investigate this case.* Then there's the Osceola Report, Cadillac PD, Wexford County... a tsunami of various reports and supplementals are associated with this case. Using one report—particularly the sketchy first responders report in this case—and the autopsy report to fashion a story does not a clear picture create. Not speaking to Michigan State Police seems like a glaring omission. Certainly not good journalism.

As far as family, the reporter spoke to nobody who had any day-to-day relationship with Janette at the time of the murder. Yes, her family loves her, but none of them were living in the area when Janette was murdered. I know firsthand that the information they have been able to cobble together over the years has been almost all hearsay, aside from an autopsy report they should never have gotten their hands on in the first place. I bear them no ill will. I'd probably be doing exactly what they are doing if my relative was brutally murdered. But that doesn't mean they're the best sources for factual information for a television report that should be based entirely on *facts*. Essentially, this reporter spoke with family and law enforcement officials who had the *least* amount of hands-on knowledge of this case, and in doing so, participated in that dangerous game of hearsay he seemed to insinuate I was playing a role in.

> 4. Trust me, I did some digging. I was told that someone is trying to write a book on Janette's murder. I was also told that his/her work hasn't been well-received by police or Janette's family.

His digging couldn't have gone that deep if the reporter didn't know he was speaking to the writer in question. As for law enforcement, I have no problem with them being less than cheerful about someone writing a book. For every unsolved homicide story being written, there's a cop who wishes the tenacious writer or journalist would go the hell away. Comes with the territory.

I am in constant contact with law enforcement associated with this case. I have always been up front with them, and I hope they have done the same with me. I did my due diligence, sat down with Chuck Davis, the Reed City Police Chief, spoke numerous times with MSP Inspector Cam Henke, I had to appear before the city council to get a copy of the Reed City first responder's report released, and most importantly, I sat down with the person who has the most knowledge regarding this case, Detective Sgt. George Pratt.

It is the job of law enforcement to solve a case; it is the job of the writer (and responsible journalists) to lift up rocks and shine a light in dark places to see what's wriggling around under there. Ours is not a surface sort of job, and if you think it is, maybe rethink your career trajectory. Our job is to dig. Thirty plus years is a long time for a crime to go unsolved. The public has the right to take a look at exactly why that is. You want to do a shitty, gratuitous job of reporting on an old unsolved murder to fill your Halloween timeslot, that's on you, buddy. But don't try to malign others for trying to get at the truth in a straightforward honest way.

Not without assuming you'll get called on it at some point.

April – December

There are thirteen pages of Michigan State Police report that were sent to me by their FOIA department which represent the nine months from April through December of 1983. The first page is dated April 1, 1983 and is two paragraphs:

INVESTIGATION:

As mentioned in the previous supplemental reports, investigation into the Janette Roberson murder is continuing with any leads being followed up on with tip information. As of this writing, approximately three hundred fifty (350) tips have been received with very few not totally completed and closed. Officers from the three investigating agencies continue to carry the investigation [into] the tips on the tip forms. Each individual contact is not being made as part of the supplemental reports.

COMPLAINT STATUS: Open.

A property report receipt dated April 11, 1983 shows Trixie Shepherd as having sent Janette's personal items back, and they were turned back over to Marion Fisher, her mother. The next supplemental dated April 30, 1983 states that "information/possible suspects due to MO has been received from the Investigative Resources Unit on several occasions pertaining to this case." It also notes that on April 20, 1983 Trixie Shepherd re-contacted Detective Pratt and "advised that the subject she visions as the murderer has light hair, a hairy chest, bushy eyebrows and a mustache. A hand-drawn composite was enclosed with her letter. She feels he used a small jackknife with a black handle."

At his request, a copy of the department profile and copies of the composites were forwarded to Det. Lt. Thomas Oakey from the MSP Third District.

The report notes that a benefit held for the Roberson family by the Reed City Jaycees provided $1,579.00, which was turned over to Marion Fisher for her daughter's family.

"Investigation continues into this case with tips still filtering in."

COMPLAINT STATUS: Open.

The May supplemental—dated May 31, 1983—states that on May 3, 1983 a letter was received from the victim's father, Ralph Fisher. *"He is upset that this matter has not been solved,"* Detective Pratt writes.

A brief redacted paragraph is included, and then the May supplemental ends with this line: *"Investigation into this matter continues however information/leads are getting fewer."*

Between May and August of 1983, Ralph Fisher, Janette's father – who was divorced from her mother Marion in 1971 – wrote numerous letters to people in positions of local and state government, including the county prosecutor James Talaske, Detective Sgt. George Pratt, as well as a senator and governor. The following is transcribed from an original draft, though it is unclear to whom this particular letter was being written.

> On January 19th, 1983 my daughter Janette G. Roberson was murdered. I'm sure you are quite familiar with this case.
>
> Being her father I am deeply concerned about her murderer being brought to justice. As you probably know, I have been to see detective Pratt concerning this. I was unable to get any information from him except that he has no suspects.
>
> There is no need for me to go into detail as to how Janette's death has affected me. It is hard to describe the grief knowing that Janette died so young and the manner in which she was killed. She was a good kid, happily married and friendly with everyone. As you are well aware this also has affected Marion, her mother, who is not in the best of health. I am not a detective and I do not claim to be one. I have conducted my own private investigation and have notified detective Pratt as to my progress.

From the death certificate Janette was killed with a blunt instrument, whatever that means. Estimated time of death was 2 to 3 o'clock in the afternoon. (From the death certificate.) How anybody could walk into a dept. store at that time of day and kill a person (and from what I have learned, she did not die instantly) also that her female organs were mutilated in some way. That someone else's blood was found near her body. Which means that she must have fought for her life, and must have inflicted some type of wound on her attacker. I wonder how much pain and suffering she had to endure. It is very hard for me to print those words when I think about that.

So what does it all add up to?

Her husband Alvin was in the store twice the day she was killed. This information I obtained from the store manager. Why wasn't Alvin at work? How did the store manager know this if he was not at the store at the time? The manager told me he was notified of Janette's death and then came to the store. I was also told by the manager that Alvin refused to take a lie detector test. (Why) Perhaps Alvin knows who killed her. And is afraid.

I also found out that Janette had frequently visited a pet shop in Big Rapids. She told this to Marion. Where she met a person who wanted to obtain some gerbils and small animals for experiments as he claimed to be a teacher or professor. From the local college or one of the schools. This person could be the one who murdered her. I went to this pet store and talked to a young man with black hair, who said he was the owner. He said he doesn't know of anyone who frequented his store who claimed to be a teacher or professor who wanted to obtain small animals for experiments. But he did have a friend who could use all the gerbils I could obtain. As I told him I had some. Perhaps this friend is the one Janette met in his store. In conversation Janette probably told him, or her, where she worked etc. All of this information I gave to Detective Pratt.

As far as I know there have been no recent violent murders in Reed City prior to my daughter's death. The whole thing smells fishy to me. Someone is either lying or covering up for someone. I believe Janette knew the person who killed her. Possibly a well-known person from Reed City or the surrounding area.

Again I will say that it seems impossible that anyone could walk into that store and kill a person (and as I said before, from the information I have gathered, it didn't happen in a moment) while there were people in that store and get away with it is beyond me.

I also realize that police have other duties and cannot devote all of their time to one murder. But if this murderer is not caught he or she may seek another victim. I don't know whether you are married or have any children of your own but if you do have a daughter and she was killed, especially in that manner then you could understand how I feel. I hope and pray that this will not be a forgotten case. I realize it takes time to solve some murders. I am not rich; if I were I would hire a private detective. I also hope you will take the time to answer this letter, as I would like to know if the investigation is continuing.

Sincerely,
Janette's Father

It is unclear where Ralph Fisher was getting his information, particularly about specifics regarding injuries and blood found near Janette's body. These aren't generally the types of specifics law enforcement shares with family that soon after a murder, *or ever*, at least until the case is solved. Whether or not any of his information is factually correct, I cannot verify. The only thing I can say is that technical observations are what one would find in a report like the autopsy report. Visual observations (in this context) are those which suggest the information was imparted by someone who had either been at the scene to witness the body, or got it second-hand from someone who had. I encountered this numerous times while researching this case; descriptions of injuries that weren't technical in nature, like the ME report, but accurate visual descriptions based on the information therein—descriptions that only people who had seen the body would know or be able to circulate. One has to ask themselves if things like this play heavily into why this case has not been solved. There's only so much damage you can do to a crime scene, so many people traipsing around the body that shouldn't have been, so much information put out there in error before a case becomes something no prosecutor would touch.

According to the supplemental dated June 30, 1983, on the first of the month information was received from the Investigative Resources Unit about subjects "with a similar MO as to what occurred in this case." Additionally, another lab report was received from the latent print unit. Also at this time, attempts were made to contact someone who'd called in a tip through 9 & 10 News. They agreed to run pleas for this person to contact Detective Pratt or another named individual however approval for the information to be run had to come from the FBI headquarters in Washington DC, for some reason. No plea was ever made because on June 6, 1983 the Cadillac MSP post received a call "distinguishable as coming from an outside payphone from a subject obviously holding his nose to talk."

What the individual said is redacted from the report.

On June 27, 1983 a card arrived at the MSP Post in Reed City addressed in care of The Roberson Family and came from Century 21 Denton Realty in Beulah, Michigan. The sender asked it to be forwarded to the family.

The last line in June of 1983 simply states "Investigation continues."

The supplemental for July dated the 31st has three short notations. The first is about a call that came in to city hall asking to speak to Marion Fisher. The call was taken by Carol Reed, the deputy clerk, but when she informed the caller that Marion Fisher was there, the woman on the phone declined and said, "No, I just want to say…[**REDACTED**]."

It couldn't have been much. It was only two lines.

On the 30th of July there is a short notation that Alvin Roberson got a new car and it lists the registration and VIN number. On the 31st a lab report came in with information about four sets of prints tested.

That month's report simply ends with COMPLAINT STATUS: Open.

The August supplemental notes an ad run in the local papers regarding the unsolved homicide. August 3, 1983: "Slightly over 6 months from the time of the homicide, a full page ad was run in The Pioneer newspaper asking for public assistance in the case. The ad was solicited from and paid for by Nartron Corp. Inc., Norman Rautiola, President."

Also on this date, Osceola County Prosecutor James Talaske received a letter from Ralph Fisher. On August 9th Detective Pratt received a call from Governor William E. Milliken's office referencing the case, as the Governor had also received a letter from Ralph Fisher. Two days later, Detective Pratt received a call from Senator Mitch Irwin's office referencing a letter received from Ralph Fisher.

There is a note that a call was received from the Tri-County Shopper's Guide about running an ad similar to the one run in The Pioneer, but when it was learned that "Undersigned [Detective Pratt] did not have any funds available to pay for the ad, they were not interested in running it as a public interest matter."

The last thing mentioned in the August report is Detective Pratt talking to the Montague County Sheriff's Department in Texas about Henry Lee Lucas and Otis Elwood Toole, alleged serial murders. "He advised that at this time he does not have any information that either were in Michigan at the time this homicide occurred. Also the MO is not their style. Lucas used to live in Michigan and was sentenced to prison for murdering his mother near Tecumseh, MI in the 1960s."

COMPLAINT STATUS: Open.

The next report is dated November 30th 1983 and begins with a note from September 1st by Detective Pratt saying it had been confirmed that Alvin Roberson "is leaving the state to return to Georgia and that he is marrying Lisa Miracle, who babysat for him after his wife died."

October 30, 1983 there is a short note that reads: *"Investigation continues, however, very little information coming in now."*

The November report mentions contact with other law enforcement officials about subjects arrested elsewhere to compare notes for possible similarities, though none appear viable. The last information in November of 1983 is regarding a report written by Officer Primeau of the Reed City Police Department. The attached supplemental dated November 16, 1983 reads: "Undersigned Officer [Michel Primeau, Reed City PD] while on foot patrol was flagged into the Speeds Auto Store by one of the salesman by the name of Jeff Cole. Undersigned went into the store and received information from Mr. Cole and another sales person by the name of Robert Murphy."

A gentleman had come into the store and asked if the pet shop was still open. When told yes, the man left, so the employees immediately flagged down a cop because they thought it was odd. I contacted Jeff Cole to get the specifics. He said a gentleman about 5'8" came into Speeds Auto Store, which was then located where Pere Marquette Deli is now—on the corner of Upton and Chestnut—and stated he was from Florida, then asked if the pet store was still in the basement of the Gambles store where the murder happened. He was told yes and then he left, purchasing nothing. He left his car parked in front of the auto store and appeared to be heading down toward Gambles.

At some point between the auto store and Gambles, the man was intercepted and questioned by Officer Primeau. Jeff Cole told me the guy was gone for about three hours before he came and retrieved his car. Officer Primeau's report says he requested the subject come to the post and have his photo taken. The man agreed, so he was transported to the State Post where he was photographed and questioned. As with much of what was being checked into regarding this case by the end of 1983, it ended up being nothing.

"Investigation into this case is being continued with the limited information that is coming in, along with the past months follow-up however no break in this case has come about."

COMPLAINT STATUS: Open.

At the end of 1983, Peter Piper—a state inmate housed at the Lake County Jail—escaped. He was in prison for CSC (Criminal Sexual Conduct) and attempted murder with a similar MO to Janette's case. He was incarcerated at the time of the murder, however Lake County Sheriff's Department occasionally brought inmates to Reed City to pick up medications, visit the doctor, pick up car parts, etc., but no record was ever found that he was in Reed City on the date of the homicide, or out of custody for any period of time when Janette Roberson was murdered. All of this was mentioned in the report.

Also at the end of 1983, the FBI in Washington DC was contacted in reference to the profile request sent to them in May by Michigan State Police. They were told it was to be completed "in the very near future."

Much if not all that was happening on the Janette Roberson case at this point was checking with other law enforcement entities and comparing notes on other unsolved murders with similar MO, to no avail. The Stella Lintemuth case is of note because it was solved not very long ago, after many years, and it was mentioned a few times in the Janette Roberson file, as far as leads checked to make sure there was no correlation between the two crimes.

Whitney Gronski-Buffa worked for *The Pioneer* at the time I was researching the Janette Roberson murder. I spoke to her numerous times about the case, and during one of our conversations she mentioned the Lintemuth case after I had expressed some concerns about how Janette's case file, three decades later, might not even be indexed and computerized. I worried that if the paperwork wasn't even on the computer system, what if the prints and other evidence associated with the case weren't all entered into whatever systems they need to be entered into, in case whoever killed Janette happened to do it again somewhere else. I knew so little about how Michigan State Police kept their very old cases organized, but it seemed to me that in order to actually solve a case, all the appropriate information needed to be organized and easily accessible to law enforcement officers who might want to check something they had against prints or evidence associated with another case. Nowadays, everything is immediately entered into computers, and that's how files are kept, but in 1983 that wasn't the case. In fact, when I spoke to the Michigan State Police Inspector about whether he would assign a cold case team Janette's case, he told me that all the files at the local MSP Post would need to be indexed and organized before the team could even start from page one and re-investigate Janette's murder, and that was ***if*** they choose it from the list of other Reed City "cold" cases.

I remember getting a little pain behind my left eyeball and thinking, "Oh, so this is what high blood pressure feels like." My pulse shot up to a dangerously high level and I could hear the *thrum-thrum* of blood circulating against my eardrums.

Really? I didn't say this out loud to the Inspector over the phone, but, *Really? We're now thirty-plus years after Janette Roberson was slain the basement of Gambles and you're telling me the file hasn't been entered into the computer yet? Is it just* her *file or are* all *the decades-old unsolved murders in Michigan lying around local MSP Posts in dank closets gathering the dappled essence of mold?*

Again, I didn't say it out loud. Not then, anyway. It would be a couple more months before I suggested to the head of the FOIA department at Michigan State Police that perhaps they wouldn't have to charge people for 84 (estimated) hours of work at fifty-five bucks an hour if they had some sort of universal rule that stated YOU KEEP ALL FILES, EVEN THE REALLY, REALLY OLD ONES UP TO DATE IN THE COMPUTER. I said it a little nicer than that, but the tone was implied.

So I'm sitting in the Pioneer office in Big Rapids with Whitney Gronski-Buffa, the reporter, and she's trying to explain to me what she was told happened with the Stella Lintemuth case. As a bit of backstory, Stella Lintemuth was 89 years old at the time she was brutally murdered. Her body was found in her bedroom beaten and stabbed with hedge clippers. She was also strangled. The cord from a light fixture was ripped off and found wrapped around her neck. Scott Elwood Graham's fingerprints were found on that cord, on the door in the master bedroom, as well as elsewhere at the crime scene.

"I covered the Graham case about two months after I started at the Pioneer. It was my first full-time reporting job, and my first step into crime reporting ever. When I started, Graham's case had already been reported on in the Pioneer for two years by Lindsey Wahoviak and Brandon Fountain, so the oddness of the case was kind of known in the newsroom. When Graham was found in California, he was in a state hospital. He had to be extradited to Michigan and that required an agreement with the governors because of a case he was involved in out there."

"A few days before the trial, I met with Frank West, then the director of Big Rapids Department of Public Safety. We met weekly, and that week we talked about this case. He was the first to really explain the fingerprint matter to me. As I remember it, Graham's fingerprints had been collected at the scene of the Lintemuth murder back in 1980, but because they didn't match any local records, they didn't provide much information to police. IAFIS (*Integrated Automated Fingerprint Identification System*) wasn't created until about 20 years later – in 1999. They didn't know it at the time, but Graham wasn't from the area. He was just passing through, riding the rails on what he called a post-break-up "odyssey," so local records wouldn't have helped anyway."

"At any rate, the fingerprints collected at the scene—taken from a wall lamp, the cord of which was used in the murder—were such good prints, Michigan State Police used them in training for years after that. Officers would run them through IAFIS to show trainees how to process them. According to West, during one such training, the prints hit for the first time ever. They linked back to Graham, who had just been arrested in California and placed in a state hospital (he was schizophrenic). I don't believe it was his first arrest, so I'm not sure why those prints wouldn't have hit sooner, but this was how West explained it to me."

"This was really fascinating to me, mostly because I was new and had never heard such a story. But about a year later, a similar thing happened with another case."

"Christopher Lauer committed a sexual assault in Big Rapids in late 2011. He raped a female friend in her apartment and threatened to kill her. When DNA from her rape kit was processed, it matched with an unsolved rape case in Philadelphia, where he had attended a conference for the hearing impaired in 2004. Lauer was convicted in both cases. "

"In both of these cases, I don't necessarily think there was any user error on the parts of the investigating officers. And, oddly enough, both cases involved crimes committed by people who were just visiting an area."

"The problem with systems like IAFIS and CODIS* is that they can only "find" suspects who are repeat offenders," Whitney explained.

> *CODIS stands for Combined DNA Index System. It is a free database, funded and hosted by the FBI, that local and state law enforcement agencies can use to exchange and compare DNA information electronically. It is a resource for matching DNA in a series of crimes, even if they are years apart and has been in existence since 1990.

"If you've never been arrested and fingerprinted, or given a sentence that requires DNA sampling, your information isn't in those systems. Even in situations like sexual assaults where the assailant isn't identified, the system is only as good as the police using it. For example, if DNA samples from a rape kit are never processed, a known problem in this country, those samples stand no chance of being linked to an assailant the next time he offends."

From *Promoting Effective Homicide Investigations* (2007):

> "As of May 2007, CODIS contained more than 4.7 million DNA profiles. The profiles are broken up into forensic profiles, where the DNA originated from crime scene evidence, and

> offender profiles, which contain the DNA of individuals convicted of sex offenses and other violent crimes. About 4.5 million profiles in the database are offender profiles. The CODIS system will identify matches between forensic DNA evidence and DNA from offenders. The CODIS system may also contain DNA profiles of missing persons, unidentified human remains, and arrestees (if state law allows)."

"Stella Lintemuth's murder was nearly 20 years cold by the time IAFIS was invented, so it would actually be pretty impressive if someone had thought immediately to run the prints from that case through this new system. Unfortunately, that's the tragedy of cold cases—in ever-shrinking police departments, they're no one's priority unless a cold-case-specific team picks them up."

"In Lauer's case, police did the right thing by entering the DNA information into CODIS, but their suspect had no priors and didn't reoffend (or at least wasn't caught in another case) until seven years later. The system worked, but it's more like lying in wait than going out to hunt."

Lying in wait, indeed.

My first question as a regular 'ole citizen with limited knowledge of what cops do on a daily basis is this: Doesn't it seem like there should be some kind of rule that you run latent lifts from possible perps of unsolved homicides through the system on a regular basis? Is this a stupid question? Because it seems like common sense to me. You have, let's say, 10 unsolved homicides on your books. Maybe you jot a little reminder on your desk calendar to run the prints you think are from the perpetrator of each unsolved murder through the database—oh, I dunno... maybe once a month; once every other month. Four times a year. Or how about this? Not all unsolved homicides are lucky enough to get their prints used for training purposes. How about we make that the RULE? Training prints all come from unsolved cases, so they get checked against the system on a regular basis and don't get shoved into a drawer or box or closet and forgotten for a few decades.

BOOM. You guys can have that for free.

You're welcome.

Now, LET'S GET BACK TO 1984...

As far as the Janette Roberson murder investigation, the year began with Detective Pratt interviewing "Dan" on January 4th in Grand Rapids. Remember "Dan"? He's the guy who had a crush on Janette and lived in the same apartment complex. His mother is the one who, but for the grace of God, was supposed to stop at Gambles that afternoon with her son-in-law, Roger Soper, to look at a bird Janette wanted to sell her.

In January of 1984, "Dan" consented to give finger and palm prints for comparison purposes. The report notes that no additional information was gleaned in the interview Detective Pratt did that day. He'd last been questioned on February 10, 1983.

On January 9th Detective Pratt received a call from the Caro MSP Post in reference to a man who was in the process of being extradited from Florida on a charge of CSC (Criminal Sexual Conduct) and assault with a knife. It was thought he might be a possible suspect based on MO, so the detective said he would submit a set of his prints to be checked once he was returned to Michigan.

On January 21st, 1984—almost one year to the day since the murder—Detective Pratt notes that he heard from Officer Finkbeiner of the Reed City Police, who'd spoken to a current employee of Gambles about another employee.

I tracked this woman down—we'll call her "Beverly"—and told her who I was, then asked about the notation in the report. She immediately said I was "barking up the wrong tree" thinking [**REDACTED**] was the killer. I told her I wasn't barking anywhere of the sort, nor was I suggesting anyone was a killer. I was merely checking into something the report said and asking her to elaborate.

"What report?" she asked.

"The Michigan State Police Report," I said. "It says, and I quote, *'From PO Finkbeiner, he talked to "Beverly" who works at Gambles about [**REDACTED**].'*" She quickly shot back that she'd never spoken to anyone about anyone who worked at the store. Then she said she was not comfortable talking to me since the case was ongoing.

"They brought some investigators from out of state to work on it," she said.

I have no facts to back that assertion up, nor have I seen anything to indicate such, but I rolled with it. I told "Beverly" I was absolutely okay if she didn't want to discuss it, that I was aware it was an ongoing investigation—albeit one that had been "ongoing" for more than three decades—and if she felt she had information that was important to the case and did not want to share it, I could respect that.

She stumbled and seemed genuinely uncomfortable, and said she didn't know why anyone would think a book right now would be a good idea. I told her Janette's daughter and the rest of her family would probably like some answers... it *had* been thirty years. She said she could understand Janette's daughter wanting to know, but sometimes these things take time and she didn't feel comfortable talking to someone she didn't know because her life could be in danger.

I may have rolled my eyes. Okay, I did. I rolled my eyes. Mainly because when people start saying their life might be in danger around a thirty-year-old-murder, I assume they've watched too many episodes of *Dateline*. But I humored her and let her continue because, despite saying she did not feel comfortable talking, she kept right on talking.

She said to tell Janette's daughter to be patient because *these things take time*. I made a mental note to tell the daughter of the woman who was brutally slaughtered that maybe she should just be more patient... like for another three decades.

"Beverly" talked about working at Gambles in the pet department. She told me she spoke to Janette every day, especially when she would water the birds in their cages and she'd promise Janette they'd catch whoever did it, someday. She said it was scary down there, but she would lock herself in the back room when she was feeding the animals, and lock herself in and out when she was working in the back room. She told me after the murder, Gambles had a policy that when a customer came downstairs, another employee would stand at the top of the stairs and watch. Didn't exactly sound like a cozy work environment. I'm not sure I'd want to work somewhere I felt it necessary to lock myself in and out of the back room every time I had to go back there for something.

"Beverly" said she worked at Gambles for a couple years, but finally left because of the "controversy." Something about the boss wanting her to work in one department, and his wife wanting her to continue working in the pet department.

"It just became too much, so I quit."

Most of what she said was vague. "I learned a *lot* of things while working down there." But then "Beverly" would say she wasn't comfortable talking about them because of the ongoing investigation. She said one day the husband and daughter of a realtor who was killed came in to show her a picture of a man to see if she recognized him, but she didn't. (We'll talk more about the realtor later. Reed City has a few decades-old homicide investigations that remain open, and the case of the realtor, Sue Clason, is one of them.)

Near the end of our conversation, Beverly confided, "I think it was a hit."

Cue my second eye-roll. But "Beverly" was serious. She said the person who killed Janette was well known and had a lot of money, but "Even rich people can't cover up everything." To that last point, I heartily agreed.

I heard the "hit" conspiracy theory a few times and it always made me cringe. Just to be clear *for the record*, I found ZERO evidence of anything close to a "hit" where Janette Roberson was concerned. There is no indication that anything even remotely resembling a "hit" occurred, except within the confines of some overactive imaginations.

"Tell her kids to be patient," "Beverly" repeated. "I want it solved, too, but I can't say something that could get me killed because I have other people to think about."

Don't we all?

Beverly also warned me that she thought it wasn't a good idea to be talking too much about it when they were so "actively" working on the investigation. She repeated that a few times in the conversation, like it might not be safe for me to be asking questions. Thank you, "Beverly." Duly noted. I wasn't sure what to make of it. I couldn't get a read on if she was just one of those melodramatic gossips who wanted to appear more involved than they are, or if she really had sensitive information that she didn't think it wise to share. One thing she *did* seem to want me to know was that she was in-the-know about the status of the investigation.

"Now is not the time, when things are so active, to be talking so much about this."

To that point, and even according the latest news report by the *Reporter-Who-Dare-Not-Speak-His-Name*, there were no plans to put a cold case team on the Roberson case. In fact, his report ended with that tidbit as he stared, piercingly, into the camera.

At that point, the last time I'd spoken with the MSP Inspector who would be responsible for assigning such a task, *he* wasn't even sure they were going to put a cold case team on the Roberson case. He was still weighing his options, deciding which from the pile of unsolved cases before him might be the most "solvable," which is concern one when deciding whether to toss precious resources at a cold case. But, you never know. Maybe there was a whole bunch of behind-the-scenes stuff going on and "Beverly" was somehow an integral part of it. I hoped it was the latter.

Back to the MSP report...

On January 23, 1984—just days after Finkbeiner supposedly spoke with "Beverly" about a Gambles employee—and again, one year, almost to the day, after the murder of Janette Roberson—information came in from a source who wished to remain anonymous.

"The source feared [he] may have been involved in the homicide of the victim in this case." The source said that this subject had returned to the area two weeks before Christmas in 1982, staying with a relative. The relative's information was given and the report notes the residence in question is in the same apartment complex as Janette and her family live.

"The victim's rear entrance of her apartment faced the same courtyard which the front entrance of the family member's apartment faced."

According to the anonymous source, the subject remained living with this relative until a day or two after Christmas, at which time he moved into an apartment that was less than a mile from the victim's apartment complex. Multiple people were questioned in January regarding this person.

At the end of the January supplemental, it is noted that the FBI profile had been received regarding the case, and is described as being *"...quite lengthy and similar to the profile completed by the Behavioral Sciences Unit/Investigative Resources Unit which had previously been done."*

In February of 1984, Detective Southworth of the Osceola County Sheriff's Department is busy interviewing people regarding the subject who was called in by the anonymous source. A detailed background check is performed on the subject, and then his mother is interviewed at length in the beginning of March.

Also in March, a brief note from Detective Pratt that said a former inmate had been "talking about the Roberson murder," but was found to have been incarcerated in the Osceola County jail at the time of the murder. On March 10th more lab analysis reports were received from the Latent Print Unit.

Meanwhile, Detective Southworth continued to question numerous people who knew the subject called in by the anonymous source. After multiple interviews throughout February and March of 1984, the first **POSSIBLE SUSPECT** is named in the Janette Roberson murder investigation in the MSP report. His name is Lee Peterson and a relative of his lived in the same apartment complex as Janette. By all accounts, the family was well known and liked. Lee had graduated from Reed City High School and had been in the army—Vietnam—and was honorably discharged.

It is also clear that he was mentally ill. One of the people Detective Southworth spoke to was a woman who worked at a local Adult Foster Care Facility. I was able to interview another woman who worked at the facility during that time, and the story she relayed was disturbing.

She maintained that Lee Peterson had terrorized multiple women who worked at the foster home for months. He would come and bang on the wall or the garage door. After a while, he started showing up around where the women lived. He'd be seen walking around the immediate area of each of their homes. According to the woman I spoke to, he was stalking them—at least three other women in addition to her—and they all worked at the same foster care facility. One of the women got so scared she bought a gun and got a concealed weapon permit. The foster care employee I spoke to said cops told the woman if Lee came at her to empty the gun. "Don't talk, just shoot."

The foster care employee told me Peterson would show up at the facility or their homes and bang on the walls. At one point, the State Police set up in the house next door to hers for three nights, hoping to catch Peterson in the act, but he never showed up while police were there.

The women—who took turns staying with the foster adults overnight for supervision—continued to get anonymous threatening calls while at work. In one of them, the woman I spoke to said she was named specifically and he threatened to kill her.

She alleges that a relative close to one of the investigators in this case said to her once, "You know this is the guy who killed Janette Roberson, right?" This family member happened to own the house next door to hers where police set up to try and catch him.

According to her, as soon as the cops left the stakeout, five minutes later Peterson would show up outside, banging on windows, walls, and doors. He kept showing up after police left. This woman lived out in the country, and she said that eventually cops found a hole dug out of the ground behind someone's back yard with newspapers for cushion. It was within view of her home. She believes that's why he knew every time cops were not around, and why they could never catch him.

She described Peterson as handsome, aggressive, and would be walking down the street near her house, talking to himself like he was having a violent conversation. She recalled an incident when she ran into him while walking her dogs. She said she had to duck into a store because he was following her.

When asked if Peterson had any link to the people who lived in the foster home or the employees, she said no, police believed he'd targeted the place because there were vulnerable women working there. When I asked how it all ended, the foster care worker said that one night Lee was apprehended in Paris, Michigan. According to her, "The place was lit up like crazy."

She wasn't sure what became of Lee Peterson after that. Her understanding was that he was put in a mental hospital as the result of the Paris apprehension. When I told her Lee Peterson was dead, the woman seemed surprised. She said she wanted to know for sure because he'd threatened to kill her. The next day I made sure to send along a picture of his gravestone. He's buried in the same cemetery as Janette Roberson.

She told me police were aware of Lee Peterson when she made her first call about him. This was when he was walking up and down her street during the "stalking" phase. She called Reed City Police and they told her they'd be right there, and to make sure all doors were locked and get to an inside room away from all windows, and under no circumstances go outside or have any contact with him. According to her, the first complaint about Peterson was to the Reed City Police, but thereafter Michigan State Police took over for the stakeouts. Three times that she could recall they sat with her at the foster home when she worked.

When I spoke with her by phone, after she'd relayed this information, she asked me if I knew Lee Peterson's mother had owned the Gambles store years previous to David Engels purchasing it. I nodded, as if she could hear me through the phone. It had been ricocheting against my skull like a ping-pong ball gone berserk since the moment she mentioned his mother's name.

He was familiar with that basement...

My research assistant was able to track down the ex-wife of Lee Peterson, who verified that he was diagnosed as paranoid schizophrenic at the Kalamazoo hospital while they were married. She remembered police coming to ask her questions about Lee in the 1980s but had no idea what it was in reference to. She assumed it was due to him being in and out of mental institutions as early as

1977. She said police were only there for a short time, and never gave her any information other than asking about his personality.

"He beat my daughter black and blue from her neck down, was charged with child abuse, and never saw her again." She maintained that Lee hated women after she left him and she didn't want to, in any way, be associated with his name, because that time in her life was very painful. She said Lee Peterson was abusive, would never stay on his medications, and was absolutely capable of violence.

"He was very sick."

The whole conversation made me sad for everyone involved, and it quickly became clear why cops went at him so hard. Lee Peterson definitely looks good on paper—for the murder, I mean. History of violence, familiar with the physical location where the murder occurred, was in Reed City during the appropriate timeframe... But could they link him to the crime scene on the day of the murder? Whether or not he was capable of violence, I had uncovered no evidence that put Lee Peterson at the scene of Janette's murder *that day*. The fact that their encounters with the man as it related to the Roberson investigation didn't begin for a full year after the murder, and he wasn't listed as someone who'd been fingerprinted with everyone else listed in the early days of the investigation as having been in the store that day, speaks volumes.

I obtained a copy of Peterson's death certificate because that is often the best jumping-off point for information. Needless to say, when his death was listed as suicide, but the immediate cause of death was due to "multiple stab wounds to the chest" I had a moment. *Multiple*? A quick Google search suggests that stabbing oneself to death isn't a popular mode of suicide. In fact, while stabbings are a relatively common cause of homicide, they're the mechanism of only about 2% of suicides, according to *The Manual of Forensic Emergency Medicine: a Guide for Clinicians*. (2010, Ralph J. Riviello) I mean, think about it. If you're going to kill yourself, you've got to have some serious testicular fortitude to stab yourself multiple times when you could just as easily wrap your mouth around a tailpipe, or take a handful of pills. Not to make light of suicide—because there's nothing light about a topic so horribly brutal—but if you're going to do it, don't do it that way. In fact, I'd suggest not doing it at all. Give it another day. Shit usually looks better in the morning.

In this case, that's glib, and let me tell you why. When you're mentally ill and suicidal, your entire thought process is such that common sense and reason do not apply. There is no figuring out why someone who is in the throes of a dissociative or psychotic episode, severe depression, or any number of mental health emergencies does what he or she does. There's pain, and then there's an abyss from which some people never return. Most of us cannot fathom that kind of confusion and despair, and in cases like this, it is best to do what good humans do and try to empathize rather than judge. I should note that I have people with mental illness in my family. I also have a cousin who was schizophrenic and killed himself. It is from this perspective that I can look at someone and understand that the person and the illness are often two different things, while physically they will always be bound together.

Lieutenant Todd Golnick of the Cadillac Police Department was extremely forthcoming as far as documentation I requested while researching this particular aspect of the Janette Roberson case. To be fair to the other entities involved, that's because the subject of my inquiry was deceased and the Cadillac PD case was closed, so Lieutenant Golnick was able to furnish me with a great deal of insight and paperwork. While he did provide some documents that Cadillac PD prepared involving the Janette Roberson murder, the bulk of what I got from Lieutenant Golnick (researched, copied, and supplied by Hope Thomson, Cadillac's fantastic Public Safety Clerk) had to do with the suicide of Mr. Peterson because the incident occurred within their jurisdiction.

August 25, 1996—thirteen years after the death of Janette Roberson—a man named Bernard Rouse walked into the Cadillac Police Department and said he had found a man lying dead with a knife beside him. An officer was sent to the scene and found the body of Lee Peterson in his apartment. The door was unlocked. The report included a list of evidence taken from the scene, descriptions of what was to be photographed, brief descriptions of how the officers handled the physical scene, and two other incident reports involving Lee Peterson—one in March, and one in May of the same year (1996)—prior to his death. The report in March was a citation for a noisy muffler/excessive fumes. The incident on May 16, 1996 was a suspicious situation/well-being check. Officers were dispatched to check on a subject that may have fallen and injured himself.

> "Initial contact with Lee Peterson required the Fire Department and EMS to assist as he had an apparent injury, dried blood near his ear and his mattress was smoldering. Lee was in need of Mental Health, yet he refused treatment. He was disoriented, over-active, talking in confused sentences, wanting to preach the Christian way. Neighbors stated he had mental problems in the past, but this was far more serious behavior."

An employee from the Mental Health Unit arrived and Lee Peterson was transported to the Mercy Hospital Emergency Room for evaluation. The following narrative (*Figure 1*) was the bulk of the report regarding the August 25, 1996 scene officers encountered when they arrived. I contacted Lieutenant Golnick by email and asked, among other things, why a rape kit was performed on Lee Peterson because it had been noted as one of the items sent to the lab, along with finger and palm prints, and serology (blood).

"Why would you need to do a rape kit on someone who committed suicide?" I asked. Lieutenant Golnick suggested I come to his office and sit down with him and he would gladly answer any questions. He thought a conversation would be easier than doing it by email, at which point I told him that I was working on a book, and my questions about Peterson had to do with my interest in the Janette Roberson investigation. He told me to come in and he'd answer any questions he could. So I did.

Lieutenant Todd Golnick is a tall, strapping gent with an amiable personality and a quick smile. I was ushered into his office as soon as he was free, and sat with him for about an hour, during which time he told me that Hope, the Public Safety Clerk, was able to locate more information for me in the evidence room, including photos of the scene if I was interested, as well as a longer version of the report. Because many of the departments I dealt with didn't go to their current computerized crime reporting systems until after the incidences I was researching, it had been difficult to get original paperwork. As it turned out, because this particular scene necessitated an abundance of caution, given the nature of the suicide, there was a hardcopy stored with the pictures, and a video of the scene, though the evidence had long since been destroyed.

The first responders had wisely called in an evidence team from Grand Rapids to handle the scene in the interest of thoroughness, which was the reason the rape kit was done. They took every possible precaution to make sure it was a suicide, given on paper eighty-something stab wounds doesn't sound like suicide. But when you look at the images, you quickly get a picture of what occurred; errant pills scattered around the apartment, fine blood spatter on the hallway walls, bathroom floor, and the kitchen counter and floor; the victim laying on the floor in the living room area, fully dressed, with what appears to be tears in his shirt over his left chest area. The officers took great care in documenting the entire scene, and it seems clear that whatever occurred during Lee Peterson's last day, it took a little while. He was wandering around that apartment, likely not in his right mind, based on the scrawled suicide note found in a kitchen drawer, which contains not even one complete, meaningful sentence. But the autopsy photos of the "stab" wounds tell most of the story. Almost all of the wounds are superficial. I'd call them scratches or nicks. Cops would probably call them hesitation wounds. What it looks like to the untrained eye is a very mentally ill man who wandered around his apartment, ingesting more of his prescribed medication than was indicated, and repeatedly stabbed himself in the chest, almost always just the tip of the paring knife found next to him piercing the skin. Secondary causes of death according to the death certificate are listed as pulmonary emphysema and haloperidol intoxication. The toxicology report listed the only other things other than the haloperidol found in his system were nicotine (heavy smoker), ethanol (alcohol), and caffeine. The fine mist spatter found on the walls and bottom of the refrigerator where he finally laid were likely him aspirating blood.

Cadillac Police Department
Incident Report

Incident No: **96-003359**
Page No: **4**

Original Narrative, completed 08/25/1996 (continued):

him.

INVESTIGATION;

I went to the above listed location which is an apartment above the Natural Food Store. Upon arriving at the apartment door, the door was unlocked. When the door was opened I observed the body of a white male lying on the kitchen floor. The body was lying in a pool of blood. Apparent stab wound was observed at the left nipple area of the victim. A paring knife was laying on the floor by the victims right hand. The kitchen floor and counter had what appeared to be blood splattered on them.

It appeared the victim had been deceased for some time. An E.M.S. unit arrived and it was agreed that the medical examiner should be contacted. Medical Examiner contact by the E.M.S. unit. An interview was conducted with Bernard Rouse, the person who found the deceased. Rouse stated he went to the back patio which is used by all the people living there. The window of the deceased victim is on the patio. The window was open with a screen in place. He noticed the TV was on. Rouse stated he remembered that the victim's Friday mail was still in the mail box on Saturday. Rouse went to the victim's door and knocked, no one answered he tried the door and it was unlocked states he opened the door and saw the victim lying on the floor.

Central Dispatch was requested to contact Det. Creed and two (2) evidence technicians. A search of the apartment revealed suspected blood on a wall in a hallway to a bedroom. The TV in the bedroom was on. Suspected blood was observed by a coffee cup rack on the south Kitchen wall. A large light tan colored pill was observed on the kitchen floor.

Det. Creed arrived and was appraised of the situation. Dr. Gregg, Medical Examiner arrived and viewed the body. It was decided to call for Michigan State Police Crime lab and sent the victim to Blodgett Hospital for a forensic autopsy by Dr. Cohle.

MSP-76 Cadillac Post was contacted for a crime scene team. Evidence Technicians Hawk and Tschirhart arrived. 35 MM photographs of the scene were taken by Officer Tschirhart. A video tape of the scene was made by Officer Hawke. Tpr. Troph, MSP-76 advised the crime lab in Grand Rapids was sending a crime scene unit to the scene. Patrolman Koenig was posted in the hallway near the apartment door. Street Patrolman Huber was posted at the downstairs door to the apartments.

At 00:30 hours on August 26, 1996, a crime scene unit led by Lt. Harold Sevenance arrived, Severance advised their Complaint Number is 33971-96. The scene was turned over to the crime lab. 09:00 hours on August 26, 1996 I was advised that the autopsy would be conducted as soon as we could get to Blodgett Hospital. I, Sgt. Hofstra and Officer Tschirhart went to Blodgett Hospital in Grand Rapids and attended the autopsy conducted by Dr. Steven Cohle and Dr. John Connelly.

Investigation of the wounds on the deceased revealed eighty five (85) superficial stab wounds and two (2) stab wounds that went between the ribs but were not deep enough to cause death. Further investigation of the stomach contents showed what looked to Dr. Connelly to be the remains of ingested pills. Dr. Connelly said he was confident the deceased died from an overdose of drugs. Autopsy was photographed by Officer Tschirhart. Blood samples and rape kit were turned over to Rodney Wolfarth at the Grand Rapids MSP Crime Lab. Autopsy results should be available about August 29, 1996.

Figure 1: Peterson incident report

Lee Peterson was a very sick man who had served our country and my first instinct is to wonder whether he was failed by the mental health system. I'd like to think that if he were alive today, he'd get better care, but I don't know if that's the case. You can't force someone who is living on their own to take their prescribed medication. It's very common for people diagnosed with schizophrenia to stop taking their medications for various reasons, including not liking how it makes them feel. The longer report revealed that Lee was being supervised, and had a home visit by a mental health worker on August 23, 1996 in the afternoon, days before his death. The man had helped him get his pills together in a pill box, yet it appears—based on what was in the container after he died—he hadn't been taking the appropriate dosage.

In addition, the mental health worker noted that he had seen 20 or 30 tablets in the haloperidol bottle when he'd visited Lee, two days prior, but only the empty haloperidol bottle was found when officers arrived.

In the end, I was not able to locate even one person that could put Lee Peterson at the Gambles store the day Janette Roberson was murdered.

Maybe that information is in a witness report somewhere, and not turned over with the file I received. Clearly a lot was held back. But I think it's more likely that Michigan State Police looked at Lee Peterson because he had a history of erratic behavior and violence, he was in town when the murder occurred, and at that point, it was the best lead they had. Police only started looking at him after an anonymous caller suggested they should, a full year after the murder.

To me that suggests that prior to that, he had not been linked to the crime scene on the day of the murder. My concern was whether his prints were compared to any latent lifts they took from the crime scene that they believed were from the perpetrator. This document from the Lee Peterson Cadillac PD file left me further concerned.

STATE OF MICHIGAN
DEPARTMENT OF STATE POLICE
FORENSIC SCIENCE DIVISION
GRAND RAPIDS LABORATORY
720 FULLER AVE. NE
GRAND RAPIDS, MICHIGAN 49503
(616)242-6650
FAX (616)242-6682

ORIGINAL

LABORATORY REPORT

Laboratory No.: 33971-96 Supp.
Received By : Doug Westrate
Delivered By : Tpr Crow Cadillac Post
Agency : Cadillac Police Dept.
Agency No. : 3359-96

Record No. : 9605759
Date Received : 08-26-96
Time Received : 05:40 AM
File Class : 900-1
Date Completed: 10-25-96
Bin : 227

Nature of Offense:

Murder/Nonnegligent Manslaughter

Evidence Received: (Evidence received directly by Tpr. Doug Westrate at the scene)

1 - Mead lined writing tablet with the top paper containing writing in blue ink and containing under the top paper:
 1 - Small piece of yellow lined paper.
3 - Latent lifts.

Processing Results:

The previously listed evidence was not processed per phone conversation with Det. Creed.

Examination Results:

The latent lifts were examined and latent fingerprints appearing to be of value for identification purposes were observed.

Automated Fingerprint Identification System:

The latent fingerprints on this case are not suitable for entry into AFIS.

Remarks:

The latent lifts were placed on file at this laboratory pending future requests.

Douglas Westrate, D/Tpr.
State Police Laboratory Specialist
Latent Print Subunit

Greg Stevens, D/Sgt.
State Police Laboratory Specialist
Latent Print Subunit

DW/GS/cmr

Public Act 35 of 1994 requires: "The investigating officer of each criminal case being adjudicated shall advise the prosecuting attorney if a forensic test has been conducted in the case."

There were a couple questions I had about it, so I got on the horn with Lieutenant Golnick again and he was helpful in the explanations. **First**—does murder /Non-negligent manslaughter equal suicide? Was that the technical term, for the purposes of law enforcement? The answer is no. Here's his explanation:

"All police incident reports get a file class assigned to them. The file class system is known as the Michigan Incident Crime Reporting Index or MICR. Keep in mind it is

an 8-hour course of instruction in how to manage them so I will only give you the short explanation here. Most times whenever we investigate a death of unknown cause it will be assigned a 0900-1 file class which is the file class for murder/manslaughter. It can always be downgraded as the investigation reaches other conclusions and in this case it does change to a suicide. By starting out as a 0900-1 file class the incident gets faster service and better attention from the crime lab as well. So in answer to your first question, the investigation starts out as a murder/manslaughter and then concludes as a suicide. This is typical when an investigator walks into a confusing scene such as this one."

Second—under PROCESSING RESULTS: *The previously listed evidence was not processed per phone conversation with Det. Creed.* Why wasn't it processed?

"Your second question is about why some items were not lab tested. Whenever we process crime scenes we gather everything we feel may potentially have evidentiary value. Then we discuss the evidence with the crime lab and an agreement is typically made on what will be processed and what will not. The lab cannot and will not test everything we collect. There are some rare occasions where that may occur, but only as the initial evidence submitted to them is found to be inconclusive or unrelated to the investigation. In other words, the lab and the investigator were satisfied that only the items submitted would be necessary."

Finally—under AUTOMATED FINGERPRINT IDENTIFCATION SYSTEM: *The latent fingerprints on this case are not suitable for entry into AFIS*. Why?

"Your third question is in relationship to AFIS (Automated Fingerprint Identification System). I am not the person to speak about this topic, however I will tell you what I know from an investigators point of view. AFIS

> *requires unknown prints that are lifted and submitted to its system for ID have a minimal amount of information in them. If the lifted latent prints don't meet that criteria, then no submission can be made. I will tell you that AFIS was a young system in 1996 and it has improved significantly since then."*

I think the most unjust thing I have learned while researching Janette Roberson's murder is that police are under no obligation to disabuse the public of any notions about who they might (unrightfully) believe to be a killer. Lee Peterson, "Dan," and Alvin Roberson were just three people associated with this case who various long-time locals were *sure* had killed Janette. One would think it easy enough for cops to publicly say, *We ruled him out*, but it isn't something they tend to do. It took over thirty years for them to do so in the case of Alvin Roberson—who arguably suffered more than anyone, other than his children. Insult to injury is the phrase that echoes in my head. *Insult to injury...*

All I can do to try and mitigate any damage done to their memories is show how police had the opportunity and means (via samples taken from all three people) to rule them out *if that was a possibility*. Maybe it wasn't. Maybe the evidence in those three cases was not as black and white as the general public tends to think it is.

I can tell you that no law enforcement entity would be considering putting a cold case team on a case where the perpetrator is dead. Not when they have a stack of other cold cases they could turn their attention to. I am certain about that. They also wouldn't be keeping reports and files so tight to the vest if they were fairly sure the dead guy did it. There would be no common sense reason for that. Not everyone police looked at committed this crime. In fact, that shining honor goes to but one person. So what are the others, the un-vindicated, *the innocent* left with but a smudge they can't ever rub away because no matter how hard they try, there will always be someone out there who can't see past it.

Something about that seems rather unjust to me. My internal monologue goes a tad further. *It's pretty damn shitty.*

Laren Thorson

Evidence Collection

I spoke with Nelson Gelinas on January 28, 2015 for about an hour, after getting his name from Laren Thorson as being the person who created Northern Counties Evidence Service. Gelinas was formerly a crime scene technician with Oakland County Sheriff's Department. He came up with the innovative idea of a mobile crime lab service after having many sheriffs in his district complain about not having a fire or fingerprint expert in the area. Gelinas had given lectures at many of the area colleges regarding fingerprinting and fire cases, and had extensive knowledge and training in the field. With the encouragement of the sheriff's departments, Gelinas put together a pitch for a mobile crime lab that would service multiple counties in the area and presented it to the area County Boards of Commissioners. Once they were on board and the project was funded, he ended up starting with twelve counties.

This was in 1979. Each sheriff's department would need one deputy to be trained as a first responder whose main purpose was to keep the crime scene from being compromised by taping off the area and making sure no one entered until the law enforcement entity assigned to the scene arrived.

Gelinas interviewed deputies from all twelve counties, finally settling on fourteen individuals who were all required to take a three week course. For continuing training, which was kept up regularly, each deputy would have to go down to Kalkaska for a week, stay in a hotel, and respond to all scenes Gelinas was dispatched to, so they would encounter various types of crime scenes. According to his recollection, Detective Southworth with Osceola County had taken the training, as well as then Deputy Chuck Davis (who is currently the Reed City Police Chief). He said he did not recall Reed City Officer Theodore Platz ever taking the NCES training, even when I mentioned that he'd helped process the Roberson crime scene at Gambles.

I asked Gelinas what was covered in the three week training each deputy took. He said they learned how to protect the scene, the first and most important aspect being taping off the area. Nobody was to be let into the area until NCES got there. Interviews could be done, he said, while the first responder awaited the arrival of the mobile unit. Deputies were taught about how to properly enter a scene, taking into account things like mud, snow, and prints—all training around maintaining a secure scene with no unnecessary traffic. The deputies learned about preserving, packaging, and marking evidence collected, and also how to testify at trial. He said it was a comprehensive course that covered everything from the time the deputy received the call, to them testifying at trial, if necessary. All of the evidence collected by NCES would then be delivered to the Bridgeport Crime Lab until the Grayling Lab was established out of necessity. NCES dealt with everything from robberies, homicides, plane crashes, fires... many different types of crime scenes. They were the first ever in the area to video crime scenes, Gelinas said, and he ran the mobile lab for three years, then Laren Thorson took over.

Laren Thorson handled the collection of evidence at the scene of Janette Roberson's murder, and was eventually assisted by officers Doornbos and Bailey, who were sent by Cadillac at the request of Sheriff Needham (Osceola County) late that night. Thorson was a ten year veteran with the State Police crime lab in Lansing. According to an article in the *Ludington Daily News* published on September 11, 1982, the service was a mobile evidence unit or "crime lab on wheels" that contracted with counties at a cost of $4,500 per year for a twenty-four hour service. "Should a county decide to contract their services, several [local] officers would be trained as a response team until Thorson and the mobile unit arrived at the scene." In addition, it covered transportation of evidence, and boasted "modern" equipment such as "audio-visual camera and recorder, evidence collection kit, casting equipment, anti-putrefication kit, ultraviolet light, halogen lights, latent fingerprint kits, evidence vacuum kit, metal detector, 35mm cameras, fingerprint camera, tools, post-mortem kit, and measuring kit. Crimes frequently investigated by the NCES are," the article goes on to say, "arsons, homicides, sex offenses, robberies, breaking and entering, assaults, kidnappings, larcenies and identification of decomposed bodies."

I spoke with Laren Thorson on Saturday December 6th, 2014. He told me he retired from Michigan State Police in October of 1976. After that, he and his wife bought a hardware store, selling it in 81. In 1982 he took over Northern Counties Evidence Service.

He said he was not sure exactly what time he arrived at Gambles the day of the murder, but it would have taken him an hour or so to get there from Kalkaska where he was notified, so it would have been at least that long after the discovery of the body. He believed Sheriff Needham had contacted him.

"When I arrived, the scene was very disorganized and nobody knew who was in charge."

He said multiple law enforcement entities were milling around among customers and employees still being held for questioning. Because of that, it appeared to him that the store wasn't even closed, that's how many people were wandering around Gambles when he arrived. He says he was approached immediately when he entered by Theodore Platz, who proceeded to take him down to the basement and do a walk-thru with him, pointing out multiple items for Thorson to take note of. Thorson says he wasn't sure of Platz' role at the scene. He just continued to point things out, "See this? Look at that..." as Thorson took pictures. He told me they weren't the only people in the basement pet department while he was doing so. After they completed walk thru, Thorson recalls saying, "Either you guys get this scene under control or I'm leaving."

It was around this time, approximately 30 minutes after he'd arrived, when they agreed to take a break and set up a command center in one of the business next door. According to Thorson, at this time Osceola Prosecutor James Talaske assigned Detective Sgt. George Pratt as lead on the investigation and questioning witnesses, with Thorson as lead on the crime scene.

"But by then it was compromised," Thorson said. "If I'm working a scene, I want it organized and I want it done in a professional, methodical manner."

I asked Thorson if he believed they got a viable set of perpetrator prints.

"We got a lot of prints, but I'd have no way of knowing which ones were from the perpetrator. My job is to take all the evidence I can find."

That doesn't sound like a situation where there was a bloody hand print on the wall with the killer's signature scrawled below it, if you catch my drift.

Thorson did recall they got what eventually turned out to be a set of prints that matched Alvin Roberson's from a countertop "...at the opposite end of the room from where she was found." That would have been the register area. Multiple people had said Alvin was in the store that day. These folks were also quick to note that wasn't normal. Flossie seemed to back that up when she said Alvin didn't come in the store much. In fact, she didn't remember seeing him at all that day. Multiple people told me the "manager" told them Alvin had been there that day. Whether they were speaking about David or John Engels is unclear, since even Flossie didn't consider John a "manager" and she was a longtime employee.

But let me pose a theory here, and you are perfectly within your rights to completely disregard it. If Janette had, in fact, been getting obscene phone calls, as reported to Prosecutor Talaske, perhaps Alvin was checking in on his wife? It may have been odd for him to stop into the store, but it was noted early in the MSP report that Alvin Roberson was laid off from his job for that week, so he wasn't working. Maybe he had nothing better to do. We'll discuss the testimony of witnesses in a little bit, but I believe it's worth noting, particularly from an investigative standpoint, that when more than one explanation for an event is possible, the best choice is usually the simplest one with the fewest assumptions. Absent facts that show otherwise, it's best not to make things more complicated than necessary.

It appears those prints of Alvin's, coupled with some "red spots"

Detective Southworth saw on Alvin's boots when he went to notify him, made Alvin Roberson the most obvious suspect, right off the bat. Spouses usually are, and that's because 80 to 90% of the time in cases like this it *is* someone very close to the victim, often the spouse significant other, or relative. Years later, we know Alvin was ruled out, according to the interview given to the press by the current Reed City Police Chief. (That would be the interview your friendly writer took umbrage with. Lots and lots of umbrage.)

When I spoke to him, Thorson mentioned that he'd heard Alvin left town right after the murder—another one of those tidbits I'd frequently heard being ticked-off as reasons locals thought Alvin must have killed his wife. In reality, he did not leave right after the murder. In fact, he left Michigan in September of 1983, eight months after the murder of his wife, according to the Michigan State Police report. Maybe I'm naive, but if you're an innocent man—and you know that, even if everyone else doesn't because, um... *you actually didn't do it*—eight months probably does feel like a sufficient amount of time to subject yourself to repeated police questioning, town gossip, and the breathtakingly painful proximity to where your wife was brutally slain.

So I'll do it, if nobody else will. I will apologize for everyone who thought it, everyone who said it—I will apologize for the entire town of Reed City, because somebody should.

Mr. Roberson, I'm sorry. I'm sorry for your loss, and the subsequent treatment you received. While I understand from an investigative standpoint that what was done had to be done, I am sorry for everything you were forced to endure. I'm sorry you lost your wife and your children lost their mother.

I'm so sorry.

1984, CONT...

Less than a half-page makes up the April 1984 supplemental report on the Janette Roberson murder. The first notation is about Ralph Fisher having moved to a different residence. Another is in regards to a detective at another post entering a LEIN message about unsolved murders in the past year.

Another three-quarter page of information makes up the next month's information for May of 1984. The first notation is about the bodies of Richard and Alida Thompson having been discovered on May 5, 1984 near a vacant residence in Rose Lake Township, Osceola County. It did not appear to Detective Pratt that the murders were related to the Roberson murder, and he noted that in the file. This crime was later attributed to Peter Piper, who killed the Thompsons after having escaped from prison and managed to evade recapture for two years. Piper actually escaped *twice* in a five year period. The second time was from the Osceola County Jail in 1988, where he'd been brought to appear at a preliminary examination on first degree murder charges in the Thompson killings. He'd already been serving a life sentence for the 1966 rape and stabbing of a seventeen year old girl. From the Associated Press, August 20, 1988:

JAIL BREAK LEAVES RESIDENTS SCARED

Associated Press

REED CITY, Mich. (AP) — A convicted rapist who is accused of slaying a young couple after he escaped from jail in 1983 broke out of jail again, terrifying residents of this small community.

Peter J. Piper, 41, stymied searchers who believed they had him surrounded Friday in a wooded area near Big Rapids, about 15 miles south of Reed City. Police captured his accomplice in the escape Friday afternoon on a residential street just north of Big Rapids. Authorities suspended their search for Piper after hunting through the woods with tracking dogs and finding no sign of him, said state police Sgt. Jim Maturen.

The area "couldn't be searched any more thorough," he said. "Once he leaves the immediate area, where's he at? There's a million places he could be. He's still on foot, as far as we know."

"We just don't have any idea where he is," Mecosta County Sheriff Henry Wayer said. "We're all going to go home tonight and sleep on it" and decide in the morning whether to resume the search.

Piper was believed armed with a handgun, Wayer said.

Piper and inmate Mitchell A. Lund, 24, a convicted burglar, escaped Thursday from the Osceola County Jail after beating and tying up a guard, authorities said.

"Both of them are considered to be extremely dangerous," Lt. Dallas Jenks, the jail administrator, said before Lund was recaptured peacefully. "I'm nervous about both of them being out of my jail, but Piper would be the one I'd be most nervous about."

Piper, sentenced to life in prison in 1966 for the rape and beating of a 17-year-old girl, escaped from jail in 1983. He was captured in November 1985 in a Grand Rapids suburb where he was staying with his sister.

While on the run, police allege, Piper killed a couple from Manton, a small town near here, and sexually assaulted three prostitutes in Grand Rapids. He was convicted of the assaults and was awaiting trial on first-degree murder charges when he and Lund escaped. Police say they never determined a motive for the May 1984 killings. Richard Thompson, 21, had his throat slit and then he and his new wife, Alida, 19, were both shot.

"I guess you could call him cunning," said State Police Detective George Pratt, who investigated the murder. "On an outward appearance, he doesn't expose his violence. He's quite well spoken, soft-spoken, and does not have the appearance of a brutal killer."

> At the Short Stop Party Store, clerk Tim Hinken said he sent his wife out of town to spend the night with an aunt after news of Piper's escape got out.
>
> "Everybody is worried, I know that," he said.
>
> Lund, who faces charges of robbing a grocery store, was in a cell next to Piper's in the maximum-security unit of the jail. They assaulted the guard and escaped after their cell doors were unlocked so they could take showers and use the telephone, authorities said. The guard, Donald Simon, was hospitalized in stable condition Friday. Piper was moved to the county jail Wednesday from the Michigan Reformatory at Ionia so he could appear at a preliminary examination Thursday regarding the Thompson killings. The hearing was postponed after a witness failed to show up.

On May 9, 1984 a tip was received from the Ionia MSP Post regarding a subject who was involved in a similar crime in Ohio and was an escapee at the time of Janette Roberson's murder. Subject was reportedly violent around women and had a wife in the Morley area.

On May 14, 1984 an inquiry was made from MSP Post #71 as to the date and location of the murder.

On May 17, 1984, there was another contact regarding the Thompson murders in reference to a tip. There was a request for a print comparison for a subject from that case to the Roberson case and a set was sent to the Latent Print Unit.

It seems all police had at the moment was the hope that prints at Janette Roberson's crime scene might match that of another unsolved crime. They sure didn't appear to have anything of value locally.

A supplemental dated July 31st is two pages worth of notations that cover June and July. The first on June 11, 1984, Ralph Fisher, Janette's father, inquired of the Traverse City post, who in turn inquired of the Reed City Post, if an arrest had been made in the Roberson homicide. He was advised they had not.

A lab report on prints came back on June 29, 1984. Then on July 9th a deputy from the Ostego County Sheriff's department requested copies of the composite sketches. He had someone who wanted to check them before deciding if they had information. They were forwarded.

On July 7, 1984 Detective Southworth of the Osceola County Sheriff's Department contacted Detective Pratt and said the Gambles store had something that may be of interest in the case. Apparently an employee, Donna Evans, contacted Detective Southworth. There is a redacted page and a half of information regarding what they found.

The next entries in the MSP report aren't until September. On September 5th, the Ostego County Deputy contacted Detective Pratt advising that he'd received a telephone call from an anonymous female who suggested they check out a *"...guy who lives near her in a flat-roofed home, empty pool, and brick front."* Detective Pratt determined the lead had already been checked, and referenced supplementals signed in February and March of 1983 by Det. Sgt. Carl Goeman. This was regarding the Kris Mills interview—the gentleman who'd passed through Reed City on his work route that day, the one who'd allegedly been scratched by a cat and a tip was called in about him.

On September 5, 1984, Detective Pratt notes that a subject was arrested by the Mecosta County Sheriff's Department on a charge of felonious assault when he shook a stick at someone in the Mecosta County Park in Paris, Michigan. Subject was lodged in the Mecosta County Jail. Given the next activity in the report is centered around Lee Peterson, and the woman who worked at the foster home mentioned him being apprehended in Paris, Michigan prior to being "locked up" in a mental health facility, I think it is reasonable to assume he was the stick shaker in question. Unfortunately, in response to a FOIA request for information, the Mecosta County Sheriff's Department said, "This report does not exist."

Many of the records I requested in reference to this case no longer exist because of how old they were. Most entities I dealt with had a time period after which records would be destroyed, and trying to get things all the way back from the 1980s proved difficult, at best. Reed City Police Department, for example, had almost nothing from that time period.

The last thing noted in September 1984 is as follows:

> PROPERTY HELD:*
> #11 – One 13"X10"X3" Ultra-Violet products Inc. box marked "Reed City" "60082-83" "24-Jan-83"; "Misc. hairs etc." containing hair, fibers and other evidence reference the homicide of Janette Gale Roberson.
> #12 – Known hair from [REDACTED]
> #13 – One [REDACTED]

All items are being held in the Post property room, UD 14's submitted. (*According to the Reed City property sign out sheet, these items were received on September 9, 1984 by Detective Pratt.)

COMPLAINT STATUS: Open.

The next item in the report is a November supplemental dated Nov 9, 1984, and is devoted entirely to Lee Peterson. Under INFORMATION the first page notes, "As previously mentioned, an extensive background has been done on [REDACTED]..."

(We know this background check was attributed to Lee Peterson because in the MSP report, one of the pages in this section begins with PETERSON BACKGROUND CONT. It was the only page in this section MSP did not redact that heading from.)

It references a lab analysis that was discussed on October 5, 1984 and then under ADDITIONAL INFORMATION: "On October 8, 1984 the Undersigned [Detective Pratt] travelled with Eldon Whitford to Traverse City State Hospital and met with Nina Rosely and Dr. Lamb. Ms. Rosely is the case worker and Dr. Lamb is the psychiatrist in charge of the case. It was learned that [SUBJECT] can differentiate between right and wrong and would be aware of what happened in January 1983. Talking with him would not or should not upset him and if he had committed the murder and <u>wanted</u> to talk about it he could."

The subject was then interviewed and the remarks at the end of the November 9th supplemental read, in part, as follows: "Nothing learned up to this point in this investigation concerning [**REDACTED**] can eliminate or verify him as the suspect."

COMPLAINT STATUS: Open.

The last supplemental report submitted for the year of 1984 is dated Dec 1, 1984 and it has just a few notations from work done in previous months. On October 4, 1984 hair samples and items found with the evidence at the crime scene were taken to the Bridgeport Lab for comparison.

On October 22, 1984, "Beverly" – an employee of the Reed City Gambles store advises that a subject was in on the 10th or 11th and said "...he hadn't been downstairs since the girl had been killed." The store owner, David Engels, told "Beverly" he was okay, "He doesn't look like the composite." No record of this subject was found as being in the Gambles store "that fatal day."

On November 21, 1984 residents of Reed City were interviewed "...regarding statements made by a former housekeeper who has confided with them about the homicide." The subjects were concerned about what she had told them. Detective Pratt notes, "I have talked to the housekeeper in the past and she professes to be a "witch" with certain powers."

The last paragraph entered in the Janette Roberson murder investigation that year strikes me as one of the most telling entries in the entire report:

"Investigative leads in this case have ceased with the exception of individual "feelings." At times, calls regarding information have been received from persons closely associated with the case, relatives, witnesses, fellow employees, or other police officers with their information, usually already checked out, but if not, investigated without any substantial information being gained."

COMPLAINT STATUS: Open.

The first supplemental of the year is dated August 23, 1985 and it is a scant two pages of notes which make up Detective Sgt. George Pratt's summaries on the Janette Roberson case from January through August of 1985.

The first line reads as follows: *"Investigative leads in this case have been little or nothing for some time."*

Detective Pratt notes that the Roberson case was presented at the *8th Annual International Homicide Seminar* held March 17-25, 1985 in Columbus Ohio as an unsolved homicide. The next mention is of Officer Finkbeiner having obtained information that a named individual had been in the store on the day of the murder and that it had been confirmed with David Engels, the store manager. Detective Pratt noted he had already interviewed the subject.

On May 13, 1985 Osceola County Sheriff David Needham contacted Detective Pratt and advised that he had seen Alvin Roberson in Reed City on Saturday, May 11, 1985 at Plumb's Supermarket. Needham ran the plate on the vehicle Mr. Roberson was driving. Reed City Police Chief Phillip Rathbun was contacted and requested to check with Janette's mother to determine if Alvin was "still around." On May 16, 1985, Chief Rathbun re-contacted Detective Pratt to say Mr. Roberson had come to Reed City to pick up his wife, the former Lisa Miracle, on Wednesday, May 8th and they left town on Saturday the 11th—the same day the Sheriff saw him. According to Detective Pratt, Chief Rathbun learned from Marion Fisher that they were living in Georgia, about 40 miles south of Savannah.

On May 29, 1985 a letter that had been received "...during the past ten days from the Investigative Resources Unit regarding [**SUBJECT REDACTED**] was reviewed. Their inquiry was if he had been looked into on this case, which the answer is NO. **[SUBJECT]** has an extensive record and was last involved in CSC 3rd Degree in Newaygo County."

On June 21, 1985: "A meeting was held at the 6th District Headquarters with Dr. Gary Kaufmann of the Behavioral Sciences Section, Det./Lt. Paul Wood and Dt. Sgt. William Bradway of the Investigative Resources Unit; D/Sgts. Barry Beck and William Morris of the Major Case Unit and [Detective Pratt] regarding the unsolved homicides in the Reed City Post area. This case was discussed with several suggestions for follow-up to be completed in the near future."

Also on that date—June 21, 1985—two copies of the Roberson report #62-113-83 were left for D/Lt. Robert L. Smith per his order so that the case could be reviewed by Detective Morris Vincent of MSP Post #63 (Mount Pleasant) and Detective James Albright of MSP Post #64 (Grand Haven).

Eight days later (the 29th), a meeting was held at the 6th District Headquarters in Grand Rapids by Det./Lt. Robert Smith. Present were Captain Thomas Meehleder, Inspector Kelley Steinbower, Det./Lt. Jon Hulsing, Detectives Albright and Vincent, Detective William Morris, Detective James Ward and Detective George Pratt.

"The investigation of this case was turned over to Detectives Albright and Vincent by Det. /Lt. Robert Smith. Attached to the post copy of this report is the synopsis of this meeting." It appears that the higher-ups decided the Janette Roberson murder investigation might benefit from a couple sets of fresh eyes, which is common when a case has gone cold.

Only two more notations are made on the August 1985 supplemental. One is regarding a subject who'd recently been brought back to Michigan from Nevada to face murder charges in Kent County. Apparently the body had never been located in that case. The subject was noted to have attended high school in Reed City and, according to Pratt, "...several inquiries, including from policemen have been received questioning whether [SUBJECT] could have been involved in any of the unsolved homicides, including the Roberson case." Detective Pratt then notes that he was advised by the inquiring sheriff's department handling the extradition that this subject had been picked up in August in 1982 by Nevada authorities and had been in prison since that time.

The last notation by Detective Pratt in August of 1985 is with regard to an insurance carrier for a Workman's Comp case paying out death benefits to the Roberson children. They simply wanted to know if the murder had been solved, and requested to be notified if an apprehension had been made.

Albright & Vincent

The next supplemental in August is signed by Detective Vincent and is dated August 27, 1985. He went to the Mecosta-Osceola Career Center and spoke with Robert Miller, the administrator, regarding the records of two students, one of whom was "Dan," the fellow who allegedly had a crush on Janette and lived in her apartment complex.

"Both of these students attended Reed City High School for one half day and they went to the Career Center in the afternoon. Their classes at the Career center were from 12:20pm until 2:45pm." The Student Services coordinator was spoken to in reference to missed time regarding the students. The Principal at the high school, Douglas Dodge, was also contacted in reference to these students.

The next day, Detectives Albright and Vincent interviewed Edna Lucha, Marion Fisher, (Janette's mother) and Jeffrey Scott Lucha. The following day, on the 29th, they spoke with "Dan."

"["Dan"] was contacted at his apartment. This apartment is registered in his mother's name and he lives there with her. When contacted by Det./Sgts. Vincent and Albright he was asked if he would go with the officers to the Manistee State Police Post to be interviewed in reference to the Janette Roberson homicide. He advised officers that he would be willing to talk to them and go to the post for the interview. At the Manistee Post "Dan" was advised of his Constitutional rights by Det./Sgt. Albright, and he stated that he understood and knew those rights and was willing to talk to officers in reference to the investigation."

Jerri Denton was also interviewed on the 28th regarding a letter sent to Detective Pratt. Detective Pratt had not opened the letter, but had forward it to Alvin Roberson. Jerri Denton, co-owner of Century 21 Real Estate in Beulah, told the officer that she had no personal contact with the Robersons, and did not know them, but read the request for reward money in the paper for the apprehension and conviction of the killer of Janette Roberson. She told the officer she sent the money because she had children approximately the age of Janette and sent it to be added to the reward money.

It appears the new guys were checking everything—even a letter that was never opened from a stranger in the hopes that something would pop out of the woodwork. I believe the technical term is called "dotting Is and crossing dead-end Ts."

The last August 1985 notation is a trip Albright and Vincent took to Traverse City on the 27th in an attempt to locate Lee Peterson. They checked one residence and found he no longer lived there. The manager of the apartments gave them an alternate address, which was a home of "mentally retarded subjects," according to the report. The manager of the home told the officers he no longer lived there, but gave them a third address. When they went to that address, they were told by an upstairs occupant that he lived in the basement at that location, but had gone on an outing and would not be home until later in the week.

September of 1985 begins with Detective Vincent checking Alvin Roberson's employment and speaking with numerous people regarding his work ethic. He received answers like *'He was very quiet and reserved'* and *'An average employee with quality work but not job quantity.'*

Kenneth Samuels told the detective he was the General Foreman at the Unitest Plant in Marion and that Alvin worked for him, having worked for the Unitest in Reed City and then moved to the Marion Plant. He was described by Samuels as being "Real quiet, real bright and intelligent, with a lot of automation application, and that he worked in the Heavy Duty Application Department rebuilding starters, generators, alternators and water pumps. Samuels told Vincent that Alvin rode to work from Reed City with Allen Foote from Chase, and gave him the name of another friend they might speak with, as well.

On September 6th Detective Albright talked to Kris Mills at the Antrim County Sheriff's Department in Bellaire. Like with "Dan," it is noted that Mills was advised of his Constitutional rights prior to the interview. Albright finally caught up with Lee Peterson on that same day, also advising him of his rights before Peterson was interviewed. The interview with Peterson is noted as having been tape recorded, with his permission. Directly after that interview, a notation is made regarding evidence being sent to the Bridgeport Crime Lab.

On September 9th, Detective Albright received a call from Detective Pratt referencing a call that had been made to the Traverse City post by a Cynthia (Trowbridge) Moore of Petoskey. Pratt advised that Moore wished to speak with the two officers who had interviewed Kris Mills in Bellaire. At that time, Detective Albright contacted Cynthia Moore in Petoskey. During that interview it was learned that her last name used to be Trowbridge and she was the girlfriend of Kris Mills at the time of the Janette Roberson homicide. She advised Albright by telephone that she had initially talked to one of the sergeants at the Reed City Post. At this time she was interviewed and it was also recorded. After the interview, the Antrim County Sheriff's department and the Bellaire Police department were contacted. The Antrim County Sheriff's department indicated they had no arrest records on Kris Mills, but they *were* familiar with Cynthia Trowbridge Moore.

Research done on iCHAT—Michigan's Internet Criminal History Access Tool—shows Cynthia Trowbridge Moore has a multi-state criminal history that includes charges of felony financial transactions, felony fraudulent activities, passing bad checks, operating a vehicle while intoxicated, driving without a license, and at one point was a fugitive from justice where an extradition was required. These crimes date back to the early 1990s through the early 2000s.

It appears, based on her multiple contacts with law enforcement involved in the Janette Roberson investigation, she wanted cops to look real hard at her ex-boyfriend.

I left a message for Kris Mills in order to get some background on his involvement in the Roberson investigation and I heard from him on January 12, 2015, about two months later. After hearing his story, it's no wonder why he was hesitant. Getting caught up in the Janette

Roberson investigation had proven a sticky wicket for him in the past. In his words, "I can't ever get away from this mess."

In 1983, Kris Mills worked for Curtis Wire products in Petoskey. He was a truck driver who hauled things like refrigerator wire and oven racks from Grand Rapids to Petoskey, which necessitated passing through Reed City by way of Old Highway 131. It was a regular route for he and his partner, who took turns driving loads. That was another thing he mentioned. "Man, it could have been him driving that day, but it was me. I was the guy stuck in the wrong place at the wrong time."

When he drove that route, Kris would stop at a restaurant called Miniers for lunch. He said he'd been stopping there for years, and based on his recollection, on January 19, 1983 he was there at approximately 12:30 or 1:00 in the afternoon. Earlier that day, Kris says he stopped at a business called Little Engines, which was on the south side of Reed City. They sold lawn mowers, chainsaws, things like that.

"I still have a picture of that lawn mower somewhere!" he told me.

Kris said he stopped at Little Engines first because it was on the south side, and went to Miniers afterward because it was on the north end of town on the way to Cadillac. When he stopped at Little Engines, he had to park his rig across the street, along the side of Old Highway 131 because of its size. He was hauling a 47 foot trailer and with the rig he believes it was around 60 feet long. You can't just slide a vehicle that size into a spot and call it a day. There's a bit of planning involved.

Kris mentioned the name of the business, Curtis Wire, was on the truck in red and white, clearly visible. He assumed that was how they tracked him down as having been in town on that day. Someone saw the truck, knew he'd passed through, and that's why police wanted to speak to him. That's not exactly the case, based on the report. Cynthia Trowbridge, his ex-girlfriend, called in a tip. When I spoke to him, he didn't appear to have put that together.

"Man, that was a bad time in my life," he said. "I lived in Bellaire back then and I had an ex who was stalking me. She was breaking into my house and the police couldn't catch her. I even took out a restraining order, but that didn't help."

"Is this Trowbridge? I asked.

"Yeah! How'd you know that?" Kris Mills asked, surprised.

I told him her name was in the report and that I was aware of her criminal history. Kris said it started like this. One day he woke up and found a note on his door that said two detectives were looking to speak to him. He had no idea what it was about, and at that time, had not even heard about the murder in Reed City. According to him, he'd never even been to the Gambles store. But the proximity of both Miniers and Little Engines, with Gambles in between, makes it perfectly understandable why cops looked at the guy. Little Engines was right there on Chestnut, near where the State Police Post was.

Kris couldn't remember if the Detectives called him, or if he contacted them after seeing the note, but they came to his home and asked him to come to the sheriff's department so they could talk to him. He was confused and didn't know what it was about, but he went with them anyway. When they got to the sheriff's department, they told him his truck had been seen in Reed City around the time a murder occurred. They questioned him regarding his whereabouts on the day of the murder, and then asked for a hair sample. Kris said he believes they also took his fingerprints. He did this willingly, as innocent men are wont to do when all they want is for cops to move past them so they can get the hell on with their lives.

After they questioned Kris, he said they took him home. Not long after that, the detectives showed up at a restaurant where he was with friends. They needed to talk to him again, they said. Kris told me it was embarrassing and he felt they were being intimidating. He said they started following him around after that and it was so bad, he had to get a lawyer. He described the whole situation as "intense." Kris told me he spent around five thousand dollars, "for nothing" because, according to him, he didn't do anything wrong, but they continued to harass him. At one point, he would no longer speak with police at all, and all communication had to go through the lawyer.

"I didn't know anything about a murder. I didn't even know where the store was, and they kept talking about a basement. I asked them what kind of idiot would kill someone and then drive away in a truck that had their work name all over it? And where did they think I was supposed to park that truck in Reed City? Did they think I drove it up to the store, double parked, then went in and killed somebody, and nobody noticed?"

Kris mentioned that he had a scratch on his face which they asked about. He told me it was from a tousle he got into with Trowbridge, she had scratched his face, though he also told me his folks had some cats, and he had some scratches from them on his hands, too. He said he later found out Trowbridge told police she had seen him washing blood out of a jacket.

"Yeah, I was! My hunting jacket!"

Kris was not aware of what the interaction between police and his employer was, but he was glad they were a good company. "Anyone else would have fired me, between the cops asking questions and the stalker ex constantly calling there."

We had talked for a while when Kris said, "I really think I may have seen the killer that day, on 131 in that long stretch by the airport."

He described the incident as follows: A car was driving really fast behind him, very erratic, and then almost hit his truck as it went to pass him. He said it was about 12:30 and he was on his way to Miniers for lunch. The vehicle was a dirty brown or blue sedan; an Olds or a Buick. Because the cab of the truck was high, Kris said he was able to see one male individual in the car and he described him as "driving real crazy, north on Old 131 towards Cadillac."

"But that's not even it!" he said, exasperated. "There's more to the story. About a year or so ago—last spring I think—I stopped at the Frankfort True Value hardware store. I moved to Alberta and was running a marina, so I sometimes stopped in that hardware store for bolts and stuff. Anyway, this time I got to talking with the store owner and he mentioned he used to own a hardware store in Reed City. I said, 'Not the one where the murder happened?' The guy said yes. I couldn't believe it!"

David Engels—former owner of the Gambles store in Reed City—owned the Frankfort True Value, at least at that time. I told Kris I knew he'd purchased another hardware store, but I thought he'd sold it.

"Not as of last spring, he hadn't," Kris replied. "Anyway I was shocked because here was this thing in my life *again*. I was just this hard-working guy who'd been in the wrong place at the wrong time, and this thing that caused me and my parents such an emotional time, and all that money... and here it is *again*, popping up in my life! So we were talking and the manager says to me, 'Oh, that case was solved.' He told me it was the boyfriend or husband—someone like that who did it. I can't remember which, but he said it was *solved*. So that's why I was surprised when you contacted me and said it was still unsolved. He told me they solved it."

"Nope," I replied, wondering why anyone would've told someone otherwise.

"Man, it's *still* unsolved? I hope they get who did it because they screwed up a lot of lives, I bet. Just like mine. I didn't do anything but work that day and all I want is closure. It should be in my past, where it's supposed to be, but it keeps popping up. First at the Frankfort Hardware, and now a book. I mean, I think it's great you're writing it, but I hope they get whoever did it so it can finally be over."

Your mouth to God's ears, Kris.

1985, CONT...

The supplemental dated September 11, 1985 shows Detective Albright making contact with some of the people whose names were given at Alvin's place of employment. Alan Foote was one of the people he interviewed, and I was able to get in touch with him. I asked if there was anything he remembered about Janette and Alvin, and if he could recall the types of questions police asked him.

"I worked with Al [Alvin Roberson] when the shop was in Reed City and met Janette a couple of times. I typically picked on her about her Southern accent. After the shop moved to Marion, I worked in the same area with Al. We became closer friends. The day she was murdered, I saw it on the news at home and called Al. I remember telling him I wanted to make sure it was not his wife. He told me that it was, and I drove into town and sat with him awhile. When I left, I went downtown and told the police that they should at least send someone to tell him what was going on, as he was completely in the dark. I don't remember if it was the next day, or the following day, but they came to question me at work."

"I remember them asking questions about Al, mostly what type of guy he was, but the thing I remember most was them asking about paint that we used at work. At that time we used a lot of red paint and I am sure it was on his shoes. He told me later that they took his work boots. I think they wanted to know about red paint to rule out what was on the top of his work boots. I also remember him having to leave work early to give them a hair sample. He was concerned about it and said there was a chance his hair may be on Janette because they slept in the same bed and used the same brush."

"What seems like months later, a different officer came to work and did the interview again. No questions about paint this time. They pretty much asked my relationship with him, and basically asked if I thought he was capable of such a thing. I remember telling them at that time, during lunch, something had come on the radio about a random, dumb killing. He [Alvin] started crying and said something to the effect of *'Has the whole world gone fucking crazy?'*"

"Al and I became closer friends after that, worked on cars together, etc., until they moved to Georgia. I doubt I have really told you anything new. Sorry, not much help."

But he was helpful, actually. With the exception of one or two people I spoke with, everyone went out of their way to be helpful. They wanted to share their memories, maybe in the hopes that all these years later their combined recollections would come together to make sense of the tragedy.

What I was left with after Al Foote's recollection is an image of Alvin Roberson sitting in the apartment and looking at his children after finding out his wife is dead, and nobody's telling him what's happening, and he's wondering what he's supposed to be doing because he has no frame of reference for what's happening to him... *What do I do? What am I supposed to be doing right now*? So he's just sitting there, paralyzed, wondering, like Al said, *'Has the whole world gone fucking crazy?'*

Picture him there. Remember, as I write this he's been ruled out as a suspect. So picture this guy you now know *didn't kill his wife*. Think about the scenario differently—think of it as your brother, or nephew, or son. How must he have felt? In the span of a day he was suddenly a single parent with two young children, his wife had been murdered, and everyone thought he did it.

It's easy to speculate. "Of course the husband did it!" I heard that more times than I can count while researching this case. Alvin Roberson seemed the easiest person to point fingers at, despite how many times I told folks that his DNA and fingerprints had been taken very early on, and if he killed his wife at her place of employment in the middle of the day, and cops weren't able to pin it on him—this man who by all accounts was a simple, quiet, hardworking man—well, they couldn't have been very good at their jobs.

The first time I spoke with Reed City Police Chief Chuck Davis, he told me that the overriding feeling in law enforcement was that Alvin Roberson killed Janette. He said at one point they thought Alvin was close to confessing, but someone walked into the room and Alvin clammed up. I'm not sure what room or who because he didn't elaborate. Chief Davis told me there were numerous things that led them to believe it could have been him, including him leaving town with the babysitter. Davis told me the general "profile" of a crime like the one perpetrated on Janette, (revenge was the word he used), was done by someone who'd "intimate" with the victim. But he did say it could have also been someone she'd "turned down."

Chief Davis worked for the Osceola County Sheriff's Department at the time of the murder, but he wasn't on duty on January 19, 1983. To his credit, when we spoke the first time at the Reed City Police Department, he probably hadn't looked at the file in years, and I have no indication he ever worked the case personally, prior to that, so what he told me about Alvin was most likely the impression he'd been left with over the years by his peers in law enforcement, having not been a part of the investigation himself.

I spoke to Detective Sgt. Southworth and was able to confirm that he also believed Alvin was on the verge of confessing at some point. He said there were a few things that made him believe Alvin Roberson was the perpetrator, including his demeanor the day of the murder, and how he left town. Southworth also told me that he recalled Detective Pratt not being convinced Alvin had killed his wife, based in part on the types of injuries she sustained. Still, he said, Detective Pratt continued his investigation in a professional manner, doing everything a well-seasoned detective does to try and rule someone out as a suspect. Cops can have a feeling but they still do the necessary work because, in cases like this, spouses are involved more often than not.

After a memorial walk was held for Janette in January of 2014, and a few new leads came in, Chief Davis went over the file with one of the Michigan State Police detectives assigned after Detective Pratt had retired. According to one of the *Pioneer* articles—post-Memorial walk—the new MSP detective stated there had been almost no tips coming in for years until that walk generated so much attention.

According to a former employee with the Osceola County Prosecutor's office, after Detective Pratt's retirement, not much happened with the case. It had technically transferred from hand to hand, but never moved out of whatever dusty confines it had been relegated to for storage.

I should also note something else Chief Davis confirmed when we spoke the first time. In 1983, Reed City officers were Patrolman, not in any way trained to handle what they found that day. Today it would be different. Today with the popularity of shows like *Criminal Minds* and *CSI: Miami*, the average person would likely pick up on problems that could be associated with things like dispatching a murder as a heart attack. The problem here is that those first responders were anticipating a person having a heart attack, not a dead body, so they weren't looking for clues, or paying attention to the same details they would if they knew ahead of time they were responding to a homicide. It is less likely that an officer who thought he was responding to a homicide would walk an EMT through a spot of blood on the floor, either—or allow a bunch of witnesses to leave the premises without being questioned.

But it is hard to justify some of the things that happened afterward. Even by 1983 standards, a Rhesus monkey could probably tell you that you don't allow that many people near a crime scene. Way too many people had access to Janette Roberson's body. Too many employees; too many cops; too many customers. Too many people traipsing around where evidence would eventually be recovered to make it anything close to a pristine crime scene.

Mistakes were made, that much is clear. I will say, however, that I don't see anything that occurred being intentional, so much as gross ineptitude and a series of unfortunate events occurring in a short span of time—including multiple law enforcement officers arriving in close proximity to one another at a scene more gruesome than most of them had likely ever encountered. You want as few people as possible roaming in and out of a crime scene. While it is unclear how long that scene was unsecured, it is clear that a few people who had no business being around that body after it was discovered made their way down there. According to Detective Pratt's notations, "...some more than once."

The fact that there were people around that body who shouldn't have been when EMTs arrived is supported by the Osceola County report prepared by Det. Sgt. Southworth. There is a chunk of that report REDACTED between the time he arrived and was led by Officer Finkbeiner to Janette's body, followed by the notation, *"At that time Officer Finkbeiner stated to the undersigned, 'You are an evidence technician, I want you to take over the scene.' At that time, the undersigned removed everybody away from the body, except EMS personnel checking the body."* It also notes after that *"Both doors to the store were then locked so no one else could enter."*

Who is this "everybody" and why was "everybody" standing around ogling the body, anyway? Where was the common sense that day?

Detective Pratt's notes say the people he learned "through investigation" had been around the body were Chief Rathbun, Thomas Hawkins, David Engels, John Engels, Angie Tillie, the Medical Examiner, and the nurse at the hospital who, according to Pratt's notes "was just passing by" as first responders arrived. Gary McGhee says she wasn't down there near the body while he was there, so when was this nurse around the body? When was Chief Rathbun down there around the body before Pratt arrived? Hawkins? He was a customer and apparently not even the store manager or owner had the presence of mind to keep customers away from the area. It is unclear which of those people were down there at what points because not one of the reports is specific in that regard. I don't think I'm going out on a limb in suggesting they damn well should be. Unfortunately, the only solid note taker, Detective Pratt, wasn't present when all that occurred, so he only had to go by what others told him and some of those "others" might not have provided the best information.

Another thing that's troubling, purely from a common sense standpoint, is the supposed back-and-forth about being an "evidence technician" in both the Osceola County and Reed City reports. After it notes that the EMS crew entered and examined the victim, the Finkbeiner/Primeau report reads: *"At this time Detective Southworth of the Osceola Sheriff's Department arrived and PTL*

Finkbeiner stated to him "Are you an evidence technician?" Det. Southworth replyied (sic) "Yes I am" and PTL. Finkbeiner than (sic) stated "I would like you to take over this scene." Det. Southworth than stated "secure the building do not let anyone leave or come into this building. PTL Finkbeiner than left the room where the victim was at allowing PTL Primeau to enter the room."

Obviously the doors hadn't been locked immediately after John Engels found the body, based on this report and Southworth telling them to "secure the scene." You don't have to say "secure the scene" if the scene is already secure. Also, horrifying grammar aside, the back and forth about Southworth being an evidence technician flies in the face of all that is normal conversation. Why was he asking if Southworth is an evidence technician?

Really? Not, "Have you called the Chief? Did anyone ring the Sheriff? Has anyone locked the doors?" Finkbeiner's initial instinct is to ask if Southworth is an evidence technician? You might be buying it, gentle reader, but I'm not. Perhaps that's because I normally write fiction and spend a great deal of time reconstruction how humans speak to one another. This back and forth—as noted by both the city and county reports—seems wildly out of focus to me. Maybe it's out of context. Incomplete is what it feels like. A whole lot missing. Like, maybe an hour's worth?

Southworth could have walked in and said, "WHY THE HELL ARE ALL THESE PEOPLE STANDING AROUND THE BODY AND COMPROMISING EVIDENCE?"

To which Finkbeiner may have responded, "SORRY WE'RE ALL JUST A LITTLE FREAKED OUT HERE, MAN! ARE YOU AN EVIDENCE TECHNICIAN BECAUSE I'M NOT TRAINED FOR THIS SHIT!"

Maybe that's happening as Gary McGhee is yelling to Pam McDonald to get the hell out of there because she's still frozen in the doorway, absolutely no help to him as he hurriedly assesses the brutalized body before him. And don't forget the birds squawking. According to EMT McGhee, those birds were making a lot of racket.

Yes, this is wild speculation, but do you see what I'm getting at? What is noted in the city and county reports generally only reflects small pieces of what *may have* been happening, but certainly doesn't track with the other reports and recollections of people on the scene. Based on how both reports are written, they suggest Detective Pratt showed up right after that conversation. Yet, we know it was around an hour later that he arrived. So what was happening during that time that is not noted in the reports?

Southworth thought enough to call the county prosecutor to the scene right after viewing it, and to me that's telling. Perhaps he didn't like what he saw when he entered the scene any more than I would have if, for example, I was the State Detective assigned to a case and I walked in to find a guy who'd been drunkenly screaming F*CK THE STATE POLICE prior to assaulting them, now helping to "process" my crime scene.

I would not like that one bit.

And another thing, who was inside watching the scene after Officer Finkbeiner "officially" turned it over to Southworth—who then immediately decided to go outside and radio for Chief Rathbun, Sheriff Needham, Deputy Kingsbury and the County Prosecutor, James Talaske... Maybe I'm not as trusting as I should be, but the officer who'd just traipsed an EMT through blood and let a bunch of witnesses leave the scene doesn't inspire confidence as far as doing things like keeping employees from wandering downstairs to catch a peek before the State cops got there and tightened things up.

It's unclear if we'll ever know exactly what happened between the times Janette's body was found and when Detective Pratt arrived, but I'm fairly confident suggesting we don't have anywhere near the full picture if all we have to go on are the first responders' reports. Glaring omissions like witnesses having been allowed to leave, no notation of the blood that was tramped through, inconsistencies as far as when the doors were locked and who arrived when... one can only hope these aren't just the tip of the iceberg.

Marion Fisher

Perhaps the person I feel like I got to know the most while researching this book is Marion Fisher, Janette's mother. She was first described to me by Terry Hall, a friend of Janette and her brother.

"I found her to be very creative, very intelligent, and very tolerant. She had her own mother move in and she tended her, plus held a job, and had a son at home all at the same time. Plus she was very active in her church. Sometimes on the way to church I'd be following and watch Marion brake and swerve to miss birds in the road."

Marion Fisher was the Reed City Clerk and Treasurer at the time of her daughter's murder. Back then it was all one position. So, in addition to all the other things she was juggling when Janette was killed, she was also playing a major role in helping to keep Reed City running smoothly.

One of the first bits of research I did for this book was to devour three years' worth of city council meeting minutes, which were printed out by Jackie Beam, the current city clerk. The bound volumes had to be lugged from storage to where they would be copied. Thirty years ago, they were kept in legal size binders, which meant legal size paper, extra-long and more bulky than the standard 8.5 X 11 inch commonly used today. The copies I received are clearly of hand typed documents, and often Marion's handwriting is at the top marked "Indexed." Each set of monthly minutes bears her signature.

Being able to get an up-close look into her day-to-day job proved an invaluable insight, even though each set of minutes only represented one meeting she'd had that day, which occurred in the evening, usually called to order at around 7:30pm by the Mayor at the time, Donald Collison. After a long day at the office, that's where

Marion was a couple times a month, taking notes, very often bobbing and weaving.

The Reed City city council, bless their hearts, they were... how shall I put it? Well, they were an *opinionated* bunch, and even though council members came and went, the core group stayed basically the same for the time period I researched.

One individual was a standout: Marjorie Brown White. I remember sitting down with Barb Westerburg, the present city treasurer, and saying, "I'd have loved to talk to her. She seemed like a pisser." Barb nodded and smiled. "Yes, she was."

Marjorie fancied herself, among other things, an historian. She wrote a book titled *One Hundred Going on Two Hundred* that commemorated Reed City's centennial in 1975. I purchased a copy at *The Old Rugged Cross Museum* in Reed City. That is where I found all of the old Herald and Pioneer newspaper articles from which I obtained a great deal of historical context about Reed City in general, as well as what was going on around the time of the murder.

Mrs. Brown White's life deserves a book in and of itself, but for our purposes, she was the councilmember who wasn't afraid to point fingers and name names in the middle of a televised council meeting. At one point, those fingers were being (dramatically) pointed at Marion Fisher. But before we get to that, we must go back almost a year prior to the murder in order to set the stage.

In an *Osceola Herald* article published on March 10, 1983—almost two months after Janette's murder, and just after his termination—former Reed City Police Officer Theodore Platz commented: "Police Chief Rathbun has stated that I have not violated any laws. Am I being terminated because of an embarrassment to the city? If so, I submit that the actions of some council members at council meetings (which are shown live on Cable 7) are far more embarrassing to the city."

I contacted Colin Hayward, who was the Chamber of Commerce secretary at the time of the murder, and he gave me a bit of backstory on the filming and broadcasting of the meetings.

We broadcast the proceedings of the Reed City city council live and in living color way back in the first days of having cable TV in Reed City. I'm believing in 1980 and 1981. We had to go West off Chestnut across from Don Patterson's home and reach up a pole and switch the broadcast wire from my home on Chestnut across the street from Vic's Market to a wire from the Nazarene Church, and after the broadcasts make the switch back. It was very interesting that many people said they NEVER watched the Council meetings, but when I would pack up the equipment and take it back to our studio in the City Hall portion of the city building, I would go out to the then Frontier Inn and later the Chuck Wagon and someone would make a comment about what happened at the Council meeting. I had to smile inside as they would have said, "We never watch the Council meetings." One of the other things we broadcast were the birthdays and anniversaries of anyone who wanted their name on a continuing loop that played when we weren't broadcasting a live or videotaped event.

During those years we also videotaped a few sessions of the County Board of Commissioners and played the video tapes on the system from my breezeway between the garage and house at 715 S. Chestnut Street. That is the place the programs emanated from, whether live or video, for the news, interviews, weather or whatever. All the video tapes were played from that location until we moved to the City Hall, as an alternate location. When we did, I had to make the wire switch on the pole across from Don Patterson's home.

I'm sorry I don't have any of those old tapes for you to watch. The Reed City Council meetings were very interesting. I had served on the City Council and when the opportunity became available, it was fun to broadcast those sessions live. Once in a while they would have a closed meeting for personnel reasons (which is allowable under the law) and the City Attorney would come and make sure the cable was disconnected from the camera and sound feed was also disconnected. The law stated that the Council had to make some type of report at the end of

> the closed meeting as to the type of thing discussed, and then they could end the meeting.

To begin my city council research, I went to the city building and picked up a thick packet of copied council minutes, binder-clipped into three sections, one for each of the years 1982, 1983, and 1984. I was hoping for some context. Murder doesn't occur in a vacuum, and even though I knew it was highly unlikely that I'd read the name of the killer on any one of those legal-sized pages, I figured you could learn a lot about a community by what they were spending their money on, not to mention what they spent time arguing about.

The monthly meetings were full of what you'd expect—street lights that need fixing, citizens coming to air a gripe or two, property assessments, votes on city ordinances, discussions about fluoride in the water, audits of the finances, bids for city work to be done... yadda, yadda, yadda—you get the idea. Not exactly riveting stuff.

But my curiosity was piqued right out of the box—high drama only three pages in and it read like a soap opera, if by soap opera you mean the city manager being summarily ousted, mid-meeting.

On February 1st, 1982 the city manager was Ralph Westerburg. He'd come from Milford, Ohio where he was city manager, and took the helm in Reed City in March of 1973. From a 2003 article in *The Pioneer* after his death, Westerburg was described as follows:

> *Phillip Rathbun:* "I have nothing but praise to say about him. Ralph was a very progressive city manager. He went out and made things happen. He developed an industrial park, created a park system in Reed City for recreation, expanded industry, started the repaving street program, extended water and sewer, I could go on and on... We will miss him, I will miss him. I bear the sadness of his loss because he was like one of the family."
>
> *Tom Meinert,* Reed City Planning Commission chairman and former city councilman during Westerburg's era: "I always had a good working relationship with Ralph. You might not get the answer you would like from him, but you always got the straight answer."

Aggressive is a word I got a lot when people described Westerburg. It's clear he knew the job was about bringing new business to the area and then promoting it. Another thing I heard a lot was that Mr. Westerburg was a drinker. A couple years into his tenure, two of Reed City's finest (names you'll now find familiar) took it upon themselves to haul him into the pokey for it. The article hit the AP, and I found it in no less than five different newspapers around the country, probably for the fact that the officers in question had arrested their boss. It's unlikely that happens with glaring regularity, for obvious reasons.

TINEL TUESDAY, MARCH 18, 1975

Officers Arrest City Manager On Drunk Charges

REED CITY (UPI) — The big question in legal circles and the coffee shops in Reed City, population 2,290, is:

Is it wise for two policemen to arrest the boss?

Officers Ted Platz and Larry Finkbeiner were suspended with pay Feb. 28 after they arrested City Manager Ralph Westerburg on a drunk and disorderly charges and held him in jail overnight until he put up $50 bond the next day. The charge was dropped by the prosecutor's office.

Police Chief Philip Rathburn suspended the two policemen but reinstated them over the weekend. Rathburn said he was informed that the city charter does not give him authority to suspend the officers without authority from the city manager — in this case the man they arrested.

Westerburg could, under the charter, according to a councilman, uphold the suspensions but declined to do so.

The case is in the hands of Osceola County Prosecutor James Thompson who said Monday that he is "investigating the incident and will make a recommendation to the council this week regarding the incident."

Thompson also said he was probing several other incidents involving arrests by the two officers alleging "abusing police authority."

Even after having been fired, Reed City hired Westerburg back in July of 1986, working part of the year from Florida. Nice gig if you can get it.

The February 1, 1982 City Council meeting began like normal, including things like a long discussion regarding an auditor's report, the previous meeting's minutes were read and approved, and the council went on to discuss local business owners' concerns about the new US-131 expressway. Then Councilwoman White asked one of the other council members why he did not ask for Mr. Westerburg's dismissal after he made accusations about him at the January meeting. Apparently there had been a question as to how Westerberg had used some personal and/or vacation time.

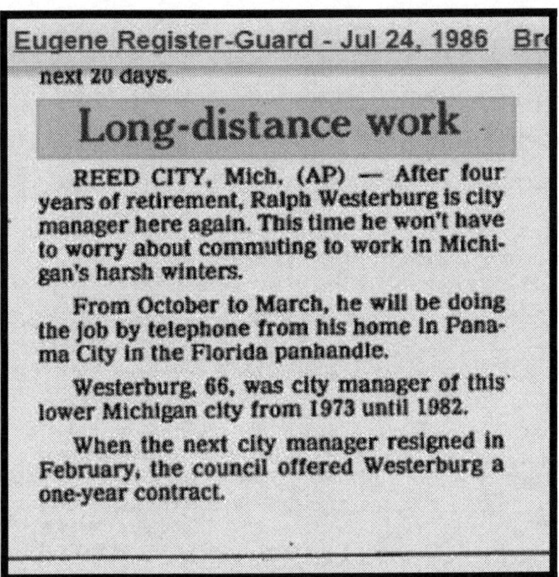
Eugene Register-Guard - Jul 24, 1986 Br

next 20 days.

Long-distance work

REED CITY, Mich. (AP) — After four years of retirement, Ralph Westerburg is city manager here again. This time he won't have to worry about commuting to work in Michigan's harsh winters.

From October to March, he will be doing the job by telephone from his home in Panama City in the Florida panhandle.

Westerburg, 66, was city manager of this lower Michigan city from 1973 until 1982.

When the next city manager resigned in February, the council offered Westerburg a one-year contract.

Councilwoman White went on to question Westerburg's authority to hire the new deputy clerk, and then she lowered the boom.

"Mr. Westerburg has been heard to say the Council doesn't run itself, he runs the council." Councilwoman White further alleged that businessmen had come to her and said, "Ralph has to go."

"Are you saying you are getting reports from business people?" Mayor Collison asked.

Councilwoman White answered that she was, and then she made the following motion, seconded by Councilman Scarborough: "We would be well advised to terminate the services of our city manager as of now, and I so move."

"Westerburg does what he thinks is best for the city, but what he does is not always for the city's good," Councilman Koon said. He further stated that it was the council's fault for letting him get away with it.

It appears this had been brewing for a while, but nobody on the council had the stones to make a motion. Nobody with the exception of Councilwoman White, who found an opening and decided to take full advantage. The Mayor was suddenly concerned about who would present the budget if Westerburg was gone, because it was due. After more discussion, a vote was taken and it carried according to the following votes: NO votes—Councilpersons Jehnzen, Marrinan, and Mayor Collison. YES votes—Councilpersons Lutz, Scarborough, Koon and White.

From the minutes, as noted by Marion Fisher: "At this time Mr. Westerburg informed the Council that they would have a real group following and that they were the ones who were going to suffer for this. He further stated that, 'As far as this town is concerned, I intend to show you what foolishness you've done. I am going to put in the paper what goes on in Reed City and what has been done by myself as City Manager.'"

Following Mr. Westerburg's statement, Larry Herring (Superintendent of Public Works) tossed his keys to Mayor Collison, and the mayor then asked if that meant he was resigning.

The mayor said there would have to be appointments made and asked for a five minute recess, after which he reconvened and informed the council that due to the fact that the City Manager had been terminated, he was appointing himself and the City Clerk [Marion Fisher] as acting City Managers until a replacement could be hired.

And then they went on to complete the meeting as if nothing unsettling had occurred. I think I may have spit coffee all over my desk in amusement as I read it. There are brown droplets all over my printed copies.

It was called to the council's attention pretty quick that the Mayor could not legally play the role of city manager. In the March 1, 1982 special meeting Mayor Collison clarified. "The Charter reads that an elected officer cannot act as Acting City Manager. The clerk, Marion Fisher, will act as city manager. Motion offered. Councilman Koon and White voted NO, everyone else voted YES."

White voted NO a lot, and often had at least one other Councilperson voting along with her. This was but the first indication that she would take issue with Marion Fisher's role in city government. For the moment, though, debt was the issue. In the same meeting, Council voted to borrow funds for "operational" expenses in the sum not to exceed $35,000. After that, Ralph Westerburg presented a request to the city to pick up one year of retirement service from his time in Milford, Ohio from the Michigan Employment Retirement System. Westerburg explained that he had intended to retire at the end of 1982 and was terminated in the meanwhile. As a result he lost about $3,000 in sick time. Then Phil Rathbun asked the council to consider *his* two years which he didn't pick up when he went to Fowlerville and then came back to Reed City. He said that he would like to regain those two years. Then the mayor appointed a group from council to start going through city manager applications, with Marion Fisher to sit in on those meetings.

So now it's March of 1982, Marion is the City Clerk, City Treasurer, Acting City Manager, and that's just the work related stuff. She's got an elderly mother at home, along with a son, and a couple of grandkids—Janette's son and daughter—who she picks up from school each day while Janette and Alvin are at work. Add those one or two monthly evening meetings, plus church and associated church functions, and it's pretty clear no dust settled on Marion Fisher.

To say a lot was going on in Reed City at this time would be a gross understatement. The city was running at a deficit. In fact, in May the Treasury Department sent a letter requesting Reed City form a plan to lower the deficit in the 1981-1982 budget. Council requested a letter be sent back to the Treasury Department asking for an extension on submitting the plan, given they were working with an acting city manager and it was usually the city manager who took the lead on such matters.

On May 18, 1982, a special meeting was called to interview James Nordstrom for the city manager position. Councilwoman White asked him what his feeling was concerning the relationship between city manager and council. Nordstrom replied, "Your city manager is only as good as your council, and vice-versa."

The mayor asked Nordstrom if he would be willing to move to Reed City if hired and Nordstrom said yes, he felt every city manager should be a resident of the city. Then the mayor asked if Nordstrom would consider combining the jobs of city manager and city assessor.

"As manager, I would say no because the funds of your city are only as good as your taxes and the assessor is a real critical person to the city," Nordstrom replied.

That was another problem. Right before the Westerburg guano hit the fan, the city had been dealing with the fact that their city assessor, Dorman Elder, was about to be forced to resign due to a conflict of interests; Elder was also the county equalizer. How that happened in the first place is anyone's guess, but it does stand out as a big no-no. In fact, according to a Pioneer article dated Jan 18, 1983 (one day before Janette's murder):

> "The Reed City City Council voted to turn over to the county, for a short-term basis, the assessing of the city in light of the resignation of former city assessor, Dorman Elder. Elder is also the county equalization director. Last year, the county commission had given notice to the city that the county would no longer allow the equalization director, or his office, to handle the assessor's job. The vote by the Reed City city council instructed City Manager Jim Nordstrom to find a new assessor within six months. The council also approved the borrowing of $30,000 by the city from an area financial institution at the best possible interest rate, to the city, with the expiration of the loan being Oct 30, 1983. "We could take the loan out from The Reed City State Bank," said Nordstrom. "I feel it would be in our best interest to borrow from a local bank than to deal elsewhere."

If you're keeping track, that would be *two* loans in less than a year. Reed City was heavily in debt by 1983.

...but we're still in 1982 and Marion Fisher is still acting city manager—and was for a total of six months, until the July 14th, 1982 meeting where James Nordstrom was voted in by council as the new city manager. Boy did he step into it. His first meeting was a doozey, mainly for how much crap was going on and the ill-will swirling around Reed City for a number of reasons. From the meeting minutes transcribed by Marion Fisher:

> Upon request from Councilwoman White, the following will be added to the June 7th meeting minutes: "Mr. Les Heyboer suggested various ways to clear up the deficits in the city budget; one of the ways was to check into the Fire Department New Equipment fund. Councilwoman White strongly objected to this."
>
> Addition noted.
>
> Councilwoman White also stated that if we ever change the way we do our Fire Department business, we'll have troubles galore. She further stated that we have the best Fire dept. in the country.
>
> Councilman Marrinan stated that he didn't feel that the auditor suggested taking money specifically from the Fire Department Fund, but that he was just talking in general accounting terms.
>
> Councilwoman Jehnzen stated that this was a very touchy subject with the Fire Department as they felt that money had been taken from their funds when it shouldn't have been. Councilwoman White agreed with this.
>
> Citizen Patricia Milligan (former city clerk) took issue with the above statement. She stated that she objected to this statement and that she had heard this before. She further stated that if you go through the book, everything is itemized, notes if it was an appropriation, or gives the date of the resolution that Council passed authorizing a transfer of funds or payment of an expense. She further stated that no money had ever been used illegally. If there were any questions, anyone could come to City Hall and check the books.
>
> Next discussion on proposed fees for tennis courts. Ken Bisbee came before council with a petition requesting no fees for the use. Mayor Collison asked Bisbee if he'd approached the Recreation Committee. Bisbee said he approached Community Ed. Dept. and they had nothing to

do with it. He further said that he came to City Hall and was told the City was responsible for the rates.

City Clerk Marion Fisher explained that she had set the rates (while acting city manager, and per minutes of an earlier council meeting) from figures left by Mr. Ralph Westerburg, and had even made them lower than his figures.

Bisbee said he felt these charges were causing tremendous ill will in the community and that *"We have too many things around town, both in and out, that have caused ill will."*

Mayor said he would turn this matter over to the Recreation Committee.

Dennis Marrinan stated that as far as he was concerned as a Council Member, the Fire Equipment Funds are not open to General Fund use; that they are a specific fund and that council would have to approve any transactions.

At this time Gerald Kienitz made an apology to Councilwoman White, Mrs. Marion Fisher, and Councilwoman Jehnzen for a statement printed in a letter that the Fire Department had previously mailed out. The letter stated that no council member objected to the use of the Fire Equipment funds, as suggested by the auditors.

Councilwoman White made a suggestion of logging all phone calls out of the Clerk's office. City Manager Nordstrom stated he was in the process of initiating an internal program to insure that each call is logged.

Discussion of the sewer project bill totaling $53,144.25. Council unanimously authorized cashing in of CD's from the Michigan National Bank Surplus Fund to finalize the payment to Dailey's Construction.

CLOSED SESSION - Police Chief Rathbun in attendance

Upon return, no action was taken concerning pending litigation.

The pending litigation was with regard to the purchase of the old city garage by Delbert Davidson—purchased during Westerburg's tenure. There was some question as to whether Davidson was properly informed upon purchase by Westerburg that there were code issues about building the dwelling around capped off sewers. The dwelling was too close to a city well for the Tool and Die, which could contain contaminated items. Mr. Davidson stated that he believed the city hid the fact that there wasn't any sewer access, and he had no knowledge of that until city workers came down and told him he didn't have a sewer.

City attorney James Thompson told council he prepared the deed at the direction of the city manager and council. When the deed was prepared, he was not aware that there was a well in the area. When the deed was signed, he realized what property it was. Thompson told council that Mr. Westerburg indicated to him that Davidson knew about the problem.

This actually ended up being a huge deal and costing the city money, despite what would be told to the press, later. (In writer-land we call that foreshadowing, folks.)

So, the council chugged along through November of 1982, elections were held, and on November 8th the new council was sworn in: Carl Holmgren, Marjorie Brown White, Michael Noreen, Iris Jehnzen, R. Clark Barto, and David Brooks. Carl Holmgren was declared Mayor Pro Tem. As an example of the type of exchanges that often included the dramatic Marjorie Brown White, I offer this:

> *"Councilwoman White questioned whether it was proper for Councilman Barto's wife being the secretary to Jim Thompson, city attorney. She asked if she would be allowed to get another attorney's opinion. She said she would write to the Attorney General to get a determination. City Attorney Thompson commented that she might not get an answer from the Attorney General. Mayor Collison stated that if Councilwoman White wanted an opinion from another attorney, it would have to be at her own expense."*

All of this is being transcribed by Marion Fisher who is diligently taking notes with what I read between the lines as a touch of wry humor and wit. I can almost picture the city attorney rolling his eyes and silently chuckling while flicking a speck of nothing off the front of his shirt. If this were a movie and I was the director, that's how I'd instruct the actor to play it; faux irritation with a hint of obnoxious entitlement.

In the December 20, 1982 proceedings—which would fall within our timeline as the day before the assault by a Reed City Police officer on two state troopers and a resident at the Buckboard Bar, for purposes of context—after returning from a CLOSED SESSION meeting, Mayor Collison stated that council had discussed the Tool and Die situation and directed the city manager to continue to negotiate with Mr. Davidson. In this meeting, it is also noted that a new Reed City Police officer is hired, and that would be Officer Michel Primeau. (He had only worked for Reed City PD for one month before the murder of Janette Roberson occurred.)

During the next meeting, which was held on January 10, 1983 (nine days before the murder), city manager Nordstrom asked Council's direction about the city hiring an attorney in the event of a possible litigation. This attorney would have to have labor-relation experience. After some discussion, it was Council's consensus to have the city manager hire a labor relations attorney if the need arose. This was with regard to the Buckboard Bar assault. If the Police Chief felt he was going to have to fire an officer, and the officer in question was going to challenge that firing, the city would need an attorney with labor-relation experience to handle the situation.

At the January 17, 1983 regular meeting (two days before Janette's murder) Marion Fisher read a letter of resignation from Mr. Dorman Elder, city assessor. Council unanimously voted to turn assessing over to the county for a maximum of six months or less, and the city would be charged appropriately. Council unanimously authorized Mr. Nordstrom to go to local finance institutions and check the best possible interest rate that he could negotiate on a $30,000 loan.

Then Councilman Holmgren asked why the city would not go ahead and hook up the Tool and Die's sewer? Nordstrom explained he would rather they choose their own contractor and expressed that if the city went ahead with the expense of this project, which would be *in the low thousands of dollars*, Flight Tool could easily say that they were not ready to open their business, therefore refusing to pay the city back for the expense. Later, in a Pioneer article, Nordstrom is quoted as saying "Flight Tool will select the contractor and is paying 75% of the total costs."

After a CLOSED SESSION the mayor attributed to negotiations between the municipal employees and the city, Councilman Noreen questioned estimating water bills, credits and debits. The city manager answered all questions, which were about adjustments on bills for overestimations on water and sewer.

(There's another bit of foreshadowing here, folks… just remember <u>Sewer & Water</u>.)

Next, Nordstrom chimed in to say that Reed City Police Officer Larry Finkbeiner had received the Citizen of the Year award from the Reed City Jaycees. Then a member of the press asked Councilman Brooks if he had forgotten his question concerning a municipal employee? Councilman Brooks replied that his question was answered in the standard procedure of the closed session. Whatever the press was asking, they weren't getting an answer, since they aren't allowed in closed session, neither is the public. It's like a super-secret meeting that only council members and the city attorney are privy to.

The press was there for information about the Reed City officer who had assaulted two state troopers and a resident at The Buckboard Bar, because the press tends to be drawn—like moths to flame (or me to Oreos)—to any misconduct around law enforcement officers. Looks like the council didn't want to pull that can of worms out in front of an audience, legal issues aside, given the RCPD had not decided what to do about the officer in question. At least not formally. Was Officer Platz suspended? Was he working? Had he already been informed of his impending termination? All questions I'd have been asking if I were a member of the press. It appears they tried, but were shut down. Not exactly a beacon of transparency, but it does remind me of that saying Nancy Grace uses on her show, *ad nauseam*: "There's no detergent like sunshine!"

Two days after this meeting, Janette Roberson is murdered in the basement pet department of the Gambles store.

February 21, 1983 is the next scheduled city council meeting and Marion Fisher is taking notes as usual, despite the devastation in her personal life. Her daughter has only been dead a month. At this meeting, "City Manager Nordstrom stated that he and Mr. Davidson of Flight Tool Company have verbally reached an agreement that he would recommend to the city council. The city would carry 90% of the sewer connection costs and 100% of engineering fees. Flight Tool would carry 10% of the cost of the sewer connections. The city will ask for bids. Nordstrom will have a written agreement prepared between the city and Davidson."

This is a drastically different deal than he told the Pioneer reporter in the article published on January 17th after the last meeting. It is unclear what turned the proverbial tides. Perhaps when faced with a grisly murder, the city decided to cut its losses and move the hell on.

But things were only getting worse. Aside from the murder that would rock Reed City, in the months to follow, embezzlement in the clerk's office came to light. There's no telling how long the folks in the city office knew about it, or how long they were scurrying around to figure out how bad it was, and what they could to do mitigate the damage. It *is* clear that the city manager doesn't mention it until his hand is forced by Marjorie Brown White in another dramatic council meeting.

(Now might be a good time to grab the popcorn.)

Dorothy Critchfield, the former Deputy Clerk, who'd worked for Reed City for over twenty years, was found to have been futzing with the Sewer and Water books. One has to wonder how the auditors didn't pick up on the inconsistencies, given the books were audited every year, but it does explain why the city was so far in debt. Not only had she been solely responsible for the sewer and water books for over twenty years, but she was also the secretary for the Andersen agency—the insurance company for the city. Based on the arrest report, an audit of the books is only done from 1980 on. That was when the city went to computerized billing. Whatever she may have taken prior to that remains unknown. I can't imagine anyone would believe she'd just started stealing from the city in the last couple years of her decades-long employment.

Multiple people I spoke to said gossip around town was that Critchfield was just the fall-guy. I have uncovered nothing to suggest that to be the case, but unfortunately it was a very short time period that was audited within the investigation done by Michigan State Police, and whatever investigation Chief Rathbun did prior to that is unknown. All of Reed City's records from that time period are gone. According to the response to my FOIA request for anything maintained on the Critchfield investigation, *"This incident is beyond the retention period that we have files on record for."*

It is unclear whether Chief Rathbun did any investigation into this matter. What is known is that Critchfield was able to steal a whole lot of money in a short period of time. One wonders how much she was *really* responsible for stealing from the citizens of Reed City.

[redacted]

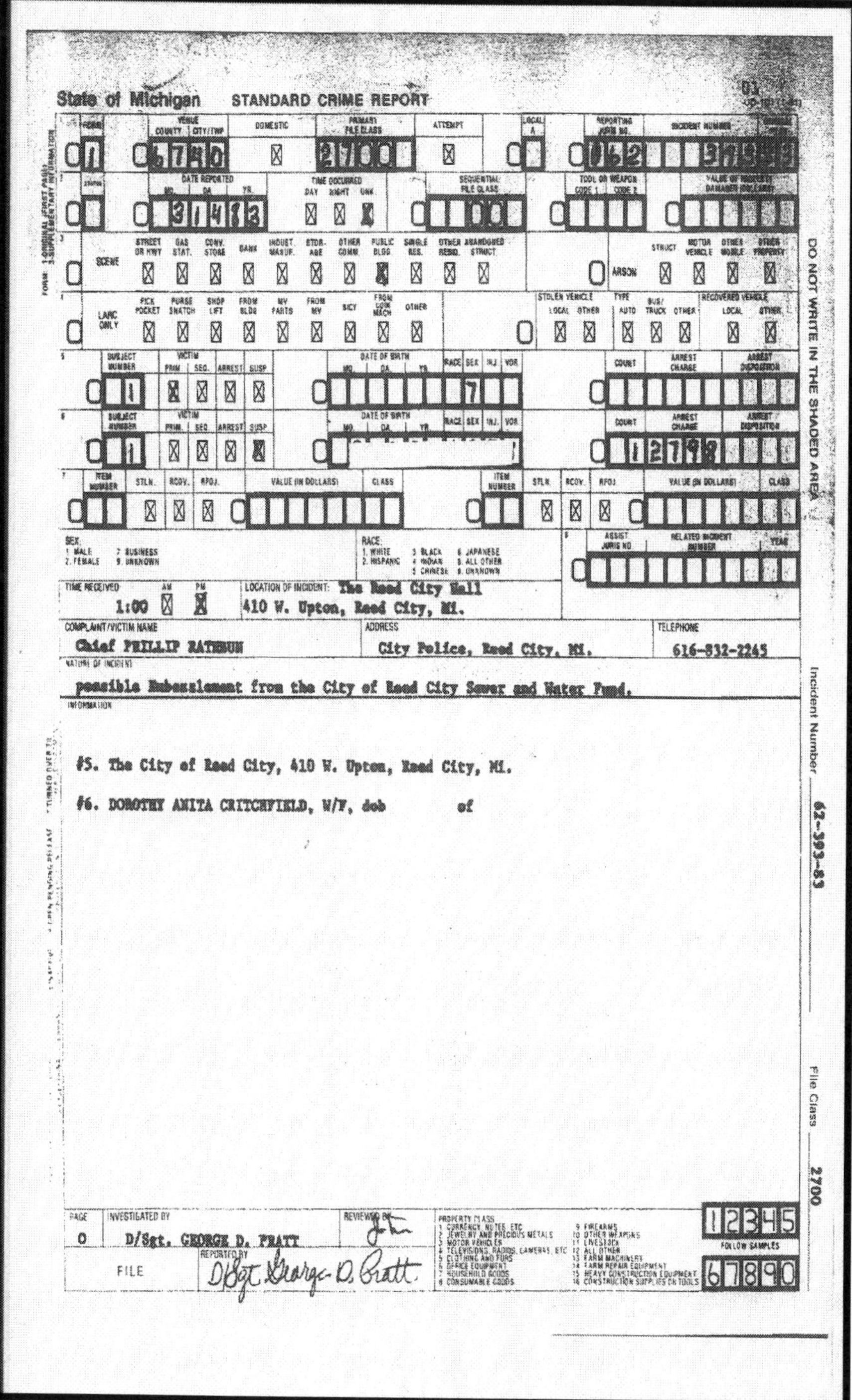

State of Michigan STANDARD CRIME REPORT

COUNTY CITY/TWP: 6780 — PRIMARY FILE CLASS: 2700 — REPORTING ORGN NO.: 062 — INCIDENT NUMBER: 393-83

DATE REPORTED: 3 14 83

TIME RECEIVED: 1:00 PM

LOCATION OF INCIDENT: The Reed City Hall
410 W. Upton, Reed City, Mi.

COMPLAINANT/VICTIM NAME: Chief PHILLIP RATHBUN

ADDRESS: City Police, Reed City, MI.

TELEPHONE: 616-832-2245

NATURE OF INCIDENT: possible Embezzlement from the City of Reed City Sewer and Water Fund.

INFORMATION

#5. The City of Reed City, 410 W. Upton, Reed City, Mi.

#6. DOROTHY ANITA CRITCHFIELD, W/F, dob of

PAGE 0 — INVESTIGATED BY: D/Sgt. GEORGE D. PRATT

FILE — REPORTED BY: D/Sgt. George D. Pratt

DO NOT WRITE IN THE SHADED AREA

Incident Number 62-393-83

File Class 2700

UD-110 (Rev. 8-79) FILE COPY

MICHIGAN DEPARTMENT OF STATE POLICE	Original Date: March 14, 1983	Complaint No.: 62-393-83
☐ Supplementary Complaint Report ☒ Additional Complaint Page No. 2	Date of Supplementary Report:	File Class: 2700

NATURE OF COMPLAINT:

Chief PHILLIP RATHBUN reports a possible embezzlement from the City of Reed City Sewer and Water Fund.

VENUE:

City of Reed City, County of Osceola, State of Michigan.

TIME:

It is believed that the embezzlement has been taking place since the City of Reed City converted to a computerized billing which occurred in February of 1980.

VICTIM:

The City of Reed City, Sewer and Water Fund, 410 W. Upton, Reed City, Mi. tx 832-2245

LOSSES:

The total amount of the embezzlement is unknown at this time, a true audit is to be done to determine this.

SUSPECT:

DOROTHY ANITA CRITCHFIELD, nee BRIAN, W/F, dob Dyed Red and Blue, R.H.. POB Ops# SS# upstairs), Reed City, Mi. tx

INFORMATION:

The suspect held the title of Accounts Payable Clerk with her employer, the City of Reed City whom she has been employed by since 9-1-59. In addition to her collecting the Sewer and Water accounts, she also would collect City taxes owed.

Recently due to a cash flow problem, City Manager JAMES NORDSTROM of the City of Reed City began reviewing deposits made on behalf of the City and discrepancies were being found. Due to this, SEIDMAN & SEIDMAN, The Certified Public Accountant Firm of 700 Union Bank Plaza, Grand Rapids, Mi. tx 616-774-7000 who does the Citys accounting were contacted. Accountants LESTER HEYBOER Jr. a partner in the SEIDMAN & SEIDMAN Firm and another employee, both CPA's, RICHARD C. REAHM began a preliminary audit.

The preliminary audit by HEYBOER and REAHM revealed what is believed to be a "lapping" scheme where money from one customer which is being paid on one date would be credited to another of a back date. Then another customer would pay and the money from this would cover the account that was first mentioned.

In a second scheme, a check dated 2-8-83 from the Reed City Hospital, check number 06359, in the amount of $2777.32 was paid to the City of Reed City for Sewer and Water services. The customer copy of the billing showed $2777.32 as being paid, however, the City's copy of the billing showed $1447.93 as having been paid.

Reporting Officer	Reviewer
D/Sgt George D. Gratt	[signature]

[redacted]

UL-110 (Rev. 8-79) FILE COPY

MICHIGAN DEPARTMENT OF STATE POLICE	Original Date	Complaint No.
☐ Supplementary Complaint Report	March 14, 1983	62-393-83
☒ Additional Complaint Page No. 3	Date of Supplementary Report	File Class 2700

NATURE OF COMPLAINT:

Chief PHILLIP RATHBUN reports a possible embezzlement from the City of Reed City Sewer and Water Fund.

INFORMATION CON'T:

Thus leaving a difference of $1329.39.

The City's copy of the Sewer and Water fund Deposit dated 2-23-83 with the Reed City State Bank shows $1447.93 as being deposited by check from the Reed City Hospital; $110.64 in cash; and fifty additional deposits in varying amounts by checks from individual City residents for a total deposit of $5494.60 less $612.00 which was to go to the General Fund for a total desposit in the Sewer and Water Fund of $4882.60.

Nineteen alleged checks totalling $1322.47 by checking the Bank's rocords cannot be found. Checking the names of the persons on the desposit slip reveals they either did not pay anytime close to the desposit date or did not pay by check.

The City of Reed City Water Supply and Sewage Disposal System Recieving Fund Deposit ticket dated 2-23-83 recovered at the Bank and passed at the time the deposit of 2-23-83 was made shows cash deposited of $110.54; and checks totallin $5384.06 with $612.00 going to the General Fund for a total deposit to the Sewer and Water Fund of $4882.60. This desposit slip is not broken down listing the names or amounts of the checks from the individuals as is the City's copy. This indicates that two deposit slips are or were being made out rather than a duplicate copy of one or the other.

As of this writing, this is the only commercial account that has been checked.

It appears that at least two different types of manipulations were occurring and additional accounting proceedures should with followup investigation substanciate this.

The Sewer and Water fund has approximately 805 participants with approximately 20 of these being commericial users with the rest being residential. The water billing depends on the meter size with the larger the size, the higher the minimum gallonage usage is allowed with the rate going up accordingly. The sewer rate is based on the amount of water usuage. A residential minimum billing (water usage under 6000 gallons) is $5.83 with a minimum sewage billing being $13.01 per quarter. The City has a rate schedule based on per thousant gallons of usuage which is used in figuring the billings. The residential quarterly Sewer and Water billing generally also reflects a $12.00 refuse hauling rate also. This is based on a contract between the City of Reed City and Tri County Sanitation Co. of Reed City for curbside refuse pickup once weekly at $4.00 per month or $12 per quarter. After a quarterly billing went out, it was noted on the bill of a due date and if the bill was not paid. a 10% late fee was added to the bill of the sewer and water fees at the time it was paid.

Reporting Officer	Reviewer
D/Sgt George O Pratt	JHA

UD-110 (Rev. 8-79) FILE COPY

MICHIGAN DEPARTMENT OF STATE POLICE	Original Date	Complaint No.
☐ Supplementary Complaint Report	March 14, 1983	62-393-83
☒ Additional Complaint Page No. 4	Date of Supplementary Report	File Class 2700

NATURE OF COMPLAINT:

Chief PHILLIP RATHBUN reports a possible embezzlement from the City of Reed City Sewer and Water Fund.

INTERVIEW WITH DOROTHY CRITCHFIELD:

When DOROTHY CRITCHFIELD was confronted this date by the Reed City City Manager and auditors of the discrepancies she admitted being involved in taking sewer and water fund monies for her own use. She acknowledged the improper handling of the Reed City Hospital check and other accounts.

At 6:40pm this date Mrs. CRITCHFIELD was met with at her home. She was advised of her Constitutional Rights which she advised she understood. She asked if she should have an attorney, and she was that was up to her, if she wanted one no questions would be asked of her until she could either hire her own or if unable to afford one, one be requested thru the Court. She advised that she wanted to talk about the matter stating that she had already talked to the others about it. She was asked if she waived an attorney being present and answered yes. She asked if she didn't want to talk about anyone part if it was okay. She was advised if during the interview she didn't want to answer a question, she wouldn't have to and if she wanted to stop answering questions, the questioning would stop. She replied that she wanted to talk about it. She was asked if she understood her rights and she replied yes. She was asked if she was willing to give up her rights and answer my questions and she replied yes, unless there was one she didn't want to answer.

Mrs. CRITCHFIELD advised that she began taking money from the Sewer and Water Fund after it was computerized, about 3-4 years ago, probably 3(feb. 1980). Her daughter was having marital problems and she gave the money to help her.

She was uncertain how much money she had taken but she thought it was around $5000. When asked if it was as much as $20,000 she said no!!

She didn't think anyone was aware of her taking the money prior to recently and she advised that no one was involved with her. She quit taking the money about a month ago but she did not recall the last amount taken or from whose account.

Mrs. CRITCHFIELD maintained she did not have any records as to how much was taken or from which accounts. It was pointed out that in dealing with over 800 accounts it would seem impossible to keep them straight but she stated that she did. It also was pointed out that if she took from one account to pay up another, the first would become delinquent and have to pay a late charge. She advised that after working at the same job for as many years as she had, she knew who the constantly delinquent people were and the others, she wouldn't notify or penalize them. She advised that there are about 100 to 120 constantly delinquent accounts and she wouldn't manipulate them.

She requested not to talk about how she actually went about manipulating the accounts until she could find the right words to explain it. She did advise that the auditors were right in how she used the Hospital account money as it had been explained to her in their meeting.

Reporting Officer	Reviewer
D/Sgt George O. Pratt	[signature]

[redacted]

UD-10 (Rev. 8-79) FILE COPY

MICHIGAN DEPARTMENT OF STATE POLICE	Original Date	Complaint No.
☐ Supplementary Complaint Report	March 14, 1983	62-393-83
[X] Additional Complaint Page No. 5	Date of Supplementary Report	File Class 2700

NATURE OF COMPLAINT:

Chief PHILLIP RATHBUN reports a possible embezzlement from the City of Reed City Sewer and Water Fund.

INTERVIEW WITH DOROTHY CRITCHFIELD CON'T:

Mrs. CRITCHFIELD advised that she had been juggling the records in all three of the City's Wards. She felt that she had kept all the manipulations in her head and they dated back as far as 6 to 8 months. Recently it had been becoming harder and harder for her to keep it straight. She advised that recently she was in the Big Rapids Ponderosa and upon seeing the undersigned, became ill and unable to complete her dinner to what she attributed as guilty feelings.

She agreed that she did change the payments and/or dates in the ledger/computer printouts of the customers money she kept.

Mrs. CRITCHFIELD maintained that she did not have any records so she would know whose accounts she had manipulated stating that she kept it all in her head and she did not want to discuss how she actually completed the manipulations.

COMPLAINT STATUS:

Open.

Submitting Officer	Reviewer
D/Sgt. George O Pratt	J.R.

The date on the MSP report attributed to the Critchfield investigation is March 14, 1983. On that date, a special City Council meeting was called and they immediately went into CLOSED SESSION.

At the regular April 18, 1983 meeting "City Manager Nordstrom stated that in the process of a budget preparation, it was discovered that there will be expenditures that far out-reach the revenues projected in the Water and Sewer Fund. Therefore Jeannette Fenner, Superintendent of the Wastewater Treatment plant, has outlined proposals for consideration to change the rate structure and rate increases."

I guess the City Manager figured they'd just raise the rates to cover what one of their employees had stolen. Where I come from, that's called *balls of steel*, my friends. *Balls of steel!*

On April 25th another Special Meeting was called and City Manager Nordstrom strongly suggested the entire meeting be open after having been served with a letter delivered by a police officer representing the Prosecuting Attorney's office.

From an article in the Herald dated May26, 1983:

> The Osceola County Prosecutor's Office is investigating an alleged violation of the Michigan Open Meetings Act by the Reed City City Council. Osceola County Prosecutor James Talaske said the matter has been referred to state police Detective George Pratt. Talaske said he has received numerous complaints concerning the city council's alleged illegal closed meetings. 'This is becoming to be a matter of concern to me,' Talaske said. 'I have very few options left.'
>
> The May 16 closed session was apparently the second time Nordstrom was involved in an alleged violation. An agenda memo sent to council members April 22nd setting a special budget meeting for April 25 stated the public would be welcome, but no public input would be taken because the meeting would be a work session. Talaske was informed of the memo and had Detective Pratt hand deliver a written opinion to Nordstrom which said all public meetings must include time for public input.

> Councilwoman Marjorie Brown White who voted against Monday's closed session said the session lasted nearly an hour and other subjects besides salaries were discussed, however, she did not elaborate.

What they were trying to do was **not** discuss in public how badly the city was in debt, and why. Going back over old newspaper accounts, there is nothing about the embezzlement in the papers. It hadn't gone public yet. But that was about to change...

Remember, this was all happening just months after the murder of Janette Roberson. Her mother, Marion, was at each of these meetings taking notes, and in the May 23, 1983 meeting, she was also taking pot-shots from Councilwoman Brown White.

First, Jim Thompson, the city attorney, read the salary resolution. Council members approved all salaries, but White and Noreen voted no on the city clerk's salary. *Really*? Her daughter was murdered four months ago and you're going to challenge her pay now? *Classy*. It is of note that the same two councilmembers voted yes for the deputy clerk's salary. The police chief's salary motion was defeated as well. Councilpersons White, Brooks, and Noreen voted no, and five affirmative votes are needed. City Manager Nordstrom stated his proposal was to make sure the Chief made more than his officers, since they received overtime, whereas he does not. Then the status of the police union contract was discussed and it was decided to wait until those negotiations were concluded to discuss the police chief's salary.

Next Councilwoman White commented that the council had never reviewed the Water and Sewer budget. It was time they discussed it. She also suggested that all citizens read their own meters. This was her way of pushing a bruise. Nothing had been widely reported about the embezzlement, and the only locals who knew anything at all were the council, city attorney, Chief Rathbun, and anyone who may have been passed the scuttlebutt straight from the council members themselves. Councilwoman White's suggestion was ignored and the city council moved on to other matters.

City Manager Nordstrom read correspondence from the Teamsters State, County, and Municipal Workers Local 214, regarding a petition for representation for the city department heads.

Councilwoman White: (to Marion Fisher) Did you start the union business?

Marion Fisher (Clerk): I do not feel I have to give out that information.

One has to wonder why Councilwoman White was instigating the woman who'd just lost her daughter in a more vicious manner than most of us can comprehend. Did she believe Marion had something to do with the embezzlement? There is no evidence to suggest Marion Fisher had any knowledge of the embezzlement going on in her office, but that doesn't mean that wasn't the gossip on the street. Councilwoman White was out there quietly telling citizens to scan their Sewer and Water bills for inconsistencies, so it isn't out of the realm of possibility that she was also suggesting the city clerk might have had a hand in the illegal actions. And she wasn't finished pointing fingers at Marion Fisher, either.

The June 30, 1983 Special Council Procedures meeting was when the "Sewer Scandal" erupted, in earnest. Mayor Collison called the meeting to order and stated that the agenda for this meeting consisted of one item only – Water and Sewer Billings. Then he turned the meeting over to Councilwoman White who read directly from her pre-prepared statement. It must have been a glorious sight to behold, in a *live broadcast*, no less.

Someone's ready for their close-up, Mr. DeMille...

Marion Fisher prepared these minutes, so you have to wonder about her mood when she typed this: "Councilwoman White, at this time, held the printout sheets of Ward 1 up one by one for the television camera."

Her daughter had been dead for a little over six months, she continued to show up for work every day, and for the flurry of meetings at night, and there she was being publicly (and not very subtly) accused of gross incompetence at the very least, and at worst, knowledge and/or participation in the embezzlement by a member of the council. It really is rather astounding when you look at it all in context.

[redacted]

202

Indexed

REED CITY
SPECIAL COUNCIL PROCEEDINGS
June 30, 1983

Mayor Collison called the special meeting of Council to order at 6:30 P.M. The meeting opened with the pledge to the flag. The Mayor directed the Clerk to show that all Council members were present, with the exception of Councilman Brooks, who was excused due to another commitment. Present: Mayor Donald Collison, Councilmen Carl Holmgren, R. Clark Barto, Michael Noreen, Councilwomen Iris Jehnzen, and Marjorie Brown White. City Manager Nordstrom was also present.

Mayor Collison stated that the agenda for this meeting consists of one item, Water and Sewer Billings. He turned the meeting over to Councilwoman White.

Councilwoman White read the following statement; When the raise in water rates was proposed, I knew I couldn't vote for such a raise unless it were justified, and this is not an attempt to embarrass anyone. After receiving many calls relative to water and sewer bills, I knew I had a responsibility as a Councilman to check out that information. I asked the Mayor to secure a printout for ward 1 billings, which he kindly did, and I discovered that approximately one bill out of three in ward 1 was incorrect. There was a total of 109 errors out of 355 accounts, and the City had short changed itself about $1200 or more. I'm prepared, at this time, to review all 109 obvious errors, but for the sake of brevity, I will tell you that the errors are so obvious they could have been spotted by a school child, and I am really personally horrified that they were not spotted and reported to the Mayor and the Council immediately. It is obvious to anyone who has seen a water and sewer rate chart that if you use 67,000 gallons of water, your sewer should be more than $18.92.

Councilwoman White then requested that copies of the water and sewer rate chart be passed out to the Council members and the media. She stated it is also obvious to anyone looking at the rate chart that sewer charges are higher than water charges, but in the last ward 1 billing countless accounts paid more for water than sewer. If we have a deficit, which she imagines is the reason for the rate increase, it is because of unpaid bills, disputed bills, and money owed the water and sewer fund from the general fund, and it is necessary that everyone pay what the rate chart states, which was not true in this particular billing.

Councilwoman White, at this time, held the printout sheets of ward 1 up one by one for the television camera. She stated that she would like some answers as to how this could possibly happen, especially at this time, and guess the answers will have to come from Mr. Nordstrom and Marion Fisher.

City Manager Nordstrom stated that he has prepared the following statement of concern which he requested be made a part of these minutes. Mr. Nordstrom read the following statement;

STATEMENT OF CONCERN

I have written this statement of concern to try to answer what I anticipate to be some of your questions for tonight's meeting.

It is my understanding that some council members have a concern about current water and sewer billings. While I am aware of the fact that billings are on tonight's agenda, I have not been made aware of any specific examples of potential problems and hence, cannot be prepared to answer your questions.

any specific examples of potential problems and hence, cannot be prepared to answer your questions.

The proper procedure for handling potential problems with City operations is to contact the City Manager with specific questions about the alledged problems. The manager can, in turn, consult his staff and properly address those operational questions. The City offices are the appropriate area to transact business.

Each councilperson has been individually contacted, encouraging them to bring their questions to myself and my staff. None, with the exception of Carl Holmgren,

203

page 2, special council proceedings, June 30, 1983.

have come to the City office or called with a specific question for my staff to research and answer. Because, with the one exception, there have been no specific questions, I can only assume that there are either no other questions or that the individuals requesting this Special Meeting are attempting to publicly embarrass my staff and myself.

My staff, given proper notificat ion of specfic questions, can properly address each of those questions in the office. To attempt to make a public specticle of my staff at a public meeting such as this one, is unethical, in bad ta te, and not in the best interest of the public we are supposed to be representing. Taxpayers are paying $60.00 for this meeting in councilperson's fees which could have been avoided if these people. Calling this meeting would have addressed this problem properly.

I feel that a viable alternative to this behavior is for the Mayor to appoint an investigative committee, as he is empowered to do via Chapter 6, section 6.8 of the City Charter, to investigate any specific water and sewer billing inconsistancies, if in fact, any exist. The committee would work with my staff and make a report at the regula r meeting of July 26, 1983.

It is my intention to cooperate with Council. My staff and I will continue to be available to answer your specific questions. I only ask that Council extend the courtesy of allowing my staff time to properly research your questions so that we may provide you with the best answers possible in an atmosphere conducive to conducting business.

I look forward to continuing to try to work with you.

Respectfully,

James D. Nordstrom
City Manager

So... the city council soldiered on, as did the Janette Roberson murder investigation.

On September 27th, 1983, Dorothy Anita Critchfield was charged, and on November 21st 1983 she was found guilty of one count of felony embezzlement, sentenced to one year in jail, five years' probation, two-hundred hours of community service, and ordered to make monetary restitution in the amount of $42,496.

That's how much she embezzled in the last couple years of her employment. Imagine how much more she could have gotten away with in her over 20 years working for the city. The possibilities are staggering.

I never uncovered anything to suggest Marion Fisher had any knowledge of the embezzlement. It was an unseemly chapter of the city's history finally closed. But the investigation into the death of Janette Roberson was nowhere near being resolved.

INVESTIGATION CONTINUED....

September, 1985; The next group questioned in the Janette Roberson investigation was affiliated with the Jehovah's Witness church she attended in Evart. After that, police circled the wagons around people who lived in Meadowview, her apartment complex.

Patricia Knapp, who said she'd been to Janette's house on a few occasions, Condra Lynn Casavettes, Jeffrey Scott Lucha, and Donald Knapp, Patricia's husband.

Detective Albright re-interviewed Marion Fisher at her home in LeRoy on September 18, 1985, according to the MSP report, "...about how she was advised of the death of her daughter, and what had happened that night." Marion told them "...she was working as the city clerk in the city building on the day of the murder, and approximately 3:45pm to 4:00pm Larry Finkbeiner of the Reed City Police Department came to the City building and told her that Janette was dead, that an incident had happened at the Gambles store. She stated that somewhere around 5:00pm, the city manager took her over to Alvin's residence on Mill Street [Meadowview Apartments] where she stayed until the police arrived, which she felt was somewhere around 8:30 to 9:00pm. She stated that during the time she was at Alvin's, she did remember Alan Foote coming to the residence and also that "Dan" came to the residence with another young boy that she did not know. She stated that the entire evening was somewhat of a blank to her, she was not sure what time "Dan" came to the residence but that he was in fact there."

The first section of interest is how she was advised of the death of her daughter. The ME report says the body was discovered at approximately 3:50pm, though there is obviously no record for the 14 minutes prior to Officers Finkbeiner and Primeau's arrival time of 4:04. It isn't written in the Reed City report what time Officer Finkbeiner notified Marion Fisher. The report flatly states that the undersigned officers [Finkbeiner and Primeau] "From 4:04 to 8:00pm did maintain building security white (sic) crime lab conducted search for evidence."

Whether Marion Fisher's notification time—per her recollection—is accurate, is unclear. Unfortunately, we only have The Finkbeiner/Primeau report to go on as far as the time they arrived. If accurate, Marion was notified minutes after Officer Finkbeiner first saw her daughter's body. He would've had to leave the Gambles store, head to the city building a few blocks down Upton, after having just turned the scene over to Southworth—who would, at the same time (according to his report) be outside making calls at his patrol car, which would have left Deputy Oyster and Officer Primeau at the scene with EMT Gary McGhee.

Whatever the specifics, it seems Detective Albright was trying to get a clear picture of exactly what happened just after the discovery of the body. Once he spoke with Marion Fisher, he interviewed Chris Casavettes. Chris's father had been a customer in the store that morning, but that is not what they were questioning him about. I spoke with Chris in October of 2014 and asked him to tell me his connection to the case, and what he remembered about the incident.

He said on January 19, 1983, he was going to a friend's house after school around 5:00pm or so. He remembers it was starting to get dark. The friends—one of whom was Patricia Knapp—had heard a blurb on the 5 o'clock news about a murder down at Gambles, and when he got there, they were all excited to find out what had happened. They wanted Chris to go down and ask Janette about it because they knew he was friends with her. So he put on his coat and headed over to Janette's. They all lived in the same apartment complex.

"Thank God the little Langworthy girl intercepted me," Chris told me on the phone. "She was running toward me from Jenny's house and she said, 'Chris, Jenny's mom's dead.'"

Chris said his sister Kelly was over at the Langworthy's at the time, and she confirmed it. But he wasn't questioned at the time of the murder. A couple years later he was living in Middleville with relatives and some state police showed up. He said their questions were mostly about "Dan." Apparently "Dan" had made a WANTED poster over at the Career Center in computer class and hung it in his bedroom window, which Chris took as "jestful." It seems "Dan" thought the police believed he'd killed Janette, and he was feeling the pressure so he acted out like awkward teenagers tend to do in situations where they have no idea how they're supposed to be acting, nor do they fully appreciate the possible ramifications of their impulsive actions. I mean, how *do* you act when this older girl you like gets murdered? One of his buddies probably should have—and likely did—tell him that putting a WANTED poster with his name on it in his bedroom window for the whole apartment complex to see probably wasn't the best way to go.

In any event, that's what police wanted to speak to Chris Casavettes about when they came to interview him in 1985. Chris told me he never knew "Dan" to be violent, and didn't see him as the type to kill someone. He said the police also asked if Janette was the type to do drugs, or if Chris knew if she was having an affair with "Dan." He told them *No* to both, as far as he knew.

I told him I'd been trying to track down Patricia Knapp, with little luck. Chris said that he didn't think she really knew Janette much at the time, but she lived in the same part of the building that "Dan" lived, so maybe that's why they were questioning her. According to Chris, he knew Janette better than Patricia did, which is why she had asked him to go check when they'd heard on the news about someone getting murdered at Gambles.

I asked him to tell me about Janette. Chris said he met her the day the Robersons moved into the Meadowview apartments. He and a friend were playing ball and wrestling in front of an empty apartment next to the one Janette and Alvin were moving into.

"I saw that Nova pull up and a man, woman, and kids got out. She was the most beautiful woman I had ever seen in my life. After she and the man went inside, I asked the kids if that was their sister. They laughed and said, 'No, our mom!'"

"Then I got to know her and she was the sweetest person you'd ever want to meet. She had an infectious personality. Just a super nice person."

I asked about the Roberson family dynamic and Chris said they were good kids and Janette was nice. Alvin was quiet and soft-spoken. He said over the years—after the murder—he watched so many of those crime shows and 99% of the time it's the husband. He always tried to figure out why, in this case, it *couldn't* be the husband. Because he didn't think it was. He said Alvin didn't seem the type. He worked a lot, mostly he seemed tired, and the relationship looked like a normal "mundane" marriage. He said he thought Alvin was a bit older than Janette, but it was clear to him that Janette really loved him. I asked if Chris had ever seen anything that made him think Alvin could have killed his wife. He said no.

Then Chris sighed and said, "You know, the only crack I ever saw was one night, I was at their house hanging with the kids and I went upstairs to the bathroom to pee. I accidentally saw Janette and Alvin in the bedroom having a serious conversation. I only heard Alvin say, 'Damn it, I never get to see the kids, anyway.'"

To his recollection, this happened in October or November of '82. That's the only sentence Chris heard from the conversation, without context, and he always tried to figure out what it might have meant. The only thing that came to mind was that in the months before, he says the kids told him they were moving back to Georgia, but it never materialized. Chris speculated that maybe Alvin wanted to go back to Georgia, and Janette wanted to stay in Reed City near her mom and brother. He said he had no idea if that was the case, it was pure speculation, but that's really the only thing he ever saw that made him wonder if it was Alvin. When they were together, they acted like a "normal" married couple as far as he could tell.

Having heard that teens from the apartment complex seemed to gravitate to Janette's apartment, I asked if people generally hung out there. Chris said yes, that she was very friendly, and they were all just sort of in and out.

In the MSP report, Thomas Hawkins (currently serving time for multiple counts of Criminal Sexual Conduct with minors) was the next interview, done by Detective Albright. Then Patricia Knapp, again, as well as "Dan," and then multiple people who lived in close proximity to Gambles were given short interviews, probably to determine if they had seen anything odd that day.

Roger Soper was interviewed on September 25th, 1985. This is the man who worked at the hospital and was supposed to stop at Gambles with his mother-in-law to look at a bird on the day of the murder. Because his mother-in-law was "Dan's" mom, some of that interview centered around "Dan."

Roger lived in Hersey, Michigan when he was younger, near the Fishers, who also lived there at the time. He knew Janette's brother and sister as kids, and he was one of the boys Marion used to drive to youth group on Wednesday nights. He didn't know Janette much because she'd moved away young and didn't come back until years later. He only remembers meeting her a few times.

Roger said Janette was friends with both "Dan" and "Dan's" mother. He told me when the police came to question him (years later) they asked why he had not made it to Gambles that day. He told them they'd just forgotten. He assumed they'd spoken to the mother-in-law and she told them the story, so they were just confirming it with him. He also remembered "Dan's" mother saying her son was "devastated and thinks everyone believes he did it."

Roger described "Dan" as slow and not good in school. He said he thought he had a crush on Janette, and although he did find the difference in their ages a bit odd since "Dan" was at her apartment so much, he didn't remember Alvin being around a lot.

I asked if he thought "Dan" seemed like the violent type.

"No. He was just... he struggled in school, didn't like it. He was a loafer."

Nobody I spoke to thought "Dan" was the violent type or could picture him killing anyone. I tried to contact "Dan" to get his version of events and learn a bit more about his relationship with Janette. I got this response: *"So you are trying to make a buck on a friend of mine (sic) death. Don't bother me."*

I could have explained to him the error of his assumption, given it is unlikely that will happen based on what I've already put into this project, but to what end? Live right, folks. That's the best defense against an ignorant accusation. One needn't worry about defending oneself if you're on the right side of the truth.

On October 4, 1984 Detective Albright mentions a letter he sent to Elke Johnson in West Germany requesting information on her whereabouts and what she did on the day of the homicide. On this date he received a collect call from Elke from her home in West Germany, and at that time she and her husband Karl were interviewed by phone. There are three pages of notes in a supplemental dated Dec 31, 1985 done by Detective Pratt which make up the last notations of the year. The date of the investigation being handed over to Albright and Vincent for re-investigation is noted, as well as when a box of evidence from the case was transported to the Crime Lab in Bridgeport by him at the request of Detective Albright. He also notes that on September 20, 1985, James Paris of the First National Bank and trust in Big Rapids contacted him in reference to information that had been requested by Detectives Albright and Vincent.

Composite sketches were forwarded to the Plainwell PD at their request, and a Detective out of Lansing send information on a subject they had arrested to compare against similarities to Janette's case. Neither lead ended up bearing fruit.

On December 2, 1985, a note was left for Detective Pratt from Trooper John Beam at the Reed City Post dated November 30, 1985 in reference to contact he had with Donald Knapp, husband of Patricia Knapp. According to Detective Pratt's notes, "Mr. Knapp reported that 'strange things are going on." Pratt forwarded that information on to Detective Vincent.

The final notation made in 1985 is a list of four property items in manila envelopes with the notation, "The above items were obtained on January 4, 1984 from "Dan" and submitted to the Bridgeport Crime Lab on October 9, 1985. UD 14s submitted."

1986

The first supplemental of the New Year is dated January 16, 1986, just three days shy of the three year anniversary of Janette Roberson's death. There are a couple more interviews done with regard to "Dan," including someone he lived with in 1985, but the next month, the February supplemental dated the 26th, the MSP report notes: "The Undersigned [Albright] officer and Detective Morris Vincent were contacted by Detective Lieutenant Robert Smith, 6th District Headquarters in reference to this investigation. He requested the officers re-contact all store employees, and re-interview them in reference to this particular homicide."

So that's what they did. Donna Evans, Angie Tillie, Flossie Earnest, David Engels (store owner), Bonnie Engels (David's wife), David Sandlin, John Engels (store manager), and then they went back the next day to speak with Bonnie Engels one more time. All of these statements have been redacted in their entirety, as have their initial interviews.

The only two lines left un-redacted in the Michigan State Police report is under the interview of John Engels on February 26th and it reads: *"In going back over the day of the incident, John Engels could add nothing further that happened that day that could help officers in reference to this investigation."*

All blank pages, and then that. I will never figure out the method to MSP's FOIA Madness.

John Engels was the only Engels I was able to speak to regarding this case, and the conversation wasn't a comfortable one, which was confusing because he had given his number freely to be contacted. Jen, the gal who would become my research assistant—but was just a curious observer at the time we spoke to him—contacted a woman who police spoke to regarding the case and happened to notice that John Engels was one of the people on her friends list on Facebook. So Jen asked for an introduction, the woman obliged, and John Engels passed on his phone number.

I hate contacting people I don't know. It makes me queasy. I fobbed off a lot of the required telephone work for this project on Jen, but in this case, both of us were excited at the possibility of speaking with anyone who'd been at Gambles that day. At that point, I'd only had the opportunity to speak to Flossie, who'd attended the memorial walk, and Gene Johnson, who'd had a brief exchange with Janette the day of the murder.

Flossie was, in fact, the one who suggested we speak to John Engels. Her most vivid recollection was of him "taking the stairs two at a time" from upstairs, where she thought he was having his lunch. When Angie Tillie came back up from the basement, distraught and unable to speak after finding Janette, Flossie had yelled, "John, I think Angie is having a heart attack!"

Needless to say, we were both confused when Jen's call was met with hostility.

JEN THE ASSISTANT: Engels won't say anything. Someone told him I'm writing a book. He doesn't wanna get sued.

ME: He doesn't wanna get sued? What does that mean? Is he planning on implicating someone? Ugh, fine...give me his number.

I'm not made for this sort of thing. I don't like putting people out. I'm uncomfortable bothering strangers. I don't even like talking on the phone, yet I've had to bother a great deal of strangers over the phone while researching this book. I happen to be the type who gets stress eczema just thinking about making an uncomfortable phone call. As I type this now, I have a huge patch of the stuff on my left hand because days ago I found out that Detective Pratt has agreed to meet, and I very much want him to like me. It's ridiculous, I know, but I have that stupid people-pleaser gene, despite all evidence to the contrary. I'm aware that most folks who've met me might think this flies in the face of everything they've ever observed, but they'd be wrong. You know that whole "don't judge a book by its cover" deal? I'm a goddamn ray of sunshine who is brash and sassy on the outside, and a quivering melted mush of marshmallow goop on the inside. You'll have to take my word for that.

I dreaded the call, but what spurred me on was curiosity regarding his tone with Jen. I was pondering someone's possible motivation to be cranky with a total stranger as I jabbed the buttons on my phone and moved into the kitchen, away from the television that my son was listening to at an ear-splitting decibel level. A female answered and I asked for John Engels. She asked who was calling and I said Jeni Decker. I heard her repeat this and then say, "I don't know."

When he got on the phone, I told him I was the writer in question. I think it is important to stop here and note that at the time I spoke to John Engels, I had absolutely ZERO intention of writing this book. I had told Janette's sister that I was thinking about basing a <u>fictional</u> character involved in a three-decades-old crime on Janette's murder, but most of it wouldn't even resemble this case because I'd already started writing the crime novel I was considering using it for as a subplot, so I'd have to weave the narratives together. Mostly, I just liked the idea of a creepy basement pet department in a store that was located in a small town, and those underground tunnels I'd heard so much about. But even that wasn't for sure. Certainly the general public had no idea about this because *I didn't even know* what I was going to do with the fictional account. As a matter of fact, that episode in my Dex Morneau series sits on my hard drive right now, half written. It got booted out of the lineup by what you're reading.

What I *had done* was written my very first FOIA request to Michigan State Police, less than two weeks prior to speaking to Mr. Engels. I didn't even realize police reports on open cases were available to the public until I read an article about a true crime writer named Blaine Pardoe, who'd covered a couple of Michigan's unsolved murders. In the article he mentioned sending requests for crime scene photos and police reports to MSP, so I emailed Mr. Pardoe and asked how he went about it. He emailed me back a copy of the letter he sent to Michigan State Police to get materials for his latest book, *Murder in Battle Creek: The Mysterious Death of Daisy Zick*. I, in turn, used Mr. Pardoe's letter—word for word—removing his information and inserting mine. So, at the time I spoke with John Engels, this would have been the only thing that existed anywhere suggesting any intent on my part to write a non-fiction account of the murder. It was not my intention to do *anything* at that time other than get more information on Janette's murder, simply because I found it fascinating.

It was only after speaking with John Engels that I thought *Maybe I* ***will*** *write a non-fiction book.* In fact, today, as I write this, I pinpoint that very conversation as the turning point. His tone during the call is what sealed the deal. I readily admit to having grown into one of those adults who doesn't like being told what to do. And it's a really bad idea to tell me *not* to do something. Telling me to let something go is probably the best way to light a fire under my ass. I've found that behind the *leave it alone* or *let it go* is usually a very good reason to do the exact opposite. Also, have I mentioned I'm stubborn?

Anyway, here I am on the phone, and I've introduced myself. I tell John Engels that I'm the writer in question, but I wasn't writing true crime. Mostly I was curious. I contacted him after talking to Flossie Earnest—his former co-worker—who specifically said to me, "Did you talk to John?"

In his conversation with Jen, John Engels said he'd heard she was a writer and he didn't want to speak with a writer because if he told her anything and she published it, he could be sued for slander. That's not actually how it works in real life, but okay... I figured I'd just disabuse him of that misinformed notion and we'd move on. I assured him that I wasn't interested in speculation regarding who he thought committed the heinous act. I simply wanted to know if he and his brother, David Engels, were at Gambles when Janette's body was discovered.

"I don't have to tell you anything, get the report."

I felt my right eyebrow make for higher ground. "Oh, I am. The request has already been sent." My inner monologue suggested I reply with *Thanks for the suggestion, Mr. Crankypants,* but I stifled the urge because my inner monologue is a troublemaker.

John Engels was contentious from the start, but never appeared to want to hang up. There were more than a few uncomfortable silences as I waited for him to hang up on me, but he never did. What was most interesting was his tone, since John Engels is a former law enforcement officer. He worked for the Saginaw Police Department before moving to the area to work at Gambles with his brother.

It has been my experience when speaking with police that 100% of the time they do more listening than talking. They want to know what *you know* and the good ones know how to get that information out of you without you even realizing they're doing it. Their tone is usually encouraging in that regard because it takes some amount of finesse in order to pull that off, but every good cop I've ever met has that particular skill set. They'll give and take just enough to "shake you down for the deets" as the kids say. That, however, was not John Engels' way.

To make him more comfortable, I assured him that I understood he was a former member of law enforcement and wouldn't expect him to share specific details about a case with me. I only wanted to establish whether he and his brother David were both present at Gambles when Janette's body was found, because I'd gotten conflicting information on that. He remained tight-lipped.

Next he questioned my motives. I told him that I'd helped work on the memorial walk for Janette and I was curious. Her case interested me in the same way an episode of *Dateline* might.

I was only asking because Flossie told me she remembered both he and David being there when the body was found, but according to a letter written by Ralph Fisher sometime after the murder, Ralph spoke to the manager of Gambles, who told him he was notified of Janette's death, and then came to the store. Whether Ralph Fisher spoke to David Engels or John Engels is unclear. He said "manager" in the letter—and according to the MSP report, that was John Engels' position—but Ralph could have used the word 'manager' to describe the owner, too. I explained all of this to John, but he wasn't budging.

Argumentative is the one word summation of my approximately twenty minute chat with John Engels. I told him we'd received some tips at the memorial walk, and I had gotten one while handing out fliers from someone who'd never spoken to police. This one, in particular, was a strange occurrence two different people relayed to me about something they saw on the corner of Chestnut and Upton right around the time the murder would have occurred.

I told Mr. Engels I had passed that information along to law enforcement officers, but when he asked me what that information was and I wouldn't tell him, he said, "Then why should I open up to you?"

"I am not asking you to open up to me. I have one question. Were both you and David present at the store when the body was found," I tried again.

"Get a copy of the police report," he repeated.

When I mentioned that people—including some in law enforcement—had suggested the initial investigation was not handled properly, he said, "People always say that. They did their best."

I told him multiple people had mentioned a cop who shared specific information about Janette's injuries with them and I found that troubling. He replied, "Finkbeiner was a friend of mine. He was a good cop. We were friends. He died too young."

"How do you know I was talking about Finkbeiner?" I hadn't mentioned anyone by name.

He responded, "It's common knowledge he was first on the scene."

I didn't have the report at the time, so it wasn't common knowledge to me, but I didn't say that out loud because he was still talking.

"People remember things wrong, it's been 30 years—who did that letter of Ralph's go to?" I was momentarily thrown off by him circling back to Ralph Fisher's letter. I told him I had no idea who the letter went to.

Then he began questioning my motives again. "So why are you doing this if you're not going to write a book?"

Why? Because I want to know. I want to know if she smiled at her killer, if she knew him, or if he took her by surprise. I want to know the last emotion she felt before she realized what was happening. I want to understand her end; I want to know how Janette Roberson's world ended. But that's not what I said. This is what I said:

"Whether or not I decide to write a fictional account is irrelevant. I want to know who killed this girl in the middle of the day, just as an average citizen." I stopped short of suggesting this wasn't Nazi Germany. Here in the good 'ole US of A we're allowed to write whatever kind of books we want to write, or not write them, *and* pick whatever fancy adjectives and adverbs we wish to use in any book we may or may not write.

"Why should I talk if everyone is pointing fingers? I know I didn't do it. You sound like you think I did it."

I never once said anything even remotely close to that but since he'd mentioned the word slander earlier in the conversation, I was quick to reply. "I absolutely *do not* think you did it. You are misunderstanding me. Flossie specifically said I should talk to you, so that's what I'm doing. I thought it would be rude not to get your side, wouldn't it? You were the store manager. Your brother was the store owner. If I hadn't called and tried to talk to you, wouldn't that be weird, not giving you an opportunity to answer questions, just like everyone else?"

"Tell me what this suspicious activity was that you say people saw," he tried again. I was tempted to ask *again* if he and David were present when Janette's body was found. See how many times we could complete the vicious cycle before one of us tossed the phone across the room.

"I can't say, but rest assured it has been turned over to police. These are all people who never spoke with law enforcement before, so I can't share it with you. I'm sure you understand that, being a former cop."

The conversation was over at that point. I have no idea why he was so contentious from the start, but I didn't expect to get that kind of reaction from a former cop. Anyone who didn't wish to speak to me just declined and that was that. I'm not a reporter. I don't go chasing people or harassing them. I respect the word no. I did my due diligence and gave every person I could track down whose name was in the MSP report (and wasn't already dead) a chance to tell me what they remembered, and most people were genuinely happy to oblige.

Near the end of the conversation I told him that—how helpful everyone had been about what they remembered, and how the residents of Reed City wanted the case solved. I was just blathering by that point, trying to end on a good note, mostly because I felt bad for having upset him. Maybe he was just having a bad day.

John Engels reply: "Good for them."

Months later, I mailed a letter to the residence of David and Bonnie Engels, asking if they would consider speaking to me. I told them I had decided to write a true crime book about the murder, and since the only interaction I had with anyone in their family did not go smoothly, I felt it would be unfair to leave my conversation with John as the only impression of their family regarding this case for the readers.

They never replied.

Profiling

> "I've been reading about sex murders and profiling. I think either our guy is a disorganized lust killer, or he wants us to think he is. He lived in the area. He's into kinky sex. Sadism. He hides it. The [**REDACTED**] injuries were to dehumanize her. He's probably sexually dysfunctional in some way."

Okay, we're not profilers so the above could very well be a bunch of crap. We don't know who killed Janette Roberson. But this is typical of the kind of message I'd get from my research assistant, Jen Carlson, on a daily basis. They weren't all about crime scene profiling, but you get the idea. We've spent over a year working on this every day—often all day, in between whatever else we were doing in our personal lives like cooking dinners and contracting roof repairs after a tornado, and dealing with kids' IEP meetings (mine), or a kid that wasn't put on the bus home after school on his first day (hers). We did a lot of debating that would sound a lot like bitching and/or arguing to the untrained ear. But that's the kind of stuff that would float into my instant messenger app on my phone accompanied by a little *ding*. We *were* talking murder—a fairly brutal, horrific murder—so the conversation topics were usually unpleasant.

Again, let me repeat, *we don't know who murdered Janette Roberson*, but we do have a copy of the fourteen page autopsy report and enough details about the scene to know that there was a sexual component to this crime. From day one, almost every newspaper article about the murder included the phrase "partially clad body," so it had to be clear to everyone that a sexual assault was involved. Nobody spends their workday partially clad. I can also say with a fair amount of certainty that Janette did not remove any clothing on her own.

I suppose now is as good a time as any to have a chat about the sexually sadistic criminal. I'm sure you're just as averse to discussing such matters as I, but after reading the ME report, it's one of the things that's almost always rolling around inside my head, even in quiet moments—what was done to Janette, what she had to endure.

Sexual sadism is so named because it describes a pairing of sexual acts with domination, degradation, and violence. Within the ME report is a fair amount of evidence to suggest our perpetrator could very well be clinically diagnosed as sexually sadistic, all fancy and legal and whatnot. Now, to be fair, there are plenty of sexual sadists out there who never do anything more than almost choke out their ever-willing auto-erotic lover. For some folks, that's Tuesday night... and that's just fine. It's none of anyone's concern if both partners are of age and consensually along for the ride.

That is not the case here. Janette Roberson was most certainly not on board with what she got. The evidence in the report suggests the perpetrator was probably known to the victim, though perhaps indirectly. Random psychos don't tend to make the kind of effort that was made here. If we were to give that kind of effort a name, it would be called suffering. This person wanted Janette Roberson to suffer. That's not stranger danger. That kind of danger lives a little closer to home.

Because this is an open investigation, I don't feel comfortable outlining specific details of her injuries, nor is it integral to your understanding of the case to have a measurement and graphic description of each injury. But it has been widely reported that she had multiple wounds and there were multiple weapons. Rage; vengeful; brutal; overkill. I'll break it down further: this guy is a real nasty piece of work.

From a profiling perspective, we're probably talking about someone with issues around women, anger, and very likely a disturbing fantasy life which propelled the action that was to follow. What kind of person does this sort of thing? Who gets up one morning and before the evening news has time to air, has so brutalized someone, her injuries were described as "beaten beyond recognition?" Who ties their shoes after brushing their teeth and somewhere between there and dinner—because our guy got away, so he actually got to have dinner that night, whereas Janette did not—so how does someone go from teeth brushing to dinner, and somewhere in between end up so brutally assaulting someone, a trained Emergency Technician is unable to complete her duties, such was her shock on seeing the body? Who is this person that police have so far been unable to apprehend? Well, he's not someone you want living next door, that's for sure.

Profiling is an art more than a science, and just one of the things that can be used as a tool during an investigation. First, you have the clues and evidence – those hard facts in the form of items found at the scene that become your jumping-off point for the investigation. You also have statistics and the study of crime itself, which help investigators put together commonalities between crimes, as well as make assumptions based on the frequency with which they find certain acts. Then you have the study of the psyche of the perpetrator, himself.

What we call criminal profiling today harkens back to the 1800s when two doctors named George Phillips and Thomas Bond used clues from the crime scenes to make educated predictions about Jack the Ripper and his personality. There is a lot you can learn about a crime based on the evidence, and there is also much to be learned from the scene about the perpetrator.

In the 1970s, the FBI formed the Behavioral Science Unit, which was established to investigate serial rape and homicides. For a period of years, a handful of agents interviewed serial murders to help them develop theories and categories for different types of offenders based on the things they repeatedly encountered.

This is where the "organized" vs. "disorganized" crime aspect comes from.

Organized crimes are generally found to be premeditated and planned. Little evidence is found at the scene. According to the classification, organized criminals are antisocial but do know right from wrong. They are not insane. They show no remorse.

Disorganized crimes are not planned, and as such, evidence is often found. Weapons, in the case of disorganized crimes, are usually weapons of convenience (found at the scene), rather than brought along with them. Generally speaking, disorganized criminals are young, often under the influence of alcohol or drugs, or are mentally ill.

The organized offender is usually above average in intelligence, methodical, and his crime is carefully planned. He likely owns a car and his crime is usually committed out of his area or place of employment. He's considered "mobile" and travels more than the average person as far as miles. Fantasy and ritual are important to him, thus he selects victims by a certain type, then gains control through manipulation or just pure strength. Though his victims will share common traits, they are usually strangers. The manipulation would include average to good verbal skills and he is socially adept. He is fully aware he is committing crimes and revels in his ability to thwart police. The organized offender is the type to keep souvenirs from his kills—often to relive the event—and would follow news reports, perhaps even return to the scene of the crime. This guy likes cruelty, enjoys torture, and sexually controlling his victim. He tries not to leave evidence behind and will usually bring his own weapon. He is aware of police procedures—though, these days, isn't everyone? He often removes the body from the scene of the crime, whether to taunt police, or prevent the crime from being discovered for some amount of time.

By compare, the *disorganized offender* is usually below average intelligence, generally a loner, not married, and lives alone or with a relative, often in close proximity to the crime scene. He is socially inept, not good with interpersonal relationships, acts impulsively under stress, and usually picks his victims from his area. In many cases, the disorganized offender will not own a vehicle but often has access to one. Unlike the organized offender, he is often sexually incompetent and incapable of meaningful sexual relationships. His favored type of attack is the blitz style, catching his victim off guard because he is not socially able to manipulate like the organized offender. Because of this, the spontaneity required doesn't allow for planning or a thought of being caught, which is why his scene will be disorganized, often called by investigators a "clustered" crime scene, where most of the activities take place in one location, including the confrontation, assault and sexual assault. Facial destruction or overkill are usually the marker of a disorganized offender trying to depersonalize his victim, as well as mutilation of the genitals, rectum, breasts, neck, throat and buttocks – which would have strong sexual significance to him.

While these are the major differences between the organized and disorganized offender, rarely are these offenses mutually exclusive. Both the organized and disorganized offender are capable of any and all type of behavior, depending on the circumstances. These are generalizations.

"The fact is that different offenders can exhibit the same behaviors for completely different reasons," Brent E. Turvey (*PhD - Forensic Scientist & Criminal Profiler*) who's been highly critical of the FBIs approach, said in an interview with *The New Yorker* magazine in 2007. "You've got a rapist who attacks a woman in the park and pulls her shirt up over her face. Why? What does that mean? There are ten different things it could mean. It could mean he doesn't want to see her. It could mean he doesn't want her to see him. It could mean he wants to see her breasts, he wants to imagine someone else, he wants to incapacitate her arms—all of those are possibilities. You can't just look at one behavior in isolation."

Profiling the offender is a way to identify a perpetrator based on the nature of the offense, as well as how and where it was committed. Just like everything to do with personality traits, aspects of the criminal's personality end up determining their choices before, during, and after the crime. When investigators combine these things with the physical evidence found at a crime scene, as well as all relevant details, timeline, and witness statements, and then compare it with the characteristics of known personality types, it is possible for them to develop a working description of the offender. In some cases, it is very general; age, possible relationship status, type of employment.

It is stated repeatedly by profilers that behavior reflects personality, and that is what criminal profiling is based on. For a homicide case, insights about the perpetrator can be found in the following areas:

- ***Antecedent*** - Prior to the act, did the murderer have any plans in place? What may have triggered the violence? Often violence is triggered by a rigorous fantasy life that the perpetrator then transfers to the victim.
- ***Method and manner*** – This includes the choice of victim, the manner, IE: stabbing, strangulation, shooting, etc.
- ***Body disposal*** - Was the body hidden or left out in full view? Did the crime take place all in one location or are there multiple scenes?
- ***Post-offense behavior*** - Injecting himself or herself into the investigation. Often perpetrators will contact media, react to media reports, or even contact investigators.

So the approach is basically this: if behavior reflects personality, by examining behavior of the offender at the scene—things that were done, things that were not done, things that were taken or left behind—investigators can glean certain information about the perpetrator. But it only works when used in conjunction with the totality of the evidence and information learned during the investigation.

Criminal profiling has been found to be particularly useful as far as serial sexual homicides. These crimes can appear random for various reasons, including how a perpetrator evolves over time, gets better at covering their tracks. Also because the motive in such cases often remains unclear, since it is only known to the perpetrator. Often, sexual serial killers commit their heinous crimes based on a rich and violent fantasy life, so their motives are known only to them. Victims of serial murders can seem random because the killer did not know them, when in fact the perpetrator chooses them for various traits. Often their significance is only symbolic and ends up being the transference of rage onto a random person.

When there is no readily reliable motive like jealousy, family issues, or the murder occurs during the commission of another crime, investigators must entertain the possibility that the perpetrator is acting out his aggression on a victim or victims based on opportunity and possible symbolic reasons known only to them within their sadistic fantasy life. As noted earlier, profiling is more of an art than a science, and its success or lack thereof depends on a great deal of things, not the least of which is the person doing the profiling and the information given to them by law enforcement.

Take for example the profile created by criminologist/psychiatrist James A. Brussel for NYCs Mad Bomber—a sixteen-year investigation that eventually named George Metesky the perpetrator.

> "Look for a heavy man. Middle-aged. Foreign born. Roman Catholic. Single. Lives with a brother or sister. When you find him chances are he'll be wearing a double-breasted suit. Buttoned."

His assessment turned out to be frighteningly accurate, other than the fact that Metesky lived with two single sisters. When questioned, Brussel explained it this way: The job of the psychiatrist is to study a person and make reasonable predictions about how they may react to a specific situation, as well as what they might do in the future. According to Brussel, profiling does the reverse. By studying someone's actions, the type of person the individual might be can be deduced.

In real life, as opposed to Sherlock Holms or exciting crime fiction, a crime is rarely deduced by one piece of evidence in an *Aha!* moment that leaves everyone in the vicinity breathless. Sure, a hit on fingerprints might cause that type of moment, but a lot must go into an investigation to get to that point.

From Sergeant Cuff in Wilkie Collins' *The Moonstone: "At one end of the inquiry there was a murder, and at the other end there was a spot of ink on a tablecloth that nobody could account for. In all my experience . . . I have never met with such a thing as a trifle yet."*

There are no trifles, not in criminal investigations. Everything matters. As Lieutenant Golnick of the Cadillac PD told me, when training his officers to document the scene, "It's not just what's there. Sometimes it's what *isn't* there. You have to get it all."

Criminal profiling is an educated attempt to suss out specific information about a certain type of suspect using all of those, as well as patterns of behavior based on leads and evidence obtained by trained, perceptive investigators. Though criminal profiling certainly has its critics—those who cite the lack of empirical or scientific evidence suggesting its relevance—it is hard to undermine the fact that having gathered all the information in the chart in ***Figure 1***, a well-seasoned investigator couldn't come up with some helpful supposition. Obviously you want everything you can get from the crime scene, as well as related police reports and forensic information, if you want an idea of who may have committed a murder. Victimology, though, is also important. The study of the victim or victims of a particular offender is of significance.

Brent Turvey summed it up well: *"In the rush to examine a criminal's behavior, it is not difficult to become distracted by the dangling carrot of that criminal's potential characteristics and forget about the value of understanding his victims."*

Victimology is essentially victim profiling. According to Turvey, the following information would be essential to victim profilers in working a case:

- Physical traits
- Marital status
- Personal lifestyle
- Occupation
- Education
- Medical history
- Criminal justice system history
- Last known activities, including a timeline of events
- Personal diaries (if known and available)
- Map of travel prior to offence
- Drug and alcohol history
- Friends and enemies
- Family background
- Employment history

1. Profiling Inputs

CRIME SCENE:
Physical Evidence
Patterns of Evidence
Body Positions
Weapons

VICTIMOLOGY:
Background
Habits
Family Structure
Last Seen
Age
Occupation

FORENSIC INFORMATION:
Cause of Death
Wounds
Pre/Post Mortem
Sexual Acts
Autopsy Report
Lab Reports

PRELIMINARY POLICE REPORTS:
Background Information
Police Observation
Time of Crime
Who Reported Crime
Neighborhood:
Socioeconomic Status
Crime Rate

PHOTOS:
Aerial
Crime Scene
Victim

2. Decision/ Process Models

Homicide Type and Style
Primary Intent
Victim Risk
Offender Risk
Escalation
Time for Crime
Location Factors

Feedback #1

Validation of Profile
with Crime/Death scene
with evidence
with decision models
with investigation recommendations

Feedback #2

New Evidence

3. Crime Assessment

Reconstruction of Crime
Crime Classification
Organized/Disorganized
Victim Selection
Control of Victim
Sequence of Crime
Staging
Motivation
Crime Scene Dynamics

4. Criminal Profile

Demographics
Physical Characteristics
Habits
Pre-Offense Behavior
Leading to Crime
Post-Offense Behavior
Recommendations to Investigation

5. Investigation

6. Apprehension

Figure 1: from *Criminal Profiling from Crime Scene Analysis* (John E. Douglas, Robert K. Ressler, Ann W. Burgess, Carol R. Hartman - U.S. Department of Justice, provided by the FBI's Training Division and Behavioral Science Unit at Quantico, Virginia. Originally published in 1986.)

Other important questions you would seek to answer regarding a victimology are as follows:

- Why was this person targeted?
- How were they targeted? Were they a victim of opportunity, or random?
- What risk was taken by the perpetrator to commit the crime?
- How was the victim approached, restrained, and/or attacked?
- What was the victim's likely reaction?

Combine the answers to these questions with the perpetrator profile and investigators may get valuable information about the motive and MO of the offender, as well as other information like their background or knowledge of police procedures, occupation, social skills, and personal characteristics. Armed with this information, the profiler can make inferences about the offender that, when added to witness accounts and crime scene information, help narrow down the suspect field.

The method of attack, or degree of force used is also revelatory. As in the case of Janette Roberson, for example, overwhelming physical assault and excessive use of force speaks to rage on the part of the assailant.

If we were to get all Jungy with it (Jungian) and you were to rule out deliberate mutilation to make victim identification more difficult, overkill can stem from a narcissistic rage and deep-seated hatred of women that the perpetrator would be hard-pressed to recognize in themselves, mostly because of their skewed sense of self-awareness.

Jack the Ripper, for example, mutilated his victims – who were prostitutes—as an expression of a suspected rabid hatred of women. Another example: Joran van der Sloot, who you might remember from the much publicized Natalee Holloway case, the student who went missing while on a school sponsored vacation in Aruba. Joran's psychological evaluation from prison suggests an immature, selfish, self-centered man-child. Angry with parents, authority, God, angry with life.

It's almost a cliché at this point, isn't it? The narcissistic psychopath or a criminal with a diagnosed antisocial personality disorder often demonstrates a low tolerance for frustration, emotional immaturity, a need for constant stimulation, and a hostile, dominating attitude toward women. These things are seen across the board with rage killings performed by males where overkill is involved, particularly when the victim is not a relation, but chosen for other reasons, or at random.

This narcissism often convinces perpetrators that they can outsmart or "game" the system. Van der Sloot, for example, had a reported compulsive gambling issue that likely reflected his highly narcissistic overconfidence that he could beat the casinos. Gambling is also something seen quite often as a way to compensate for the need for "constant stimulation."

Lying, too, is common in the antisocial or psychopathically narcissistic offender. Again, "gaming" the system, because what is lying if not "gaming" life by forcefully altering the facts to suit your own needs? Some other sparkling traits of the psychopathically narcissistic offender are manipulation, deflection of responsibility, impulsivity, rationalization, deceitfulness, conning, lack of remorse, pervasive disregard for the rights of others, physical aggressiveness, sadistic cruelty, irresponsibility, grandiosity, absence of empathy, and malingering, just to note a few.

Malingering is lazy, idle, indolent. I had to look that one up. But it makes sense if you think about it. *You do it. I'm gonna sit over here and be right and justified about everything I do or say and if you challenge me, you won't like the results.*

So, yeah, not your basic hug-monkey. You don't want to deal with the psychopathically narcissistic human if possible because they don't feel the rules apply to them. In fact, they tend to get darned touchy when you suggest they do. Imagine what someone like this would do if he came on to you and you were a married woman who nervously chuckled in an effort to fend off his unwanted advances. Maybe he thinks you're laughing at him. That wouldn't be good. Many an attack have started that way; a psychopath set off in a rage by a trifling offense that upset his delicate sense of it's-all-about-me. *My* wants and needs.

So, how does all of this relate to the murder of Janette Roberson, you're probably asking. Well, for starters, the answer to the whodunit exists within the confines of all these questions. Let's look to victimology. As far as physical traits, she was of small build and is regularly described as shy. She was married, had two children, and her lifestyle, according to everyone I spoke to, suggested nothing out of the ordinary that would cause her to be at great risk to be victimized. Essentially, she was a nice, normal housewife. Her occupation was that of a store clerk who was good with animals. She has no prior criminal history, her education was elementary at best, and no medical history to speak of that would play into her murder. By all accounts, her last known activities were working, although according to Flossie, her co-worker, Janette left the Gambles store at some point earlier that morning after what she said was a call from the school. She had no drug and/or alcohol history, no enemies that anyone was aware of, and her employment history in Reed City was noted as a short stint at Nartron before she was laid off and began working at the Gambles pet store. As for family history, her parents were divorced, and at the time, the only relatives (other than her husband and kids) that lived close enough to be a day-to-day part of Janette's life were her brother and mother, Marion Fisher.

Nothing about her history suggests any issues large enough to result in murder. She wasn't a drug user, she didn't work in a high-risk job—meaning she wasn't surrounded with less than stellar folks on a daily basis like you would expect with, say, a prostitute. That's the type of high-risk job that regularly puts you in harms' way. Where Janette worked was so off the beaten path that it pretty much rules out a random attack, in and of itself, but when you take into account the very personal physical assault, and the length of time it would have taken to inflict so many injuries, particularly given this occurred in a public place, the suggestion is that the perpetrator was at least somewhat familiar with the store and pet department. That is not to say that the perpetrator planned the attack. Blind rage could have been the thing that literally removed the perpetrator from the immediate realities. He may not have considered anything other than meeting his need to violate. Maybe he knew the pet department wasn't exactly a high-traffic area and that's why he found himself down there alone with her in the first place, having taken the chance to be alone with her.

Every customer I spoke to who was in the pet department that day describes it as being slow and most of them never even ran into other customers, except for Jan Palumbo, who only recalls seeing other customers down there right as she and Venus were about to leave; a group that suddenly collected down there out of nowhere like they were all together.

This crime wasn't a "knock her over the head and get the hell out of dodge" type of crime. It was much more than that, though the risk assessment would suggest the perpetrator did take a great deal of risk, given the attack occurred in a store in the middle of the day. This didn't happen in a location where her attacker had complete control of the situation.

As far as injuries, while we don't know the exact order, it is very likely that Janette was quickly incapacitated and the remainder of her injuries were inflicted while she was unconscious. There was no screaming heard by employees, otherwise they'd have come running downstairs to her aid. Having been down in that basement, one thing I can tell you with certainty is that if she would have screamed, someone would have heard. While I was down there I could hear every word spoken upstairs, and every footfall on the creaky wood floor.

I don't believe she even had time to scream.

Janette Fisher married Alvin Lee Roberson on Aug 14, 1971. She was just shy of her sixteenth birthday. They had been married eleven years and had two children when she was murdered. Most the time she had coming to her was stolen. None of us are promised tomorrow, I guess we understand that, at least at some point. I just don't think she was even *there* yet. That place where you realize there's only so much time. She was at that age where time means little because it seems like there's so much of it spread out in front of you like the limitless possibilities of an open highway.

Where did the time go that day, January 19, 1983? There's an awful lot of it unaccounted for, as far as I'm concerned. Gene Johnson—*I know this store better than you!*—said at one point Officer Finkbeiner told him he was the last person to see Janette alive, except for the killer. I didn't believe that when I spoke to him, but after having talked to Blanche and Jan and Elke and Karl and Flossie, it may well have been the case, based on the times they were all there.

No other customers I spoke to saw Janette later that day. Since all of the employee interviews remain redacted, we have no way of knowing the last time any of them saw her, either.

The autopsy report says Janette was last seen at 1:25, but where did that information come from? I always assumed it was from a receipt because it's a pretty specific time. (The newest entry into the MSP computer system by Detective Sgt. Stephens lists the time of the crime occurring as between 1:40 and 3:50.) I hope Michigan State Police have some proof someone saw her then. It would certainly help with the timeline. But what if they don't? What if that's the last sale on the receipt log from her register and another employee rang someone up down there? It appears Angie rang up Jan, based on her description.

Let's take the 3:50 time as the time Janette was found because it does seem to correlate with what Mr. and Mrs. Kooiker said about having come straight from school letting out. What went on in that basement—around her body—from 3:50 when the report says she was found, until the first dispatch at 4:06, according to Gary McGhee's EMT report? The Reed City Finkbeiner/Primeau report says they arrived at 4:04, which would have been before the dispatch even went thru, if Raymond Haight dispatched that call in the order he says he did.

Ten minutes is a long time to wait before calling police. If that time of 3:50 is accurate, that's 14 minutes before the report says Officers Finkbeiner and Primeau got there. What were the employees and customers in the store doing for those 14 minutes? Tom Hawkins, Elke, David Engels, John Engels, Flossie, Angie... what's going on before—according to Raymond Haight—David Engels calls the Osceola County Sheriff's Department and says there's been a murder in the basement, because that's when everyone starts arriving. The Osceola County deputies are running out of the Sheriff's Department, the EMTs are hopping into the ambulance, Haight is calling the State Police Post, and it's 4:06 when the EMTs arrive and Officer Finkbeiner is standing at the front door sending potential witnesses on their way. What was going on for those 14 minutes before the wagons had circled?

Go stand in the center of your living room for 14 minutes and see how much time that feels like. Run outside, down your driveway, stop, count to sixty, and then run back inside. How long did that take? Get a firm grasp on how long that much time is and then ask yourself what you think might have been happening for that long, prior to anyone calling police. Also, keep in mind that there are three law enforcement entities, city, county, and state police all within two minutes or less from Gambles. *Literally*.

What were the employees doing? The list Detective Pratt gave of the individuals he learned "through further investigation" had been around the area of the body "some more than once" isn't that long.

So what were *they* doing in those ten minutes? This would have been after Angie ran up the stairs panting, pointing back down toward the stairs so that Flossie had to scream for John Engels, who came barreling down from the second floor, taking them two at a time.

Where was David Engels when John ran down those stairs from wherever he was eating lunch? Flossie didn't call David Engels, she called John Engels. And where was Thomas Hawkins? Elke? It appears Bonnie Engels had gone home before the body was discovered, or at some point before Detective Pratt got there because there is no mention of her being there when the body was found.

As far as I can tell, nobody remembers seeing Janette after around 11:30 when Janette met Gene Johnson at the center of the store and asked if she could help him. Every time a customer went looking for her in the pet department after that, she wasn't there. Karl brings the gerbils in around 10 or 11. No Janette. Maybe this is when she was gone, having responded to the call from the school like she told Flossie. But she comes back and has her encounter with Gene Johnson at 11:30 or thereabouts. Last he sees her, she heads downstairs. Around noon, Blanche goes down there looking for her "Ick," no Janette. Next, Jan and Venus go there around 2:00, until sometime before four o'clock, no Janette. Elke was there right around that time, even though Blanche doesn't remember crossing paths with her, despite Elke saying she was up and down those stairs three or four times, continually asking the female clerk where Janette was, and being told she's probably at lunch. Everyone kept telling customers Janette was *probably at lunch.* Was being an employee at Gambles so relaxed that break time was an hour, two hours… or more? Karl alleges the store manager told him Janette was probably at lunch when he was there the first time with those gerbils. Angie apparently told Elke the same thing when she returned with them the second time. It certainly doesn't seem like anyone knew where Janette was at any time that afternoon, except for Gene Johnson.

And then there's that blood. Let's talk about that blood Gary McGhee walked through on the way through the pet department, which he only noticed when he came out of the back room after having attended to Janette. Nobody else saw it. *Nobody*. Blanche, Jan, Venus, Elke... all of those ladies down there in that final couple of hours during the crucial 1:40-3:50 time period. None of them saw it. Both Jan and Venus, as well as Elke claim to have been there for a considerable amount of time looking at the fish and that's the area Gary McGhee describes it as being. There couldn't have been much time between when Jan and Venus left and Elke returned with those gerbils, and from then on she was there until Janette was found. Yet, all of those people walking around looking at those fish tanks right where that spot of blood is and nobody, *not one of them* saw it? Yet, she had been killed and was likely laying back there deceased when those last few women were in the pet department. Certainly she was already dead when Elke was there. So if the blood was on the floor in the pet department already, because the killer had already come and gone, why didn't any of them see it? So many questions; not nearly enough answers, and I'll admit, that blood bothers me. So I got back with Gary McGhee one more time and asked him if it was big enough that someone else should have seen it.

"To my recollection it was about 6 ft. outside the doorway. It really wasn't a 'puddle' of blood per se; it actually was a spot of WET blood. I would say about the size of a slice of bread but no bigger. As I said, I did not see it when I went in the room, but noticed it when I left. I was not looking at the floor when I went in there. I do not remember seeing any footprints in it, but there was a chance that I had stepped in it and that was why my boots were taken. It was my 'assumption' then (and always has been) that the initial assault took place where the blood was located and that she walked or was dragged/moved to where she was found. I can't explain why no one else saw the blood."

"I know this store better than you!" Is it possible that's the last thing anyone said to Janette, aside from the killer, if they exchanged words? God I hope not. It sounded like a bit of an abrupt exchange, and by all accounts Janette was rather shy. Gene was joking, but even if she took it as such, I'd like to think something kinder, softer, maybe less off-putting was the last thing someone said to her before someone else viciously took her from this Earth. According to Gene, after that Janette said she had something to take care of downstairs and down she went. He never saw her again. Did anyone else? The killer did. That much we know.

2014 – PRESENT DAY

When we got that whole, "If you want the rest of the file, give us six thousand dollars and we'll see what we can do" my assistant and I started limiting the scope of our FOIA requests. For example, we'd ask for all of the interviews and files generated by Detective Southworth (Osceola County) but were later transferred to MSP, according to Osceola County's FOIA denial letters. The response from the MSP FOIA Department would go something like this: "Give us about three hundred and fifty bucks and we'll look, but you're probably going to get mostly blank pages because that's what we've been sending you in your recent requests, hadn't you noticed?" Same with the simple question of the Reed City State Police dispatch log for the day. "Oh, that'll take us about three hundred to search for. We'll give it a go!"

Really? That log, if it exists, can't be more than a couple pages. But that's basically the gist. No matter what we asked for, it was going to set us back about three bills to search for what we wanted, and once we received what we'd asked for, they'd check off a few exclusions and give us mostly blank pages. So we decided to work backwards. I sent a request for everything they had done on the Roberson investigation from Jan 1, 2012 to the present (which was December 2014 at that time.) Three years. I got three pages.

What those three pages gave us was that they'd narrowed the time Janette Roberson was murdered to between 1:40 and 3:50pm, and that the investigators had identified several possible suspects and/or persons of interest, but there was not sufficient evidence to issue an arrest warrant for anyone.

The last page lists the STATUS as Open.

[redacted]

Michigan Department of State Police
ORIGINAL INCIDENT REPORT

ORIGINAL DATE	INCIDENT NO.
Thu, Jun 12, 2014	063-0002680-14 (67)
TIME RECEIVED	FILE CLASS
0920	78000

WORK UNIT	COUNTY
MSP MT PLEASANT	Osceola

COMPLAINANT		TELEPHONE NO.	
PATROL			
ADDRESS: STREET AND NO.	CITY	STATE	ZIP CODE
3580 S ISABELLA ROAD	MT PLEASANT	MI	48858-
INCIDENT STATUS			
Open			

62-113-83 JANETTE ROBERSON HOMICIDE

INFORMATION:
This on-line AICS incident report was generated to document further investigation, tips, and leads regarding the murder of Janette Roberson on 01/19/1983 at the Gamble's Store in downtown Reed City, MI. The purpose is to keep all further records in an on-line format.

The original investigation is documented on MSP Reed City Post incident 62-113-83. The original investigation is currently in an "inactive" status. Several possible suspects and/or persons of interest were identified by the original investigators; however, there is no sufficient evidence to date allowing the issuance of an arrest warrant for any particular individual.

A memorial walk was held on 01/19/2014 by friends and family members of the victim in order to re-generate public interest in the case. A few tips were called in as a result of the walk.

VENUE:
OSCEOLA COUNTY, REED CITY
114 W. UPTON AVE.
AT OR NEAR: GAMBLE'S STORE

DATE & TIME:
WED, JAN 19, 1983 AT 1340 TO 1550

CONTACT VICTIM'S SISTER:
I was contacted the the victim's sister, Lana Lockhart, on 03/31/2014. I provided Lockhart with an update on the investigation and advised her she could contact me with any tips she may learn of. Lockhart advised there is going to be a picnic at the park in Reed City on 08/02/12014 in hopes of gaining more information regarding her sister's death.

FOIA REQUEST:
I was contacted by Carla Jones of the Michigan State Police Freedom of Information Unit on 06/9/2014. Jones advised there has been a FOIA request for all documentation, photos, and video related to this investigation by Jennifer Decker (Lopez). Decker is requesting these documents stating she is a writer and wants to write a book about the case.

Jones advised they have photos in Lansing; however the original report states there are polaroid pictures and a video tape. She requested I locate these items and bring them to the FOIA office to be copied for their file. I located several polaroid pictures and a video tape at the Reed City Detachment. I transported these items to the FOIA office at MSP Headquarters. Kimberly Dowling of the MSP Photography Unit scanned the polaroid pictures and returned the originals to me. The VHS tape was turned over to Carla Jones for a copy to be made. She will contact me upon completion.

The Detective seemed happy to furnish crime scene photos to the FOIA department for scanning. I was subsequently charged for them, I sent a money order, and then I waited. I never got the photos I paid for that Carla Jones was preparing for me. I got a letter, instead, saying my request had been denied (the one they'd already approved) and on the back, this is what they checked out as a reason for the exclusions:

DENIAL OF RECORDS:
Denial is based on the following provision(s) of the Freedom of Information Act. MCL 15.243, Sec. 13(1).
(All that apply will be checked.)

☑ (a) Information of a personal nature where the public disclosure of the information would constitute a clearly unwarranted invasion of an individual's privacy.
☐ Telephone Number(s) ☐ Address(es) ☐ Date(s) of Birth ☐ Physical Characteristics ☐ Driver License Number(s)
☐ Other: ______

☑ (b) Investigating records compiled for law enforcement purposes, but only to the extent that disclosure would do any of the following:
☑ (i) Interfere with law enforcement proceedings.
☑ (ii) Deprive a person of the right to a fair trial or impartial administrative adjudication.
☐ (iii) Constitute an unwarranted invasion of personal privacy.
☐ (iv) Disclose the identity of a confidential source, or if the record is compiled by a law enforcement agency in the course of a criminal investigation, disclose confidential information furnished only by a confidential source.
☐ (vi) Endanger the life or physical safety of law enforcement personnel.

☑ (d) Records or information specifically described and exempted from disclosure by statute.
Statute: Crime Victim - William Van Regenmorter Crime Victim's Rights Act.

☐ (m) Communications and notes within a public body or between public bodies of an advisory nature to the extent that they cover other than purely factual materials and are preliminary to a final agency determination of policy or action.

☐ (n) Records of law enforcement communication codes, or plans for deployment of law enforcement personnel, that if disclosed would prejudice a public body's ability to protect the public.

☐ (s) Unless the public interest in disclosure outweighs the public interest in nondisclosure in the particular instance, public records of a law enforcement agency, the release of which would do any of the following:
☐ (i) Identify or provide a means of identifying an informer.
☐ (ii) Identify or provide a means of identifying a law enforcement undercover officer or agent or a plain clothes officer as a law enforcement officer or agent.
☐ (viii) Identify or provide a means of identifying a person as a law enforcement officer, agent, or informer.
☐ (ix) Disclose personnel records of law enforcement agencies.

☐ (u) Records of a public body's security measures, including security plans, security codes and combinations, passwords, passes, keys, and security procedures, to the extent that the records relate to the ongoing security of the public body.

☐ (w) Information or records that would disclose the social security number of any individual.

☐ Your request is denied under the authority of Section 13(1)(a) above. However, if you provide a notarized, signed release of information from the individual to whom the records pertain, you will receive that information to which the individual signing the release is entitled.

☐ To the best of the Department's knowledge, information, and belief, under the information provided by you or by an other description reasonably known to the Department, the public records do not exist within the Department.

☐ Based on the information you provided, we are unable to locate any records pertaining to the incident you described. In order for us to continue processing your request, please comply with the following items. To ensure proper handling of your request, please include a copy of this letter with your response.
☐ Specific location (i.e. city, county)
☐ Michigan State Police incident number
☐ Names of those involved in the incident
☐ Specific dates (i.e. date of incident)
☐ Name of driver and their birth date or driver license number
☐ Date of birth

☐ The report you have requested has not yet been completed and filed. Please resubmit your request in 30 days.

ADDITIONAL COMMENTS: MCL 780.758 - A refund for 157.14 will be processed and forwarded to you within 3-4 weeks.

According to the William Van Regenmorter Crime Victim's Rights Act, of 1985 (780.775 - Section 25):

> (1) This article shall take effect October 9, 1985.
> (2) This article shall apply only to crimes committed on or after October 9, 1985.

Janette Roberson was murdered on January 19, 1983.

I appealed, of course, noting the Act did not apply, as well asking how releasing the redacted photos could deprive anyone of a fair trial, or interfere with law enforcement proceedings, given they'd allowed them to be released in another open MSP case.

The above is from a Michigan State Police case that remains unsolved, and is from the same time period as Janette's case (1980s). The point here is that choices made within the MSP FOIA department are not uniform, nor is their application of exemptions. In one open case they will send redacted photos with no issue whatsoever. In another, they will withhold them all – even though it stands to reason not every single picture would fall under the exemptions they applied in the letter. They are applying denials and exemptions in a blanket manner, which is specifically a no-no with regard to the Freedom of Information Act.

Here is the final denial I was sent from Michigan State Police regarding my request for crime scene photos (specifically noting I understood they would need to redact the body of the victim).

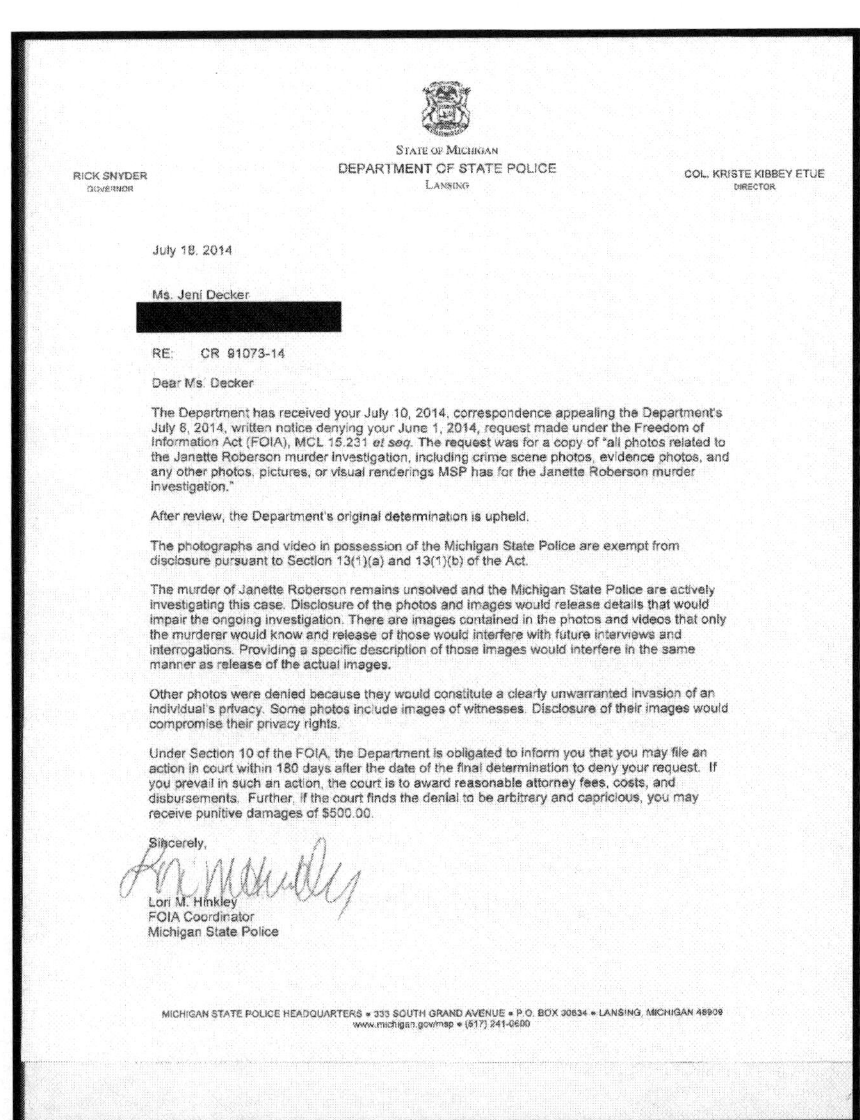

STATE OF MICHIGAN
DEPARTMENT OF STATE POLICE
LANSING

RICK SNYDER
GOVERNOR

COL. KRISTE KIBBEY ETUE
DIRECTOR

July 18, 2014

Ms. Jeni Decker
[redacted]

RE: CR 91073-14

Dear Ms. Decker

The Department has received your July 10, 2014, correspondence appealing the Department's July 8, 2014, written notice denying your June 1, 2014, request made under the Freedom of Information Act (FOIA), MCL 15.231 *et seq.* The request was for a copy of "all photos related to the Janette Roberson murder investigation, including crime scene photos, evidence photos, and any other photos, pictures, or visual renderings MSP has for the Janette Roberson murder investigation."

After review, the Department's original determination is upheld.

The photographs and video in possession of the Michigan State Police are exempt from disclosure pursuant to Section 13(1)(a) and 13(1)(b) of the Act.

The murder of Janette Roberson remains unsolved and the Michigan State Police are actively investigating this case. Disclosure of the photos and images would release details that would impair the ongoing investigation. There are images contained in the photos and videos that only the murderer would know and release of those would interfere with future interviews and interrogations. Providing a specific description of those images would interfere in the same manner as release of the actual images.

Other photos were denied because they would constitute a clearly unwarranted invasion of an individual's privacy. Some photos include images of witnesses. Disclosure of their images would compromise their privacy rights.

Under Section 10 of the FOIA, the Department is obligated to inform you that you may file an action in court within 180 days after the date of the final determination to deny your request. If you prevail in such an action, the court is to award reasonable attorney fees, costs, and disbursements. Further, if the court finds the denial to be arbitrary and capricious, you may receive punitive damages of $500.00.

Sincerely,

Lori M. Hinkley
FOIA Coordinator
Michigan State Police

MICHIGAN STATE POLICE HEADQUARTERS • 333 SOUTH GRAND AVENUE • P.O. BOX 30634 • LANSING, MICHIGAN 48909
www.michigan.gov/msp • (517) 241-0600

In Janette's case, there is ZERO information in any of those crime scene photos that only the killer would know. Not with the parade of folks we know trampled around in that back room. According to Detective Pratt's notes, quite a few people were in the vicinity of the body, and most of those listed were not law enforcement. They were employees of Gambles *and* customers, as well as a nurse who walked in off the street, not to mention the customer who is now serving time in jail for sex crimes.

As far as the paragraph about "witnesses" being in the pictures, this is interesting because we have a list of the "witnesses" who were around the body from the MSP report, so how in the name of *Sweet Baby Jesus* would any of those "witnesses" be covered under any invasion of privacy exclusion? We already know who they are. In fact, one could argue—and I *would* argue if I were standing before a judge—the public has a *right* to know which witnesses were allowed so close to the body and crime scene that there were pictures snapped of them.

Here's a question: At the point pictures were being taken of the scene, why were "witnesses" still milling around the body, anyway? That was over an hour *after* the body was discovered. The MSP report states that Detective Pratt and Laren Thorson both took pictures, so why were the witnesses not cleared from the scene by that point?

It is troublesome issues like this that lead the average person to wonder why so much of the report is being held back. As I stated in my FOIA appeal to the Reed City city council, "When a public entity withholds information, this leaves a reasonable person's mind to wonder if, in fact, something is being covered up. Absent facts, the entity responsible for that kind of public perception is the one who decides to withhold the record in the first place. The core purpose of the Freedom of Information Act is to provide information that contributes significantly to the public understanding of the operations of government. The people have a strong interest in knowing how those who were sworn to protect and serve handled the crime scene in an extraordinarily brutal murder that occurred within a mile of three different law enforcement entities in the middle of the day."

Right after the photo denial, I got a call from Inspector Cam Henke of Michigan State Police. He told me they were thinking about putting a cold case team on Janette's case, but they had not yet decided. He could only say that their next case would come from the Reed City unsolved homicide cases, although he told me he hadn't made that announcement to his team yet. They were in the middle of wrapping up a case on another unsolved homicide and it had yet to go to court. They were, however, going over the Reed City cases, reading them to familiarize themselves with each one. We know they went over Janette's, and based on a letter the sister of Esther Gaffney received (another of the unsolved homicide cases), Detective Sgt. Stephens was going over hers, as well.

But the most recent pages from the Roberson file indicate that it was in an "inactive" status at the time of my FOIA request, hence, they would not have had legal cause to exclude items based on the possibility of releasing documents somehow interfering with any "open, ongoing" investigation. There's a legal standard that must be reached to prove a case is open and ongoing, and I'm fairly comfortable stating Janette's case wasn't there at that point. In fact, my request asked for all activity on the case from 2012 to present (2014) but there appears to have been no activity, other than Janette's sister making a call to inquire as to the status, and my request for documents. Three days after my request, MSP changed the status to "open."

I asked Inspector Henke how he would determine which case they would choose. He said there were multiple determining factors, but they look at solvability first—meaning, which case gives them the best chance of getting a bad guy off the street. That makes sense. You don't wanna throw a bunch of resources at a case that doesn't look like it has a good chance of being resolved. Taxpayers get touchy about wasted money, and higher-ups like to have nice, tight clearance rates.

"What if the case you're looking at, you determine the most likely suspect or person of interest has died? Would that lower it on the list from which you are choosing?" I asked.

Inspector Henke indicated that would probably lower it on the list, because even though they do want to give families closure, generally they want to try the ones where they have a good chance of solving (closing) the case and putting someone away. So that's where we were. The promise of a possibility that Janette's case might get looked at again. *Maybe*.

A few months later, my assistant made a couple email contacts with Detective Sgt. Mike Stephens, trying to ascertain where the case stood. When she asked for specificity she received this reply:

> *"Yes, the investigation is ongoing. There has not been a "cold case team" assigned as of yet. I have conducted several interviews, talked with Chief Davis and retired D/Sgt. Pratt on several occasions regarding this case, and continue to review the evidence for any other possible avenues. Hopefully this helps, thank you again!"*

Because they continued to maintain the case was *ongoing*, every denial of records request we submitted relied heavily on excluding items because their release may interfere with an open, ongoing investigation. My next FOIA request was for everything done on the Janette Roberson murder investigation from 2000 to 2012, where we'd left off. Again, I was working backward, while my assistant filed another request, hers for the last few years of the 1990s. We also asked to know the page count associated with each of our requests, because having been told the report was comprised of approximately 5,000 pages—though they were able to supply us with only a few hundred—obviously we wanted to know where all those pages were. I won't come right out and say I don't believe them, but as an illustration, the report released in 2014 by the government regarding the torture done by the CIA was around 6,000 pages. I have a hard time believing Michigan State Police generated almost as many pages on their investigation into Janette Roberson's death. Maybe they did, but what I want *as a taxpayer* is accountability. Show me the money. Show me the pages. Show me around five thousand pages of work associated with this case. You don't have to tell me what's on every page, but I damn sure want to know that if you were going to charge me almost six thousand dollars for what I was told was approximately five thousand pages, those pages actually exist, and it wasn't just a ploy to get me to go away.

DON'T MAKE ME GET ALL GLENN CLOSE IN FATAL ATTRACTION ON YOU PEOPLE bellowed my inner monologue.

For a while, three hundred dollars or so seemed to be the sweet spot. We got quoted around that amount a lot, often for one item, such as the Reed City MSP Post dispatch log for January 19, 1983.

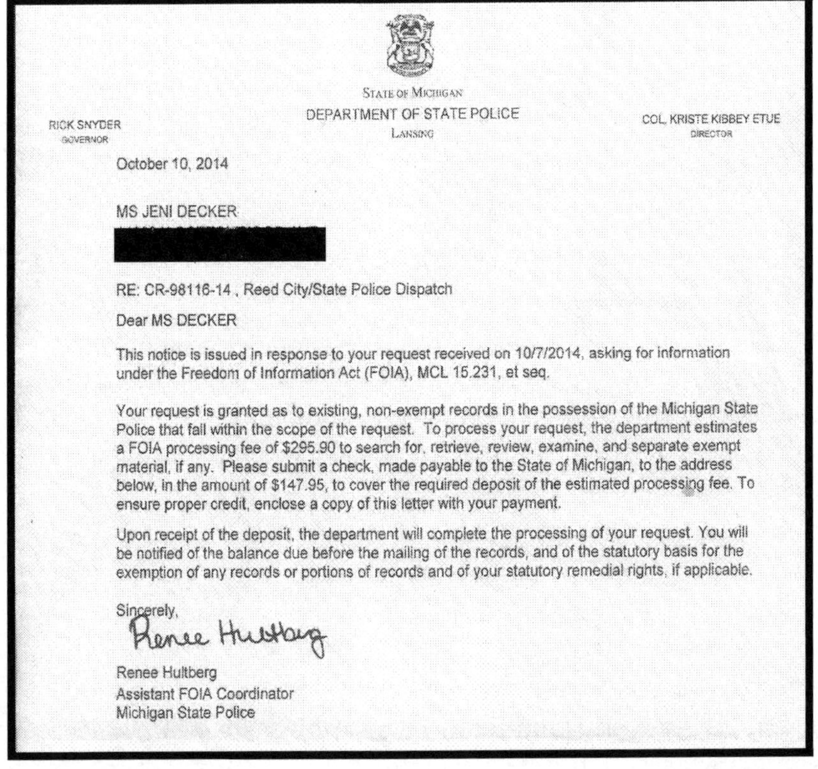

STATE OF MICHIGAN
DEPARTMENT OF STATE POLICE
LANSING

RICK SNYDER
GOVERNOR

COL. KRISTE KIBBEY ETUE
DIRECTOR

October 10, 2014

MS JENI DECKER

RE: CR-98116-14 , Reed City/State Police Dispatch

Dear MS DECKER

This notice is issued in response to your request received on 10/7/2014, asking for information under the Freedom of Information Act (FOIA), MCL 15.231, et seq.

Your request is granted as to existing, non-exempt records in the possession of the Michigan State Police that fall within the scope of the request. To process your request, the department estimates a FOIA processing fee of $295.90 to search for, retrieve, review, examine, and separate exempt material, if any. Please submit a check, made payable to the State of Michigan, to the address below, in the amount of $147.95, to cover the required deposit of the estimated processing fee. To ensure proper credit, enclose a copy of this letter with your payment.

Upon receipt of the deposit, the department will complete the processing of your request. You will be notified of the balance due before the mailing of the records, and of the statutory basis for the exemption of any records or portions of records and of your statutory remedial rights, if applicable.

Sincerely,

Renee Hultberg

Renee Hultberg
Assistant FOIA Coordinator
Michigan State Police

Remember, that doesn't even mean you'll get the items you requested, only that you're paying for them to look for it. As time went on, though. The prices got higher. This was October. By the following January, the quotes on sections of Janette's file got even more ridiculous and prohibitive. Lest you think state agencies would *never* do such a thing, consider this. In 2009, the Michigan Department of State Police wanted to charge the Mackinac Center for Public Policy $6.8 million for a Freedom of Information Act request regarding the state's handling of federal homeland security grant money from 2002 to 2009. Yes, I said **million**. I would have framed that letter and put it on my wall.

According to an article on August 9, 2011 from *Michigan Capitol Confidential*, when the Mackinac Center for Public Policy requested two years' worth of salary and benefits information for CEOs at the Muskegon Area Transit System, the County of Muskegon said they no longer had the 2009-2010 information and the 2010-2011 information would cost $300.

> "Either Muskegon has the world's most expensive employee or the world's most expensive copier," said Patrick Wright, senior legal analyst for the Mackinac Center. Wright said it is "economic stonewalling." (cont...)

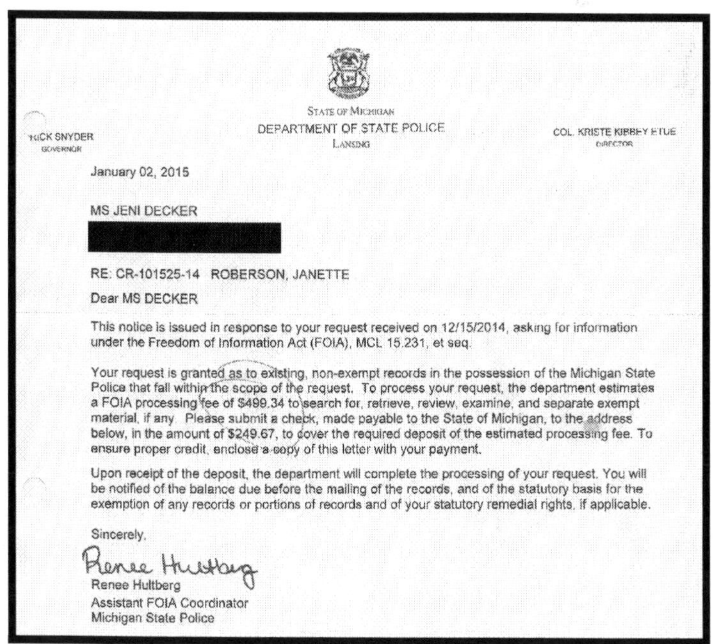

STATE OF MICHIGAN
DEPARTMENT OF STATE POLICE
LANSING

RICK SNYDER
GOVERNOR

COL. KRISTE KIBBEY ETUE
DIRECTOR

January 02, 2015

MS JENI DECKER

RE: CR-101525-14 ROBERSON, JANETTE

Dear MS DECKER

This notice is issued in response to your request received on 12/15/2014, asking for information under the Freedom of Information Act (FOIA), MCL 15.231, et seq.

Your request is granted as to existing, non-exempt records in the possession of the Michigan State Police that fall within the scope of the request. To process your request, the department estimates a FOIA processing fee of $499.34 to search for, retrieve, review, examine, and separate exempt material, if any. Please submit a check, made payable to the State of Michigan, to the address below, in the amount of $249.67, to cover the required deposit of the estimated processing fee. To ensure proper credit, enclose a copy of this letter with your payment.

Upon receipt of the deposit, the department will complete the processing of your request. You will be notified of the balance due before the mailing of the records, and of the statutory basis for the exemption of any records or portions of records and of your statutory remedial rights, if applicable.

Sincerely,

Renee Hultberg

Renee Hultberg
Assistant FOIA Coordinator
Michigan State Police

Figure 3: Charges quoted for Roberson file from 2000-2012

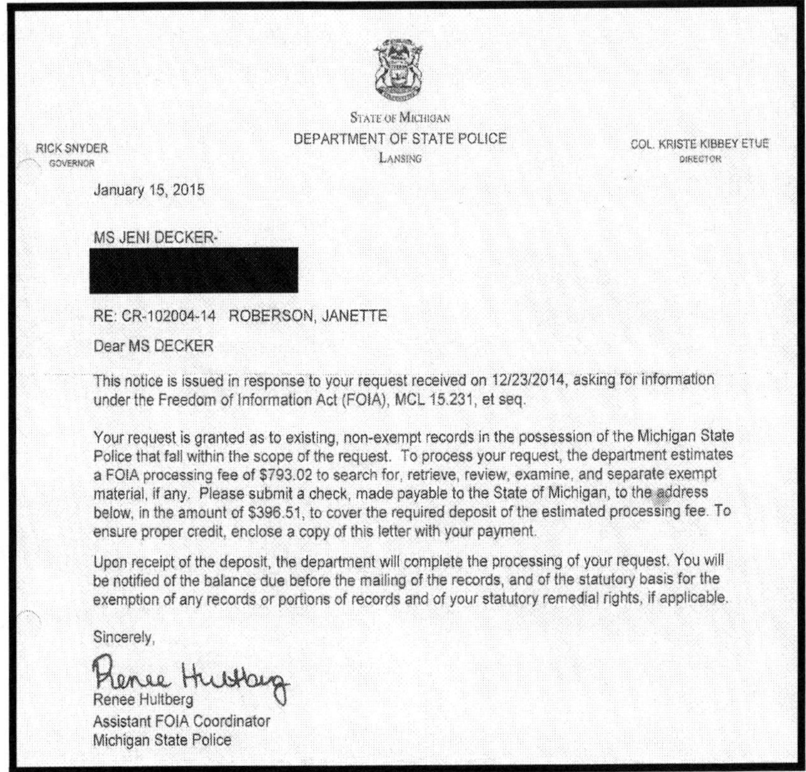

STATE OF MICHIGAN
DEPARTMENT OF STATE POLICE
LANSING

RICK SNYDER
GOVERNOR

COL. KRISTE KIBBEY ETUE
DIRECTOR

January 15, 2015

MS JENI DECKER-

RE: CR-102004-14 ROBERSON, JANETTE

Dear MS DECKER

This notice is issued in response to your request received on 12/23/2014, asking for information under the Freedom of Information Act (FOIA), MCL 15.231, et seq.

Your request is granted as to existing, non-exempt records in the possession of the Michigan State Police that fall within the scope of the request. To process your request, the department estimates a FOIA processing fee of $793.02 to search for, retrieve, review, examine, and separate exempt material, if any. Please submit a check, made payable to the State of Michigan, to the address below, in the amount of $396.51, to cover the required deposit of the estimated processing fee. To ensure proper credit, enclose a copy of this letter with your payment.

Upon receipt of the deposit, the department will complete the processing of your request. You will be notified of the balance due before the mailing of the records, and of the statutory basis for the exemption of any records or portions of records and of your statutory remedial rights, if applicable.

Sincerely,

Renee Hultberg
Renee Hultberg
Assistant FOIA Coordinator
Michigan State Police

Figure 4: Charges quoted for Det. Sgt. Southworth's interviews

> "They are throwing up a high dollar request hoping people would go away rather than fight it and that way they can keep the information hidden," Wright said.

When we finally got a response to our requests for information on Janette's case starting backward (mine from years 2000 to 2012, my assistant's the last two years of the 1990s) we were both quoted prices of almost $500. Eventually, it dawned on us. It was right there in a short email from Detective Stephens, we'd just failed to pick up on it.

> "I generated the new case number in order to document any leads and follow up I have conducted as the original investigation was documented in an off-line format."

Off-line meaning none of it—*not one word* of the Janette Roberson murder investigation file—had ever been entered into the computer. To that point, we just assumed when Michigan State Police went to statewide computerized reports, at least *that* portion of her file had been entered. We'd been laboring under that assumption simply because it seemed unheard of to even think nothing from the file had ever been brought into the digital age. I even emailed Shannon Banner, the MSP Manager of Public affairs, to find out when they went to computerized reports.

> "Our current report-writing system AICS (Automated Incident Capture System) was first used in 1995 as a standalone application. In 1997, it became a mainframe application allowing us to be able to access reports via query as we do today. Prior to AICS, there was a program called Enable that was used for a short period; however, it was mostly a word processing application. I do not have an exact timeframe for when Enable was used, but prior to Enable, reports were typed using a typewriter.

I can't believe it took me so long to figure it out—the ridiculously high FOIA request estimates we kept getting. Those ladies weren't stonewalling us. They literally had no access to the information I wanted from where they were in Lansing, until someone at the local State Post went through it all. Every one of our requests would mean that someone at the local post would have to fetch what we wanted, manually, probably rifling through boxes, then scanning and sending it to Lansing. That still doesn't explain why it would take 84 hours and almost $6000.00 dollars to do, though. Once we opened up this can of worms, I can only imagine the scanning, indexing, digitizing frenzy happening at the local Post. At least I hope. I can't fathom the file remaining in that state after so many queries in its regard. Surely it was time to usher the Janette Roberson murder investigation case file into this century.

How can you even work a case that's three decades worth of pages in boxes? I know that Jen and I had to index all of our material and keep it in a manner that we could access digitally. I have a box and four binders worth of material regarding this case, and my hardcopies are so worn from frequent flipping through that I've had to put support rings on some of the worn pages to keep the hole-punch area from further ripping. Yet still, everything is backed up digitally for ease of access. I wouldn't be able to keep track, otherwise.

The realization was gutting. Not because it seemed impossible we'd ever get the rest of the file—whatever that included—but it defied logic to think a case that wasn't even on the computer system would be chosen to re-investigate over one of the other Reed City "cold" cases that were more recent and already computerized. Some of those might have "named suspects," which would presumably put it higher on the list of solvability. According to Detective Stephens' June 12, 2014 entry—the very first computerized entry on the Roberson case—the initial investigators had identified "several possible suspects and/or persons of interests." What if one of the other cases had *actual* named suspects, or better evidence, and nobody let witnesses leave that crime scene, or walked through evidence?

I remembered Inspector Henke saying that in order to "bring it up to date" the file would have to be completely indexed before they could even consider re-working it. That's months of work before they could even begin reinvestigating it. He'd told me, months earlier, only I'd failed to grasp the realities.

I could almost feel Janette's case sliding further down the priority list.

Reed City's unsolved homicides

According to Michigan State Police, from 1970 to present there are 7 unsolved homicides attributed to the Reed City MSP Post, (now Mt. Pleasant – the Reed City building is currently a detachment). I started researching what goes into the solvability of a case in an effort to determine if I thought Janette's had a chance, based on what I knew, which, admittedly, isn't as much as I'd like.

In 2007—using information collected from a conference which included more than 100 law enforcement and related personnel including chiefs, commanders, detectives, crime scene personnel, crime analysts, prosecutors, and defense attorneys—The Police Executive Research Forum, in conjunction with the *US Department of Justice Office of Community Oriented Policing Services* put together a report titled *Promoting Effective Homicide Investigations.* This was a collective effort to determine strategies for raising the national clearance rate by pinpointing areas of concern.

What is a clearance rate, you ask? Well, a clearance rate is the percentage of cases that are closed and it is determined by dividing the total number of homicides reported in a year by the number of arrests and "exceptional means" homicides. An *exceptional clearance* is made when an investigation has established an offender, there's enough information to support an arrest charge, and the location of the offender is known, but there is a reason outside police control that prevents arresting, charging, and prosecuting the offender. This happens, for example, if the offender has died.

While the number of homicides in the US has fluctuated since the 1960s, the number of homicides being solved has decreased in that time by around 30%. What this means is that, while the crime rate varies, the cases getting closed are markedly decreasing—something that doesn't bode well for communities. From *Promoting Effective Homicide Investigations:*

> In 1965, the average national clearance rate for homicide was 91%; in 1976 it was 79%; and in 2002 it was 64%. The decline in clearance rates may be the result of organizational changes in law enforcement agencies, including changes in the structure and placement of homicide units, decentralization, lack of resources, substantial turnover of experienced personnel, poor working relationships with prosecutors and crime labs, inability to keep pace with advances in forensic technology, and poor procedures for processing and analyzing evidence. Additionally, backlogs and heavy caseloads within crime labs and coroners' offices may reduce investigative effectiveness. The length of time it takes to get results of DNA analysis leaves offenders on the street to perhaps kill again or become victims themselves.

Unsolved homicides have significant negative impact on family and friends of victims, but also the community. In order for residents to feel comfortable cooperating with officers during an investigation, there must be a level of trust with local law enforcement on the part of the community. A lack of trust can foster the opposite, and a lack of willingness to cooperate on the part of possible witnesses can hinder an investigation.

> "Unsolved homicides effect communities by lowering the public's confidence in police, increase fear in the community, and affect officer performance. Of course, the most important consequence of an unsolved homicide is that a killer remains free, able to commit additional murders. ...as a result, police may encounter reluctance and resistance from possible witnesses who fear retaliation from an offender still on the loose."

Another negative effect too many unsolved homicides risk is invalidating any possible deterrence effect. When the clearance rate decreases, it tells criminals our justice system is unable to hold them accountable—that they can literally get away with murder. When the public sees this happening on a regular basis, any hope of deterrence being a factor in someone not committing a crime can be expected to deteriorate. To complete the vicious cycle, all of this contributes negatively to officer performance due to lack of resources, morale, and pressure from their superiors and the community.

Cold case units play a large part in breaking the cycle illustrated above. But how do they decide which case(s) from the pile to tackle first? The answer is solvability. Remember, there's usually not just one old, unsolved case investigators are dealing with. In some places, the cold case pile is literally that, *a pile*. At some point, as sad as it is, this pile of unsolved cases—each with a victim and grieving family behind them—must first be organized into a list, at the top of which sit the cases that give the investigators the best chance of positive results.

Case closed! That's what everybody wants, another bad guy taken off the street.

The criteria used by the Las Vegas Metro PD when choosing cold cases to re-investigate includes a five point solvability scale. Their **Level 1**—top priority cases—have a named suspect, forensic evidence (DNA, latent fingerprint, firearms ballistics), witness identification of the suspect, and physical evidence that connects the suspect to the victim (photos, writing, fibers). This gives investigators a great deal to work with.

Level 2 cases would have all of the above *except* a named suspect, but would still require physical evidence connecting the suspect to the victim. This means, they have all that stuff to work with, but no suspects or persons of interest have been identified.

At **Level 3**, the suspect is unknown and while there might be physical and forensic evidence, there are no witnesses.

Levels 4 and **5** both have an unidentified victim and little or no evidence. Suffice to say you don't want the case you're rooting for in the Level 4-5 range.

It has to be a gruesome task for investigators, picking and choosing who you will put all of your effort and resources into getting justice for, when it is something every victim and their family deserves. When we say resources, though, we mean money and manpower, and the only way to effectively make those decisions is to pick the cases you believe have the best chance of being closed.

Does viable physical evidence exist? Are there any witnesses? Is the suspect living, dead, or incarcerated? Is there an opportunity for multiple clearances (meaning, is this a possible serial killer)? Has the case been presented to the prosecutor before and been denied for any reason? Once investigators answer all of these questions, they prioritize their list of unsolved cases based on the answers.

North Carolina's Charlotte-Mecklenberg PD has a process that's been touted by the Department of Justice as having a good track record for cold case clearances. They have also received international awards. A civilian review team (retired members of law enforcement with differing areas of related expertise) review each case based on a set forth criteria, and then present each at a monthly meeting to the entire cold case team according to a strict format:

-victimology
-summary of crime
-Medical Examiners report
-evidence and/or property collected
-lab reports
-witness locations
-parallel investigations
-potential suspects
-recommended follow-up

The case is then discussed with the entire team and a solvability rating from 1 to 5 is assigned. When available, former detectives on each case are present because they're an invaluable resource, particularly on very old cases. Some things don't make it into the official reports. There will always be subtle nuances and small details that only the former investigators on a case will be able to convey. As they say, sometimes the devil truly is in the details.

So the civilian review team has done the initial legwork for active investigators. At this point, a DNA lab staff member is assigned to the team to get evidence processed as quickly as possible. The next step is meeting with witnesses again. Particularly with older cases, this is important because often with the passage of time, folks who were once reluctant to talk are now willing to cooperate. Time passes; people age. Where once a witness was afraid to come forward, now they're older and enough time has passed for them to process it. They may decide there's no longer a reason to remain quiet.

Engaging the community is important. Tapping into knowledge that others may have through personal relationships or secondhand gossip might shed light where there was once only murkiness. Police use media resources to their advantage as well. Human interest stories featuring details of the case and interviews with family generate interest from the public and get folks talking about the case again, sharing what they remember.

From the standpoint of investigators, the evidence itself is something that has to be seriously considered. With older cases, before DNA was regularly performed, certain evidence may not have been collected at the scene because many of the tests done today were not in existence years ago. Some testing uses up the evidence, and there may not be any of a specific piece left to analyze with newer technologies. Then there is deterioration, as well as the all-too-often destroyed evidence, gone forever to the passage of time or need for space. I was heartened to read, however, of more than one instance after it appeared that was the case, where agencies contacted the coroner's office to find they'd kept their own samples stored and were happy to help. That, however, is the exception, not the rule.

When I spoke to District 6 Inspector Cam Henke and he told me the next cold case he assigned a team to would be from the Reed City list, we discussed solvability as being one of the key determining factors. I wanted him to choose Janette's case and I was trying to assess, based on solvability (and what little I knew) whether it had a shot. I wanted her to have that shot. *The shot*. The next one, like right now. Let's get this done.

Pick her. *Pick Janette Roberson*.

It feels bad to write that, now. I wanted him to pick Janette's name from the list of others I'd gotten from the Michigan State Police, but behind every one of those unsolved cases is someone who would wish the same for their loved one. Each case, at its heart, is about a person, and those people have names.

Pick Sue; Pick Nick; Pick Esther... I can almost hear their family members' pleas. I kept a list of the open homicide cases attributed to Reed City on my desk—Burton Scott, Janette Roberson, Sue Clason, Thomas Hancock, William Essex III, Esther Gaffney, and Nicholas Beebe—and decided to learn more about each case because they, too, deserve justice.

On June 26, 1979, Marilyn McLachlan walked into the Reed City MSP post and reported her 25 year old son, **Burton Scott**, missing. She said no one had seen him since Friday evening, four days prior. He'd been last seen dropping someone off at the Evart Lounge Bar. She said his car was currently parked "on the north side of the barn, out of sight" in a place it wasn't normally parked. Also, a person who had been living with her son at the time was now gone, along with some of Mr. Scott's possessions, including two guns and a couple chainsaws. A search of the victim's property was made after police found no signs of violence in the trailer home. The body of Burton Scott was found approximately 20 to 30 yards behind the trailer lying face down in a small, wooded ditch with an apparent gunshot wound. Trooper Clifford A. Baker—who was at the scene with the mother of the victim and a family friend—then contacted Detective Sgt. George Pratt for assistance on the case. When I spoke to Detective Pratt, I asked him about the Burton Scott case and he told me the friend who'd been staying with Mr. Scott had been the primary person of interest, but he had disappeared and they were never able to track him down.

Sue Clason—a realtor with Century 21 in Cadillac, Michigan—was murdered while showing property in Osceola County on September 11th, 1984. Because she was another attractive female murdered around the same time as Janette Roberson, there have always been rumors that the two crimes could have been committed by the same perpetrator.

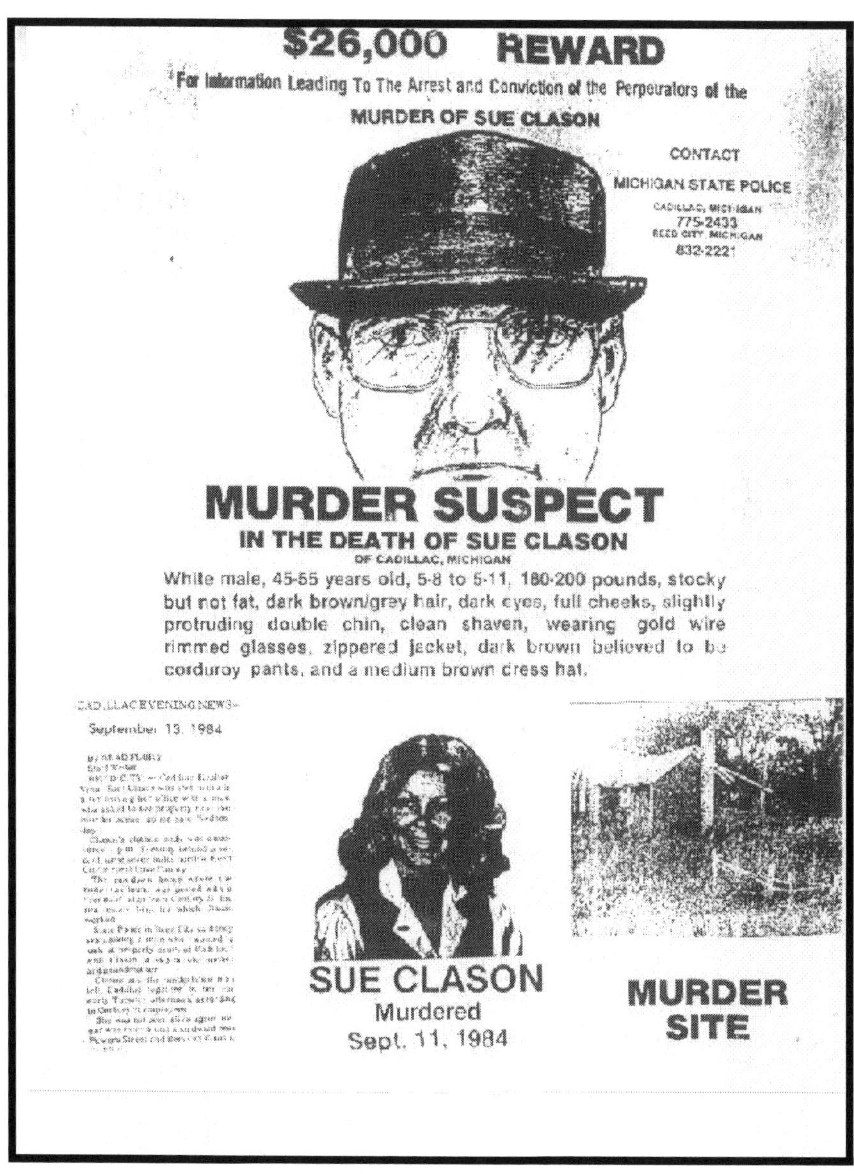

At one point, Clason's murder was thought to possibly have been attributed to that of a man by the name of Gary Robbins. According to a *Pittsburgh Post-Gazette* article on April 30, 1988, Detective Pratt said he was looking for information that would put Robbins in the Reed City area when Sue Clason was murdered in 1984. "We realize it was a long time ago, but this fits the pattern we've found."

From the *Pittsburgh Post-Gazette*, April 19, 1988: Detective Sgt. Pratt said "...the divorced Clason escorted the man, described as 45 to 50 years old, well dressed and between 180 and 200 pounds, to a remote parcel of land near Cadillac, Michigan. Her body was found the next day with a gunshot wound in the head."

"Mrs. B" lived across the road from the property where the realtor escorted the man pretending to be a potential buyer and saw both Sue Clason and the man who killed her. Mrs. B's granddaughter told me that her grandparents' house overlooked two ponds and the front of the house was mostly windows with a great outdoor view. Her grandmother told her that on the day in question she was cleaning the front living room and noticed a car pull into the property for sale. She grabbed her binoculars to get a look at what was going on and noticed a man and woman getting out of a car. After that, Mrs. B went back to her cleaning, but shortly thereafter heard a shot ring out. As the day wore on, she felt as if something wasn't right. So much so that when her husband came home from work, she asked him to go over and check it out. As husbands often do, he told her it was probably nothing.

So Mr. & Mrs. B went into town and had dinner, but it ate at her the whole time, *that shot*... When they got home she again asked her husband to go check things out. He headed out to feed the geese and ducks on the pond and then decided to humor her, jumping into his truck and driving over. He was looking at a group of deer in the field when he almost ran over what would eventually be identified as the body of Sue Clason.

Mrs. B's granddaughter told me that her grandmother lived in fear for a very long time, a loaded gun never far from her side.

When I spoke to Detective Pratt, I asked him about Sue Clason's case and he said it was determined her murder was *not* attributed to Gary Robbins. Based on the "25 points of similarity" mentioned in a *Pittsburg Post-Gazette* article, the MO of the perpetrator in the Clason murder must be similar to that of Robbins. Most of his victims were blindfolded, muzzled, tied up, raped and tortured before they were killed by the man who presented himself as an out-of-towner looking for real estate.

Sue Clason had multiple injuries, including evidence of manual strangulation and a gunshot wound. The cause of death was listed as a single gunshot wound to the head; manner of death, homicide. The perpetrator of this crime was seen by multiple people, including fellow employees at the Century 21 office in Cadillac, Michigan. One of the employees, "Gail K," was later put under hypnosis "as a means of developing additional leads."

From the police report: "The session, which lasted from approximately 1:45 to approximately 3:18pm including the pre-session and post-session briefings, was recorded and will be transcribed. Under the hypnosis, Mrs. K was able to take herself back to the early afternoon of September 11th and provide information as to what occurred at that time."

"The suspect was described under hypnosis by Mrs. K as a white male in his fifties (like her father), not real tall 5'11" at most, heavyset—stocky not fat—like he may work outside or exercise, a little round heavy set face, he wore a dark brown hat like a dress hat with a narrow brim that curled up on the edges and was indented above the brim forming a rounded point in front, he had on gold colored wire-rimmed glasses with rectangular lenses with rounded corners, dark eyes but not blue, a tan colored zippered close to the throat waist-length jacket, dark brown believed to be corduroy pants, brown colored lace-up oxfords that were nice looking but dusty, he carried the paper with Sue's ad in his left hand, his hands were clean and large, his hair was dark brown with gray in it and it curled around on the back of his neck/hat—it was mid-collar in length—he looked like he needed a haircut, it was unruly, he spoke in a low soft gravelly voice."

"In addition to being quite explicit as to what occurred while the suspect was in the office, Mrs. K heard Sue ask him what his name was and she said '—ON Whitm?—something that starts with a WHITmmmm, JOHN WHITMAN?' Under hypnosis Gail thought she saw Sue writing something down on her yellow pad described as from Michigan Bell Telephone with Century 21 on it. Sue asked him where he was from and he said Jackson. When Gail was asked the name she heard the suspect say, she said JOHN WITNER (sp?)"

"As Mrs. K was involved in the original composite, she was asked if she would change any details of it. While still under hypnosis she looked at the composite she previously made and said the face should be rounder, cheeks puffier but not fat, thinner lips with a droop at the ends like a frown, wider nose at the bridge, a change in the hat with the brim rolled up on the edge, and the different style with it being pulled down touching the ears causing them to stick out."

The last line in the November 1, 1985 supplemental (a little over a year after the murder of Sue Clason) is as follows: "Although several tips are yet to be followed up, there are no good leads in this case at this time."

Thomas Hancock—On Monday November 20, 2000 the postmaster of the Idlewild, Michigan post office was dropped off for work at approximately 8:35 in the morning. He entered through the rear entrance and began the task of preparing for the day when he looked out the front window and saw what looked like someone lying on the ground. He went out and checked the person for signs of life, and upon finding none, called 9-1-1.

The Lake County Sheriff's Department was the first to respond, then contacting Detective Sgt. George Pratt to assist. From his report: "The body of a fully clothed white male with trauma around the facial area was found lying on the ground partially obscured by a cluster of cedar trees on the southwest corner of the building. The snow that had been accumulating and that of the previous days had melted beneath the victim and approximately 4 to 6 inches away from the body."

At approximately 10:18am, the Lake County Central Dispatch was contacted by Annette Hancock, reporting her husband missing. "It was learned that the Hancocks lived on Logan St., which was less than half a mile from the crime scene."

From Mrs. Hancock it was learned that Thomas Hancock, who was a carpenter by trade, was home all day the previous Sunday, and he'd watched a football game. She said he had about six beers, gotten ready for bad, having put his pajamas on, and later decided to go out for more beer. She remembered telling him it was almost

10pm and he'd have to hurry because the store would be closing. She described him as 6'1", 165 to 170 pounds, brown hair and a moustache, and his left hand was wrapped in an Ace bandage due to a recent accident with a saw.

That morning Mr. Hancock's wife found his truck parked in front of the Idlewild Party Store where she thought he was going to get beer. Everything was covered with snow and she didn't see any vehicle tracks or footprints in the area.

Thomas Hancock was last seen at the Red Rooster Bar the night before. According to the bar owner, William McClure, he'd been in twice that day, once between 4:30 and 5:00pm, had one beer and left, then returned that night between 9:00 and 10:00pm, drank two beers, "Came in alone, sat alone, and left alone."

William (Billy) Essex was four-years-old at the time of his death on April 2, 2001, which was originally attributed to a house fire. At autopsy, the child was found to have blunt force trauma to the side of the head that the medical examiner said was not indicative of having been caused by falling debris. When asked during an interview on the date of the incident how she believed the fire started, his mother told police, "That stupid, fucking lighter" was the cause of the fire.

Everyone in the home that night, except Billy, escaped the fire. There were two adults present, with the rest of the occupants being minors. According to the Michigan State Police report, following the autopsy on April 3, 2001 by Dr. Stephen Cohle in Grand Rapids, it was determined that the victim received a severe blunt force trauma injury to the left side of his skull prior to the fire. The next day, a search warrant was obtained and evidence was collected, including a gas can sitting just inside the door of a shed on the property.

The day after the autopsy, a search warrant was obtained and evidence was collected. *The Cadillac News* reported on June 6, 2003 - **Story unfolds in arson, murder case:**

> During testimony on Thursday, Sgt. Mike Jenkinson, a Michigan State police officer currently assigned the fire marshal division in West Branch, recounted his findings at the scene. Jenkinson said he processed the bedroom

containing the victim first. After spending the entire day in that room, investigators concluded the fire and death were accidental. Two days later, Jenkinson received the autopsy report showing the victim sustained blunt force trauma to the head. Investigators returned to the scene. This time, he discovered traces of gasoline located underneath a melted inflatable mattress in a separate room and a cigarette butt in the bedroom. Although Jenkinson doesn't believe the cigarette butt would be capable of starting such a fire, he said other accelerants such as paper and clothing could. Based on these findings, Jenkinson testified the house had two fire sources. He stated also that he believes Forgar set the fire in the living room and Taylor set the fire in the bedroom.

Dr. Stephen Cole, a forensic scientist, testified about autopsy findings conducted on Essex's body. The prosecution presented evidence showing blunt force trauma to the victim's head. Despite the evidence of head trauma, the actual cause of death was carbon monoxide poisoning. His blood showed 87 percent saturation of the lethal gas. During the testimony, Cole stated that 50 percent saturation is enough to be lethal. Cole stated also that falling objects from above would not be substantial enough to cause Essex's head injury.

The prosecution alleges that Essex was struck by a blunt object, such as a baseball bat, and left unconscious as the house burned. He later succumbed to the poisonous gases.

The defense argued the accidental death was caused when falling debris from the burning house struck Essex in the head rendering him unconscious.

According to a *Cadillac News* article published on October 10, 1983, the murder and arson charges were dismissed for lack of evidence.

Charges were brought when investigators found trace amounts of gasoline in the living room. Further investigation found inconsistencies in the testimony of Taylor and Forgar. Murder charges came about when medical examinations found Essex had suffered a blunt

> force trauma to the left side of his head. In Grant's ruling, she stated there was little evidence to connect Taylor and Forgar to the arson. In addition, she stated the prosecution did not have sufficient evidence to determine either defendant played a role in Essex's injury.
>
> The defense argued that the head injury was caused by debris that fell as the roof collapsed. Grant also stated brain injuries may have resulted from the intensity of the fire. Prosecuting Attorney Sandra Marvin said it is too early for the county to consider the case closed.

This case didn't go to trial where jurors get to hear all of the facts and make a determination. This only made it to preliminary hearing where two lawyers interview a handful of witnesses before a judge. If the right witnesses aren't presented, if the witnesses fail to adequately explain themselves, if the judge doesn't understand the testimony, if not enough evidence is presented... there are a great many reasons why a preliminary examination will end in a dismissal.

Here are two facts to consider:

1. Michigan State Police considers this a homicide, not an accidental fire.
2. Karen Taylor adamantly maintains this was an accidental fire and she did nothing to cause injury to her child.

Now, Common Sense taps me on the shoulder and asks why they didn't just send it to court and let a jury sort it out, but the problem is that it appears the Judge felt the Prosecutor did not meet the burden in District Court to prove arson even occurred.

Former Osceola County Prosecutor Sandra Marvin believed it was Dr. Cohle's professional conclusion that the blow to Billy's head occurred prior to his death. It was their further position that by the time the rafters fell from the ceiling, Billy would have been dead from the toxins created by the fire. She also believed she had presented enough evidence on the elements of arson to have the case bound over to court to let a jury decide.

As for the Defense—we must remember this case never made it past the preliminary examination phase, and the fire occurred in 2001. That's fourteen years with no subsequent charges. The defendant maintains this was a horrible moment in their lives, but she had absolutely nothing to do with the death of her son. In fact, in her very first interview on scene that day, she says one of her children said, *I sorry I play with the flower lighter* as they took shelter in a car outside the house while the fire was still burning. This lighter was later found and, according to the Circuit Court documents, had no flint and was inoperable.

A great deal of the Defense statement of facts centers around what they clearly believe was a violation of standard procedure. They maintain the Fire Marshal did not preserve evidence on the first day because he believed at that time the fire was accidental, but that changed when he received the autopsy report results and learned of Billy's head wound. Their argument of law hinged upon their belief that the elements of felony murder were not met, nor was the Prosecutor able to meet the **bindover standard** regarding the arson.

> *"Probable cause requires a quantum of evidence 'sufficient to cause a person of ordinary prudence and caution to consciously entertain a reasonable belief of the accused's guilt.'"*

Something to note here is that the statements of fact come from the appeal which was in Circuit Court. Essentially the Prosecutor believed the District Court Judge abused her discretion. The Circuit Court Judge, though, "cannot merely substitute his judgment for that of the District Court Judge," the Defense attorney argued. "...an appellate judge must form his judgment solely from the printed word." So the Judge hearing the appeal could only use the printed pages from the lawyers in front of him to make his judgment about the appeal, not the facts of the case, whatever those are/were. Only the arguments by each lawyer and the District Court's ruling.

Both arguments are compelling, but I keep coming back to one thing. *The gasoline*. The Fire Marshal said when they pulled up that air mattress, "it was such a strong overwhelming odor when we lifted that material off the floor it about knocked you off your feet, it—it was strong."

Both the Prosecution and Defense note that multiple areas in the living room tested positive for gasoline. I like facts; I like science. While I cannot tell you how and when Billy sustained his head injury, I can say there shouldn't have been gasoline found in the living room of that house. Not so much that the fire marshal describes it *overwhelming*. That was never addressed by the defense. By law he doesn't have to. All he has to do is show that the State has not met its burden.

Still, it bothers me. *That gas.* In an interview done by the *Gladwin County Record & Beaverton Clarion* in 2011, Mike Jenkinson, the former fire marshal had this to say when asked, "In your years as a fire marshal are there any fires that stick out in your mind?"

> "The fire that sticks out the most in my mind was a fatal fire that involved a 4-year-old boy. There were some suspicious factors right early on and we ended up working that scene about 18 or 19 hours straight. Then, after we got the autopsy results that showed the boy had sustained a blow to the head prior the fire, we got a search warrant and spent another 18, 19, 20 hours the next day."
>
> "We had one of the—in my opinion—leading forensic pathologists in the country and he concluded the boy was beaten over the head and it was a debilitating injury and he would have been rendered incapacitated. The thing that we found was that the initial fire was staged. There was no question about it. They tried to make it look like some cigarette started the fire in a clothes basket. And clothes don't burn that readily. Then on top of that we had a couple accelerant detection dogs come out and between their findings and our lab results we found gasoline all over that house. At the preliminary exam, when all was said and done and all the evidence was provided, the judge said the pathologist was full of crap, that a board must of hit the kid's head even though we clearly showed the only thing that had hit the kid in the head were some ceiling tiles and they are not

> going to crush his skull two-inches deep. And then basically [the judge] said the gasoline didn't matter because everyone has gasoline in their house and she dismissed the arson and murder charges against these people. It went on appeal and the circuit judge didn't necessarily agree with the decision but didn't feel the district judge abused her position, and as a result the two people that killed this boy and set the house on fire are walking the streets somewhere and I think of that case dang near every day. It's disgusting."

Pretty strong words, almost a decade after the fact. But at the end of the day, another thing we have to ask ourselves is this: Should the State be able to continue to call something homicide if they are ultimately unable to prove it? I don't know what happened to little Billy Essex in those early morning hours. Maybe they *all* got it wrong - the investigators, the firefighters, the Prosecutor, the Medical Examiner - but I do know that Billy Essex lived and died and a great many people who never even knew the little boy *have not forgotten*.

Esther Gaffney was murdered sometime between July 10th and July 12th 2004. Her body was discovered having been shot in her secluded home following a weekend of moving preparations. The home was partially burned in an apparent attempt to cover up the crime. When I spoke to her sister, Ruth Wagner-Belisle, she said Esther and her late husband Charles Gaffney (former Detective Sergeant with Michigan State Police) were both good marksmen and lived on 80 acres of hunting property.

At the time of her murder, Esther was in the middle of a move to Cadillac to be closer to her church. She'd had some garage sales in an effort to get rid of things she wouldn't have room for and had an auction scheduled for just days after her murder.

"Anyone who knew my sister well knew what a special person she was," Ruth wrote in a tribute. "She was intelligent, fun to be with and totally open and honest in her dealings with others. With Essie it was strictly *What you see is what you get*. There was no pretense about her. If she felt strongly about an issue, even if it was controversial, she'd state her mind in no uncertain terms. Neither did she shy away from taking positions of leadership, whether in her church or in other organizations with which she was involved."

From a September 6, 2004 article in the *Cadillac News*:

> Esther Gaffney's daughter, Pat Gaffney of Lake, said much of her thoughts have been dominated by what she saw and experienced on Monday, July 12, when she entered her mother's Tustin area home and discovered her body. "When I found her, I didn't know she was shot," she said. "There were definite signs of fire."
>
> Detective Pratt has declined to comment about the type of weapon used in the crime. Pat Gaffney said all the plastic items inside the secluded home, including the alarm clocks, radio and other items melted from the heat of the attempted arson of the home. There was soot and smoke damage to the things inside.
>
> "Very little was actually burned up," she said. Pat said she tried to use the phone in her mother's bedroom to call police but the phone did not work. She ran outside and found a neighbor who called the authorities.

Three years later from the August 1, 2007 *Cadillac News,* it appears leads had run dry.

> The Gaffney home, located about two miles north of Tustin, sat on 80 acres — the nearest neighbor at least a quarter mile away. What happened that weekend of her death is still unknown. Gaffney was found by a relative on Monday, July 14, 2004. An autopsy later determined Gaffney died of a gunshot wound. The assailant also attempted to start a fire in the Gaffney home. Three years later, the family is still waiting for answers. To aid the investigation, family members are offering a $10,000 reward in addition to $5,000 already being offered for information that leads to the arrest and conviction of the person responsible for her death.
>
> "We want some closure and hopefully this will jar somebody's mind or get some snakes to crawl out from

> under some rocks," said Kathleen Stadtfeld of Manton. Stadtfeld is one of three of Gaffney's children.
>
> Det. Sgt. George Pratt with the Michigan State Police Reed City Post said there's not a lot of update about the investigation. "We've not classified anyone as a suspect," Pratt said. "We've looked at many different avenues but no specific person has been identified as a suspect."

Eighteen year old **Nicholas Beebe** was shot through a window on May 12, 2006 at his residence. According to Beebe's mother, he was sleeping on one of the couches in the home, with his girlfriend asleep on the other when she was awakened by what she described as the sound of "firecrackers."

"It's a slow process as with any major case," said Osceola County Undersheriff Dave Fowler in 2006. "The key emphasis is going to be thoroughness instead of rushing to judgment." Police had a ton of leads, Fowler said.

What Richielene Beebe remembers from that awful night almost nine years ago is that it was Mother's Day weekend and she got a call around three in the morning from a relative of Nick's girlfriend. "Nick's been shot..."

She jumped out of bed, didn't even change the jogging pants she had on, got into her car, and drove the ten miles to Nick's house. She found an ambulance parked on the corner.

"Are you going to Nick Beebe's? Are you looking for the boy who was shot?" she asked them.

They told her they couldn't enter the scene until police had secured it for entry.

"I'm his mom, I'm going in..."

Of course that was her response. That's exactly what I would have said if my son was in there and I was told he'd been shot. She confided that at that time, it never occurred to her Nick was dead. She thought there had been an accident or something. She figured she'd be following an ambulance to a hospital and sitting at the Emergency Room all night. The enormity of the situation hadn't yet hit her. She pulled up to the house and there was a police car in the driveway. She went to the back door and two deputies shined flashlights on her as she went to step inside. They told her she couldn't come in.

"That's my son. He needs me. I have to see him." She still didn't know.

The deputy told her to go stand by the police car but it was dark and she didn't feel safe so she sat in her car and waited. I can't even imagine what she must have been feeling. My kid has been shot and you want me to *wait*? I'm certain every instinct in her was screaming to *get inside that house right now*, but instead she was sitting in her car alone in the dark. *Waiting...*

Sometime in the days to follow, she got the story from Nick's girlfriend. She said Shiann Ankney told her she was awakened by a "firecracker noise" and then she heard a vehicle drive away outside. She tried to wake Nick by shaking him but he wouldn't wake up.

In 2009, three years after the murder, Osceola County sought assistance from Michigan State Police. I submitted a FOIA request to the Osceola Sheriff's Department for their first responder's report from the date of the incident. It was denied in full.

"The Sheriff's Department has indicated this is an open case and the records cannot be released at this time. They have indicated you may call them at (231)832-2288 after some time passes to obtain a status update."

"It's a small town. A lot of people don't want to speak out of fear," Richielene Beebe told me. "Friends of friends... that's how small towns are. But somebody knows something."

It was heartbreaking listening to all of these very personal stories from family members who are still so raw and anguished over the lack of closure. Every one of these victims deserves justice and their families deserve to know what happened to their loved ones.

People are good, people are good—some days I have to repeat this to myself on a loop over the echo-chamber of grief and sadness, lest I get pulled into its undertow.

Detective Sergeant George Pratt

From the *Cadillac News*, March 1, 2012:

OSCEOLA COUNTY – It wasn't long ago that Osceola County said goodbye to the long-standing Michigan State Police Detective Sergeant George Pratt when he retired after more than three decades on the job.

It was a short break, as during a county commissioner meeting earlier this month, Osceola County Undersheriff Justin Halladay asked commissioners to approve a new position that would allow the hiring of an as-needed special investigator and consultant. Unanimously supported by the commissioners, the position went to Pratt, a familiar face in the area – and he has already been put to work. Some passing motorists travelling near LeRoy during the recent police investigation of the bank robbery that occurred at the Citizens Bank might have noticed Pratt at the scene, for instance.

Halladay said Pratt was utilized during that investigation, and on complaints filed during the recent arraignments of the suspects arrested for those crimes, Pratt was listed as one of the witnesses. The position will be limited to 500 hours per year, and the new OCSD investigator will only be used when need. This is the first time the county has utilized such a position, although years ago there had also been an as-needed special detective in the county.

Commissioners justified the approval because of the closing of the Reed City MSP post and the new MSP operations. Other than Pratt, the closest detective is located in Mount Pleasant.

Most of the time I was researching this case, even when I was in the thick of it, I really never believed I would get to meet Detective Pratt. First, I knew he wasn't all that happy about any of the file being released. As Inspector Cam Henke told me when we spoke, "George is old-school." He said it with a chuckle, as one generation does when they are explaining something that so perfectly illustrates a generation gap. Back in the day, records didn't get released. Today, there are fairly stringent laws on the books allowing for the release of police reports—even in open cases—under specific circumstances, and a long list of exceptions the State can apply if they believe the information should not be released.

Many Michigan FOIA cases have gone all the way to Michigan's Supreme Court and been upheld. Spend an hour (or twelve) like I did reading the court documents in such cases and you'll see how a well-oiled mechanism for relief works, in action. Maybe it's just the researcher in me, but I love reading cases and case law. Most people who are denied don't take it that far. Past the point where you apply for a document, are denied, appeal, are again denied, and then have recourse in the form of the local court system. Larger entities looking for documents and are refused, for whatever reason, have the time, patience, inclination, and most importantly, the money to take their case to court. They have lawyers on staff who froth at the mouth for a chance to argue a case involving the rights of *The People*.

The average person does not. There's only so much money an intelligent human will fork over in the interest of getting information, only to get a bunch of mostly blank pages before you realize you're not getting what you want, so you better get your case law ready—as I did when I appeared before the Reed City city council to get the Reed City PD report released for the first time.

That was nervous-making, let me just say. I'm not a good public speaker, so I try not to do it whenever possible. In this case, it was the only way to get my hands on the reports filed by the first responders to Janette's crime scene. Doing so was important, yet I understood the risks. Small towns don't like wave-makers. Add to that, the perpetrator of the heinous crime I am writing a book about has yet to be arrested. If he's out there and dialed in, I'm guessing he knows about the writer asking all those questions about a murder he thinks he got away with and isn't too pleased about it. I said as much to my friend Katy Knight a couple days before I appeared in front of the council. She's lived here all her life so she gets it.

"Well then, as I see it you have two choices. You can tuck tail or you can stick your neck all the way out." She's a smart girl. Since tucking tail wasn't an option, mostly due to my innate stubbornness, neck out it was. Katy even came and sat with me to show her support. Since I wanted to puke the entire time, her presence was truly appreciated.

I learned the outcome a few days later from an article in the *Cadillac News* that no less than twelve people called, phoned, texted and private-messaged me about having seen. It was an elating, yet very short-lived victory. While I am happy we got at least part of that report because it helps illustrate inconsistencies, I learned a few things that made me a tiny bit more jaded as a human being. First, I got those documents from Osceola County turned over "in the interest of full disclosure" by the City attorney. You remember the ones I'd been asking the County for, repeatedly, and was told they didn't exist? I'm just going to say it. That made me sad. Knowing that it appears to be okay to flat out tell a fib like that by an actual law-enforcing body, well... it's not right. How can you ask us to play by the rules and obey the laws if you who are tasked to enforce them are not willing to do so, yourselves? *Tsk-tsk.*

I SAID TSK-TSK.

Second—I've learned that fighting local government is a dicey proposition, particularly if you live there. You know the old saying, right? *Don't shit where you eat.*

The Federal government gets all the press, but it isn't remotely as important to our day to day lives as our local governments. How things work is the same at the smallest level, all the way up to the Oval Office. For any elected position, some stuff has to be done for the person wanting the position to receive it. I think it's fair to say a bit of glad-handing, bargaining, bullying, and bullshitting is often needed to earn a position where you make decisions that affect the citizenry. We hold elections to determine some of these folks, others are appointed by the former, and sometimes that incestuous-but-not-in-a-literal-(gross)-way relationship becomes a little sticky.

Then there's the relationship between city government and local law enforcement, which one could argue isn't always what it should be. Often residents become alienated from both entities, but if you look at that real close, what you get 100% of the time is a problem that originates at the ballot box. If you don't show up, don't expect things around you to go the way you think they should. In a great many small towns, a tiny percentage of people make the decisions about how the area is run, and a good hunk of the citizens don't even know who those people are.

I knew who *I* was. I was a gal who'd only lived in Reed City for about 8 years when I took on this research project. What that meant at a very basic level was that I had zero position of strength from which to pull a court appeal out of my ass. Arguing in front of an actual judge rather than the city attorney, police chief, and councilmembers is a bit more daunting. You need a real lawyer who knows they're doing. I prevailed in front of the city council but I wasn't as confident about navigating the court system.

At some point, I got as much of the Roberson file out of Michigan State Police as I was likely to get, until enough time passes and an entirely different crew is manning the printers. I felt confident I knew as much as I was going to know about the case, as well as what was going on in Reed City in January of 1983, so I thought *What the hell*?

Rather than call him—which I always feel puts people on the spot—I fashioned a written plea to Detective Pratt and mailed it. I never expected to hear back from him but it occurred to me that it would be disrespectful if I didn't at least give him a chance to turn me down. I'd given that opportunity to pretty much everyone else, and he was arguably the most informed person regarding the Janette Roberson investigation.

Old-school detectives keep their info tight to the vest. They aren't crazy about the immediacy of social media, and I can't fault them for it because things like the ME report getting out—which happened here and was truly unfortunate—can compromise the integrity of their case. No good detective wants to put years of effort into something only to have interested parties, however well-meaning, torpedo their work in one fell-swoop. I'd been told Detective Pratt was none too pleased about someone having gotten their hands on the autopsy report and summarily passing it around like candy, so I couldn't help but think he'd be less than charmed by someone writing a full-length book about the murder after having obtained a bunch of reports he thought shouldn't have been released in the first place. His motives are simple. He'd like to maintain the integrity of the case in the event of a later prosecution.

Imagine my surprise when he mailed me back in very timely fashion, and agreed to sit down with me, with one stipulation. He was not willing to divulge any information that would compromise the case. As soon as I read the letter, I developed a case of heartburn that did not go away for weeks. I was excited, nervous, nauseous... my stomach and bowel ran the gamut of emotions.

In the meantime, I compiled a list of questions, keeping in mind that we would not be talking about evidence, or anything that remotely circled the wagons around specifics of the case. It was a delicate balance—trying to keep my questions limited to things I believed he could answer, while still hoping to get some insight that would be important to telling Janette's story. I'm not an investigator. I'm not a journalist. I'm just a gal that's good with her words who happened to develop more than a passing interest in an old murder case. Unfortunately, once Janette's story sunk its teeth in, there was no getting away from it, and I wanted certain questions answered out of fairness to other parties—to her family, and to the community who had been so giving of their time. I hoped to at least provide as much information as I could about the young woman who was slain in the pet department and left a husband, two children, a mother, siblings, and an entire city mourning her loss.

After I completed my ten page list of questions that I assumed would cause him to cringe when I pulled them out, I did a bit of research on the man himself. His signature was at the bottom of a great many of the police reports I'd compiled while researching this case. I found this on the Michigan State Police news release page:

State Police Sergeants Receive Meritorious Service Awards
January 27, 2003

Lansing - The Michigan State Police Board of Awards is pleased to announce that Detective Sergeant George D. Pratt and retired Detective Sergeant Gary E. Shaffer have been awarded the Michigan State Police Meritorious Service Award. They are credited for diligence and perseverance under uncommon circumstances for going beyond what is typically expected of law enforcement officers.

On July 20, 1979, Diane Fay Chorba was reported missing by her relatives after not hearing from her for approximately two months. Her family was aware that she had moved to the Luther, Mich. area and was romantically involved with a married man.

Pratt and Shaffer were asked to interview the married man and his wife to try to determine the whereabouts of Chorba. During their interview, the married man and his wife told Pratt and Shaffer that Chorba had been the victim of the ill-fated flight 191 that crashed in Chicago, Ill. on May 25, 1979, destroying her body making it impossible to identify her. Before polygraph tests were conducted to verify their story, the family moved to Oregon.

In the following year, Pratt contacted the Oregon State Police and requested they re-interview the couple, which they did. However, further investigation proved unsuccessful, and once again they refused to take a polygraph test to support their story. Several years later, Pratt and Shaffer learned that husband and wife had separated, and he again requested that Oregon State Police interview the two suspects. Once again, no new results surfaced.

In 1999, Pratt and Shaffer flew to Oregon to re-interview the suspects themselves. They decided to make an unannounced visit to the wife, which resulted in a complete confession implicating her ex-husband in the shooting death of Chorba. With assistance from the wife, her ex-husband was extradited back to Michigan where he was found guilty of Chorba's murder.

In awarding the Meritorious Service Award, Pratt and Shaffer are credited for their perseverance in solving a 22-year-old murder. The Michigan State Police Board of Awards recognizes that if it were not for the dedication and professionalism of Pratt and Shaffer, this crime may have never been solved.

Pratt enlisted with the department in 1965, and was a graduate of the 59thTrooper Recruit School. He has served at the Ypsilanti and West Branch posts, as well as working narcotics and organized crime for what is now the Criminal Investigation Division. In 1974, he was promoted to detective sergeant and in 1977 he was assigned to the Reed City Post. A native of Scottville, Pratt currently lives in Reed City.

Shaffer enlisted with the department in 1968, and was a graduate of the 70thTrooper Recruit School. He retired from service in March 2001. A native of Haslett, Shaffer currently lives in Stevensville.

In a 2001 Herald Palladium article about the investigation, Shaffer said:

"You just have to keep after it, keep in contact with the people who know something about the case. You keep going over and over it, and finally, you get something. In this particular case people stopped being defensive about it. That's usually what happens on a cold case: Eventually you convince somebody to come around and be truthful, or somebody remembers something and it leads you to another person, another detail, a whole series of things... Usually, what it boils down to is a group of people working together who put their heads together and come up with the right answer," he said. "I've been very lucky to have worked with a lot of people who have done that."

From a Ludington Daily News article dated Feb 19, 2001 about the apprehension in the Chorba case:

> Pratt, who has been involved in the investigation since the start, said it felt good to see that some closure may come in the case. "I am certain that Diane's family feels the same way. You always want to solve every case, yet you can't become emotionally involved because you have to do your job. All the cases you can't solve bother you."

Regarding the February 2008 slaying of a Luther, MI man, when interviewed after an arrest had been made, Lake County Prosecutor Mike Riley said this: "Det. Sgt. George Pratt was in charge of the investigation. He's the kind of cop you want to investigate a crime."

From a *Herald Review* article on January 17th, 2012:

> Detective Pratt began work with the MSP at the Ypsilanti Post after recruit school. Previous to this, he worked part-time with the Scottville Police Department. In 1967, he was moved to the West Branch Post until January 1974 when he joined the Criminal Investigation Section and served in Detroit in the narcotics and organized crime unit. In 1977, he was transferred to the Reed City Post, and has been in this area ever since.
>
> "One of the most satisfying features of my work has been closing cases and getting bad people out of the community and behind bars where they can't do any more damage."
>
> And on the other hand ...
>
> There have been cases that have not yet been resolved.
>
> "Unfortunately, there are cases we've worked on for years that we've not been able to close," Pratt pointed out. "There are several in this area."
>
> That doesn't mean investigators haven't done everything they could to bring vicious criminals to justice in those cases. It simply means they couldn't get all of the required elements to move those cases into the court system.
>
> "We may have ideas, but we don't have the required proofs," he said. "I've worked on one case since 1977 – in Lake County – but we haven't been able to bring it to trial."

> "The Gamble Store case still is on many people's minds in this area. We've investigated that incident for years. We have reopened it many times to use new methods or technologies that weren't available back then."
>
> "It's frustrating, but I can say we did the best we could. We never ignored any avenue of investigation or tip from the public. We followed, and will continue to follow every lead. We simply don't have what we needed to close some cases."

From embezzlement to murder, bank robbery to most recently helping track down stolen exotic animals, Detective Sergeant Pratt has worked a long and varied list of crimes over his career. In fact, as of this writing, he is the longest serving enlisted person *ever* in the Michigan State Police.

I was pretty jazzed that he agreed to sit down with me. From the moment I sent my plea, until I walked in the front door of the Sheriff's department—after having the car alarm signal my arrival to all of Reed City proper by way of seven loud bleats before I could find the key fob—my stomach was in a state of turmoil.

On the day in question, I situated myself in a chair across from him. We were in one of those box-like rooms where they interrogate the bad guys. You know the ones. It's exactly like you've seen in every grainy minute of security camera footage of people being questioned, except in my case, I wasn't afraid I was about to be arrested so I didn't have to fake a good cry or hold my stomach and rock in the chair while moaning, "I didn't do anything, I swear!"

"How many years did you work for the Michigan State Police?"

"46 years, 3 months." Succinct; to the point. Detective Sargent George Pratt answered my first question in exactly the manner I would have expected from someone who'd been described to me as "proud," "private," and "a good man." I felt like I'd gotten a slight read on him, based on what I found to be a good set of case file notes—at least the ones I was privy to between the hunks of redaction.

I looked at my notes and jotted his response down, trying to stifle a smile. It wasn't happening. I smiled a lot when I talked to

Detective Pratt, I think because I found him charming, and *that* was a surprise. He was present in a way you appreciate from someone you're speaking to about a topic of interest. He listened and answered a lot of questions, and only once said, "I'm not going to respond to that." It wasn't delivered in a harsh or intimidating manner, quite the contrary, merely a statement of fact. He wouldn't be commenting on something he felt was too specific to the case and could interfere with the ongoing investigation.

"What do you like about being a detective? What about the job is suited to you?"

"It's intriguing, fulfilling in most instances, and it's not a regular 9 to 5 job. There are different types of cases, so it's not always the same thing."

When I asked Detective Pratt if there were any misconceptions about this case that he'd heard over the years, he said there were so many misconceptions about this case, there's no way he'd ever be able to list them all.

We talked a bit about witnesses because I told him one of the many things I learned during this whole thing was that witness accounts, while often tantalizing, don't seem very reliable. You hear it all the time. But I now had the benefit of experience. Right off the top of my head, I think about Jan & Venus, and about Elke. Based on the times they remembered having been in the Gambles pet department the day of Janette Roberson's murder, they should have run into one another, and all claimed fairly lengthy visits. I don't doubt their statements. There seem to be a great deal of commonalities. Nobody could find Janette. Nobody heard or saw anything strange. Elke said she had to go up and find an employee, just like the other women did. I just think the times they recall could be a bit off. Jan and Venus may have left a little earlier, and maybe Elke came into the store just as they left or were leaving. But you have to ask yourself, if that one thing is remembered a bit off, what else could be?

"Witnesses—not by design, but by nature—are only 22% accurate," Detective Pratt told me. "When you're talking about eye witnesses, based on position, noise in the area, there are many things to consider about how reliable they may or may not be. It is the same when information is passed from one person to another. Some things may get passed along accurately, but not always the complete picture."

From policechiefmagazine.org (***Failures in Criminal Investigation*** by D. Kim Rossmo, University Endowed Chair in Criminology, and Director, Center for Geospatial Intelligence and Investigation, Department of Criminal Justice, Texas State University, and Detective Inspector (retired), Vancouver Police Department, BC, Canada)

> A witness to a crime must observe, interpret, remember, recall, and then communicate information to a police investigator who, in turn, must understand and record it. Each stage has the potential for error. People are influenced by experiences and expectations, and different people view the world through different lenses. What witnesses think they see is a function of what they expected to see, what they wanted to see, and what they actually saw; the more ambiguous the last, the greater the influence of the first two factors. Similarly, what people remember depends upon what they believe. The human brain does not objectively record data, and memories are subjective interpretations that are seldom reinterpreted, even when information changes. People tend to remember those facts consistent with their theories, and forget those that are not.

There is a great deal that goes into the validity of each aspect of a witness's statement. Not only does the law enforcement officer have to take in the information, but then he or she has to judge the information and ask questions accordingly. There's a bit of the psychologist in being a good investigator, of that I'm certain. This isn't a job that everyone can do, questioning witnesses. I'm horrible at it. I always think of things I should have asked a day or a month later. Detectives don't have that luxury. They understand the stakes.

> Clear and rational thinking is not easy. ...human brains are not wired to deal effectively with uncertainty. People therefore employ heuristics—intuitive rules of thumb—to make judgments under such conditions. A heuristic does

> not have to be correct most of the time, as long as it promotes survival. While a street police officer's intuition may sometimes be wrong, it is still an unwise thing to ignore. While these mental shortcuts work well most of the time, under certain conditions they can lead to cognitive biases.
>
> Cognitive biases are mental errors caused by this simplified information-processing technique. They can result in distorted judgments and faulty analyses. There have been many murder cases in which detectives were led astray because the crime appeared to be something other than what it was. Tunnel vision—one of the leading causes of wrongful convictions—results from a narrow focus on a limited range of possibilities. Focusing on the first likely suspect, then closing the investigation off to alternative theories is a recipe for disaster.

"If someone were to ask you why this case remains unsolved after all these years, what would your response be, Detective Pratt?" I asked.

He chose his words precisely. "The answer would be that we have not achieved the necessary information to be able to prosecute it."

"Is there a DNA profile from Janette's crime scene that you believe to be the offender in CODIS?"

Again, very precise wording. "We have mitochondrial DNA."

"Fingerprints run through IAFIS?" I chirped, still riding the high from the DNA question. My internal monologue was screeching OH MY GOD THEY HAVE DNA!

"We have some unidentified prints." More precision.

Detective Pratt tried to explain DNA evidence to me for the purposes of a criminal trial, and how that timeline had evolved in Michigan. He said that in 1990 Michigan first began defining laws as to collection of profiles, and he recalled that it wasn't until 1996 or 1997 that DNA was approved to be used in this state, if the labs where they were tested had been accredited. He also said that at some point, procedural questions arose, and it was not until 2001 that the Frye Test was achieved with regard to DNA use. Basically, in order for the government to introduce conclusions and opinions based upon a novel scientific procedure or technique (like DNA or other technologies when they become available) it must meet the Frye standard by establishing that the technique and the principles behind it are generally accepted in the relevant scientific community.

I think the general belief from the perspective of the average citizen was that when DNA testing was "discovered," suddenly lawyers were tossing the fruits of its labor around court like the televised giveaways on *Oprah's Favorite Things*.

"You get a perp's DNA tested, and YOU get a perp's DNA tested, and YOU get..."

It wasn't even universal from state to state. Guidelines had to be established, laws had to be written, and a great deal of behind the scenes work had to be done so DNA could be legally used for the purposes of a criminal trial. You know that saying about the wheels of justice turning slowly? It's the same when experts want to bring new technologies into a courthouse and use them to try and convict or acquit someone. To be fair, it is kind of important they get it right.

Because Janette Roberson was murdered before DNA was being used as evidence in court, her case, as with many in that time period, was not one where a bunch of evidence was collected with the idea of testing it for DNA. In fact, collection procedures in that regard did not even exist. So the fact that they have, over three decades later, mitochondrial DNA *at all* is a plus.

But. There's always a but, isn't there? Detective Pratt was likely purposeful in his answer to that question because the answer said a lot more than just those mere words. As it turned out, my excitement-high regarding the DNA information lasted about as long as it took me to get home and Google "mitochondrial DNA."

Perhaps the simplest explanation I read was this: Nuclear DNA is BluRay; Mitochondrial DNA is VHS.

Mitochondrial DNA is only a small portion of the DNA in a eukaryotic cell. Most DNA is found in the cell nucleus. According to *When DNA Won't Work* (Visser/Hampikian, 2012, Idaho Law Review) "Mitochondrial DNA has far less statistical power and it cannot be used to search convicted offender or forensic databases in CODIS for matches."

Let me repeat that: <u>It cannot be used to search convicted offender or forensic databases in CODIS for matches.</u>

What that means is that there will be no exciting CODIS hit that positively identifies one specific individual as Janette Roberson's killer based on DNA they took from the scene—unless somehow new testing of old evidence proves fruitful. That's not how it works with mitochondrial DNA. CODIS uses nuclear DNA samples.

However, mitochondrial DNA can assist investigators if they have developed a list of potential donors to be compared to the analyzed evidence. Like fingerprints and other evidence, mitochondrial DNA is an important part of the puzzle. It is maternally inherited, so all of a woman's offspring, her siblings, her mother and other maternal relatives would have the same mitochondrial DNA. For instance, investigators have been known to approach a family member for a sample of their DNA to test against that of their relative—who is a suspect in a case—to find out if they have the same maternal DNA. If that was found to be the case, it could be extremely probative evidence.

Essentially, mitochondrial DNA almost always supplements other information, and is rarely the only evidence used in a case. A homicide could likely not be prosecuted with only mitochondrial DNA because it cannot identify a single person. Because nuclear DNA and mitochondrial DNA are different, they cannot be compared against each other, either. Mitochondria live inside a cell wall, not in the nucleus, so it has an entirely different DNA sequence. Sperm cells don't contain mitochondrial DNA, for example, but you can get it from hair.

Mitochondrial DNA passes from mother to child, unchanged, and remains unchanged as cells divide to form a human. A mitochondrial DNA match between two people doesn't mean they have the same mother or maternal grandmother, only that the chain of ancestry has entirely female ancestors. Also, you would not be able to distinguish between two male suspects who were related with the same maternal line based on mitochondrial DNA because it would be identical. However, there are types of microscopic analysis that can be done on the hair itself which could distinguish differences between sibling hairs.

So there you have it. *DNA for Dummies*. You're welcome.

Next, in an effort to understand the dynamic between the different law enforcement entities involved with Janette's case, I asked Detective Pratt why the press goes so often to Chief Davis if MSP has the case. He told me that when he retired, he handed the case back over to the Reed City PD because Michigan State Police had been called to assist the city police on the Janette Roberson investigation, since they were the first responders. Because Reed City PD does not have detectives, MSP continues to maintain an assigned detective to assist on the case.

I asked about the 9 & 10 News report that got me all hot under the collar. I said that as far as I could tell, it was the first instance where anyone went on record to say that a suspect in Janette's case had been ruled out. I asked Detective Pratt if that was something law enforcement discussed releasing beforehand. He said he was not part of that process, so he did not know who made that decision or why. (Remember, he'd graciously agreed to sit down and talk with me, but other than occasionally answering questions for the press, and working with the new investigators when needed, this is no longer his case.)

"I don't rule anyone out until the perpetrator is apprehended," he said.

I looked down at my page and saw the next question. *Has anyone else had been ruled out, like Lee or "Dan?"* Then I looked back up at him. "So I guess I don't need to ask my next question." I think he caught sight of it on my paper. He smiled.

"Was there ever a thought to releasing information from the FBI profile?" I asked. "In your report it was noted to be *'...quite lengthy and similar to the profile completed by the Behavioral Sciences Unit/Investigative Resources Unit which had previously been done.'* So if you had two reports that said similar things, why not release some part of that information to garner leads?"

"The analyses those reports provide are investigative tools. If you release all of your tools, you no longer have them."

This may sound strange coming from someone who fought tooth and nail to get every page of every report I could get (and bitched when I couldn't), but I liked him even more for being that staunch old-school detective. In Detective Pratt's world, you don't go passing out pages of reports on investigations that are still open. I can respect that because I absolutely understand he is coming from a place of wanting to protect the integrity of a case that he and others have worked very hard on. The case already has its challenges, it doesn't need more.

Next I asked if he gets feelings about suspects in those first hours at a scene, like gut instincts regarding who he feels a suspect might be. "You get those feelings, but you have to keep your mind open and not focus on a specific individual."

I took a deep breath. "Okay, so I'm not sure why the FOIA team is withholding it, so I'm just going to ask. Do you remember when you were notified of a homicide at the Gambles store?"

Detective Pratt nodded. "I was notified by the prosecutor at the time and I responded immediately. I believe it was sometime after 4:30, so almost hour after she was found."

All that wrangling with the MSP FOIA department; I must have asked them for that information a dozen different ways and Detective Pratt answered it as easily as he'd answered every other question. I wasn't sure whether to feel chagrined or amused so I smiled and thanked him.

"Why was Prosecutor Talaske called?" I asked. "According to his report, Southworth called him. Was it common back then for the prosecutor to be called to crime scenes?"

This one he answered more broadly and I suspect that is because he wasn't there when the prosecutor was called, so he had no firsthand knowledge and could only speculate as to why he was called, or what had happened prior to his arrival. Detective Pratt didn't appear to be the speculating kind, and certainly not when it came to why someone else had done what they'd done.

"Well, there are a couple schools of thought about calling the prosecutor to the scene. Some feel that by doing so they become a witness, so it makes it difficult for them to then prosecute a case."

"So you don't know why they did in this case?" I tried again.

"I have no independent knowledge of why they called, no."

I was able to follow up on that last question with the man himself—former Osceola County Prosecutor James Talaske—shortly after I spoke with Detective Pratt. Mr. Talaske said he couldn't remember who called that day—he seemed to remember it being someone from Osceola County— but his secretary took the call and told him he needed to get down to the Gambles store because there was a murder. At that time, his office was just down the street near the city building, and his residence was not far from there. He often walked to work, but he couldn't remember if he walked that particular day. He said he arrived at Gambles, went downstairs and into the back room. He saw Janette's horribly brutalized body, then turned around toward where the boiler area was and saw, in his words, "...the entire Reed City Police department, half of whom weren't in uniform, and about half the Osceola County deputies." He didn't recall seeing Chief Rathbun but he did specifically recognize city officer Theodore Platz, who was wearing a cast on his arm, and Deputy Kingsbury of Osceola County.

"Why are you all standing around down here?" is the first thing he wondered aloud. Then he immediately asked, "Has anyone contacted Detective Pratt?"

Talaske recalls hearing one of them say, "Why?"

His response was clear. "Have any of *you* ever investigated a murder?"

Talaske said he wasn't at the scene more than five minutes. He left, walked a couple doors down to the law office where David Porteus worked at the time, and called Detective Pratt. This, he confirmed, was where the meeting happened that Laren Thorson mentioned.

Talaske told me the floor in the back room of the pet department was dusty and dirty, there were shoe prints everywhere, and that those first responders had probably walked all over any possible footprint evidence.

"Why did they call you in the first place?" I asked, dumbfounded. "What was the purpose?"

"I don't know. There was no real purpose. I think to rile me. Maybe they thought I'd get sick at the sight of a dead body. But I'd seen dead bodies before. I really don't know the reason they called me."

I told him that I was under the impression Theodore Platz was suspended from RCPD at the time and Talaske said he believed he was. In fact, he recalled an arrest warrant sitting on his desk at that time for the Buckboard incident.

"Detective Pratt has taken a lot over the years about this case. I think people blame him for it not being solved. That isn't the case. He's a good detective. There may have been more to work with if that scene was handled properly."

Another thing Mr. Talaske was able to verify was the animosity that existed at the time between the various law enforcement bodies. He said around that time it was so bad, city officers were doing traffic stops on deputies. "There was a lot of tension."

"Can you tell me what Ted Platz' role was at the scene?" I asked Detective Pratt.

"He had been a patron of the store on two occasions that day. He was a Reed City officer..."

"Do you know who called him to the scene?" I asked.

"I do not. It could have been Chief Rathbun but I have no independent knowledge. Officer Platz may have been trained to work with Northern Counties Evidence Service regarding processing."

At the time of this interview I hadn't talked to him, but when I later spoke to Nelson Gelinas, the creator of NCES, he told me Mr. Platz hadn't taken the training, to his recollection. He recalled Detective Sgt. Southworth and then Deputy Chuck Davis, both with Osceola County, having taken the NCES training.

"I guess I'm curious how you become the head of a probation department after assaulting two officers and a bar patron."

What I wanted to say was that if my Puerto Rican husband did exactly the same as off-duty Officer Platz did that night at the Buckboard, it would likely not have ended with him becoming an Osceola County probation officer. But I did not say that because something told me snark wasn't the way to go with Detective Pratt.

His answer was reasonable and measured, and centered around the fact that Officer Platz had only been convicted of a misdemeanor, so there was nothing to disqualify him from getting that position. That is factually accurate, I concur. *However*, I think it is fair to note that no taxpayer would be out of line suggesting that someone with issues around aggression may not be their first choice as the person to lead offenders successfully toward the path of the straight and narrow. But to any argument that one *could* successfully do the job after assaulting three people and paying their debt to society, I would pose this question: Should they have the opportunity to do so? Over all the other candidates for the position who *hadn't* assaulted two state troopers and threatened to kill one of them, I mean?

I, personally, would suggest that someone who'd scream racial epithets in public, however drunk, and threaten to kill a fellow member of law enforcement repeatedly might not be my first, second, or third choice for probation officer in my fine city, never mind head of the department. But that's just my opinion, and you know what they say about those. Some asshole will always think yours stinks.

"Do you know why this call was dispatched as a heart attack?" I asked Detective Pratt, once we got past the discussion of misdemeanors.

"I have no idea why it was dispatched as a heart attack," he said, simply.

I went on to tell him that dispatcher Raymond Haight had, in my second call to him, suggested that maybe it was done to avoid issues with radio traffic, hoping that would nudge Detective Pratt into offering more, but he just shook his head, indicating he did not know.

"Do you believe the scene was compromised in a way that could make prosecuting any future case more difficult?" I asked.

"No, inasmuch as there are no pristine crime scenes. All scenes have something you wish had not occurred, so it's something you come to expect."

"Are you confident that everyone who was allowed to leave Gambles after the body was discovered, but before you arrived, has been tracked down and questioned?"

"I hope so," he said. "We tracked down between 125 and 150 people who'd been in the store, and that was described to us as being a slow day."

"So, was that the reason for the press release mentioned in your report? The one with the line included that stated: *'Officers are asking that anyone, whether you have been already contacted or not, (underlined) please contact the Michigan State Police, Reed City...'?"*

Detective Pratt nodded. "Yes."

I looked down and checked my notes. "The dispatcher mentioned someone who was grabbed on a bus, a call that came in not long after the first call when Janette was found. Do you recall who gave the information that led to that person being checked out? Haight said the individual was described as having run out the back door in an army coat toward where the bus picked up down by the Osceola Inn."

"There was an individual from a bus who was brought in and questioned that day, and later released, though I am not sure who provided that information."

"What about the sketch. Was that of a perpetrator or witness?"

"Well that depends. Those were actually drawn by different sketch artists of individuals seen in the store that day, as described by different people. If you notice, two of them look very similar, and we have learned the identity of the person in two of those sketches. But it wouldn't necessarily be relevant today. The way people look changes. It was something that was important to the case thirty two years ago, but not necessarily relevant now."

I realized my questions were all over the place when I saw the word **embezzlement** in bold on the page. "I did research other things happening in Reed City around the time of the murder, and one of those was the embezzlement in the city Sewer and Water fund. Dorothy Critchfield. I was wondering why your investigation of the stealing only went back to 1980. The audit, I mean. I think that's when the office went to computerized billing. But she worked for the city for over twenty years. Can you tell me why it would only have been a couple years that were audited? And was she the only person involved?"

"Well, you have to remember there is a statute of limitations, I believe seven years, if I'm not mistaken," he said. "To my knowledge, she was the only person involved."

"Do you know if Chief Rathbun did his own investigation of that embezzlement before turning it over to Michigan State Police?"

"I don't know if he did or not. I suppose you could get that information..."

"I tried. Apparently Reed City doesn't keep records that old, based on Chief Davis' FOIA response."

Specifically the RCPD response said: *This incident is beyond the retention period that we have files on record for. It appears this incident was actually handled by the Michigan State Police. I certify no such records are found with our department.*

"So, Chief Rathbun publicly stating he was "out of town" until his death. Why do you think he distanced himself from this case?"

"I don't know that he distanced himself from the case. I have no knowledge of where the *out of town* came from, or where he was when he was contacted. But he was doing things as Police Chief that day. I know he went with the city manager to notify the decedent's mother."

"But in the MSP report, when Albright and Vincent went back to speak with Marion Fisher, Janette's mother, she said Officer Finkbeiner notified her at the city building. Was that office next to where the city police department is now?"

"I have no knowledge of whether Officer Finkbeiner notified her at any point, but I know Chief Rathbun went with the city manager to the city building where she was. It was located where the courthouse annex is now."

That would have been a few blocks straight down Upton Avenue from the Gambles store.

I told him I was confused about the order of the different officers arriving, since Osceola County is literally right down the street, running distance, yet the city police apparently arrived first, despite EMTs being first called. Detective Pratt said to his recollection, the Osceola County Sheriff's Department sometimes dispatched city police back then, and sometimes the State Police Post did. He was under the impression Osceola County had dispatched this call, as Officer Finkbeiner's report suggests. But he had no personal knowledge of the order of people dispatched to the scene. He was not notified until almost an hour later.

Then I asked him about the other discrepancy between his report and the Reed City report. The question of Mr. Kooiker and where he was when Officer Finkbeiner arrived. Detective Pratt said he noted Mr. Kooiker at the front door when *he* arrived, but had no knowledge of who was or was not at the door when Officer Finkbeiner arrived on scene.

I told Detective Pratt I wanted to do a chapter in the book on the other unsolved homicides attributed to Reed City and then asked a few cursory questions about two I had done a little reading about prior to our meeting.

"The realtor, Sue Clason. I noticed you were interviewed in a few articles because at the time, there was a thought it might be linked to that of serial murderer, Gary Robbins, who had done similar things in other states. Is that still a possibility?"

"No, her case was not attributed to him."

"Burton Scott; 1979. Just reading the report, it looks like the person that was staying with him who disappeared right after would be a likely suspect. Police never located him?"

"No. To our best belief he was involved, but he disappeared right afterward, we had no name for him, and he was never located."

During my research, I had read that any fingerprint hit notification would go to the submitting law enforcement agency, meaning whoever submitted any prints to be tested against latent prints from the scene. So I asked Detective Pratt who would receive any hit notifications for Janette's case.

"Either the Reed City MSP Post detachment or Reed City Police Department," he said.

Then I asked him about the Lintemuth case, and my curiosity around how those prints hit. I repeated what I had written in my letter to him about how a reporter had gotten some information from Frank West out of Big Rapids.

"Director of Public Safety," he said, apparently familiar with the name. "Well, I can tell you that trainees wouldn't be using a piece of evidence from an open case for training. I am familiar with this case because I worked it. I know the prints were submitted and triggered a standard AFIS hit. But there still has to be an independent verification. I received notification of the hit. With the name and information provided, I was able to place the subject in Baldwin the day prior to the [Lintemuth] homicide. I acquired prints from the Lake County Sheriff's Department of the subject, along with other known prints from Minnesota and Illinois, and submitted those for verification."

I scribbled furiously, taking his information down word for word because he was pacing his answer with my writing in a way that made it clear he wanted each of them on record. Because it felt like I was missing something, I called Frank West later to get clarification.

"The prints were on file with MSP and over the years they would resubmit through AFIS to check, but early on they would hit a dead loop. They'd just keep searching the Michigan files with no connection to the national database because it wasn't available yet. And they wouldn't be using actual evidence with prints on it to train, understand that. It would be a digital copy of the prints. By the way, that offender was arrested days before the Lintemuth murder."

From an article in The Pioneer on September 1, 2010:

> Lake County Sheriff Robert Hilts testified that Graham was in fact in the area in 1980 days before Lintemuth's murder. Graham spent a few nights in Lake County jail after he tried to sleep in the bathroom at the sheriff's office. Graham

> was released on April 22, 1980, the day before Lintemuth's body was found. Hilts, who was working as a correction officer in 1980, arrested Graham and completed his booking on April 20, 1980.

West continued. "But even if they took his prints, if they were unaware he'd committed a murder, while they may have kept the prints on file, they wouldn't necessarily have been put through the system later. There would be no way of knowing the cases were related. Think of it like this. If someone was arrested for shoplifting back then, their prints may have been taken, but once that case was completed, there may never have been a reason to enter the prints into the system."

"I believe MSP still uses them for training because they were such good prints. The case itself was textbook. Everyone involved did a wonderful job processing the scene. But the crime occurred before the technology was available. It was one of those cases where, you know, you're sitting there having coffee one day and decide to run the prints. That day was a lucky break. I think they even got multiple hits because Graham had reoffended by that time in multiple states."

"Detective Pratt," I asked, nearing the end of my list of questions. "What do you think it would take for Janette's case to be solved?"

"Information. Physical evidence linking the perpetrator to the crime."

"You've been doing this a long time. Has any case ever gotten to you? I wonder how you do it. I mean all of it, *all* these cases." It seemed overwhelming to me.

"You deal with different types of crimes. You have to place them in perspective to keep your ability to pursue the case you're working on until it leads to a conclusion."

I knew how invested I'd become in Janette's story, in finding out who did such horrible things to her. I'd be a broken person if I had to deal with that all day. Hers was just one case. Detective Pratt did this for 46 years and 3 months with the State Police, and after a brief retirement, he's now doing it again for the Osceola County Sheriff's

Department. The stuff you have to look at, the people you have to deal with when you work in law enforcement—the liars and shady folks and druggies, and people who can take a knife to the soft flesh of another human, or shoot someone point-blank in the head... how, without it breaking your soul, how do you do it?

How do they do it?

I couldn't resist trying once more to get him to rule out Lee Peterson. I knew he'd said he didn't rule anyone out, but if there was any way I could say *This guy didn't do it,* I wanted to do that. Something about Lee Peterson made me sad. Maybe because I have mentally ill loved ones. I have a cousin who was schizophrenic and killed himself. His journey had been tough. I couldn't imagine a murder accusation on top of it.

"See, I want to ask you something specific, which I know you can't answer. It's about... well, it's about Peterson. I know they had his blood and prints, based on the Cadillac report, but Lieutenant Golnick said that if he'd never committed a crime, they wouldn't be in the system."

I had no idea if they were even able to get any of his prints for comparison in Janette's case because the Cadillac report I had said the set they took at autopsy was "*not suitable for entry into AFIS*."

"Well, I can tell you he *had* committed a crime," Detective Pratt said as he met my gaze. I felt my eyes widening. I knew that was farther than he had to go. He was trying to meet me half way and I found it sudden and unexpected. So they had his prints to check against latent lifts at the crime scene.

"Here's what you need to understand," he said. "Fingerprints cannot be dated. If you find a set of prints at a scene, you can't tell if they were put there yesterday or five years ago. There have been prints that survived for one-hundred years. So even if you have a suspect and find their prints at a scene, that doesn't mean they are the perpetrator. The prints may not have even been put there that day. But you may not be able to rule them out that way, either."

"Just like you may *not* find the prints of a person at a scene, and it can turn out they *were* the perpetrator," I said.

Detective Pratt nodded and smiled. He could tell that I understood. It was that explanation coupled with the knowledge of the mitochondrial DNA that swiftly brought into focus why, in this case, it would be difficult to rule anyone out until a perpetrator was apprehended. There were quite a few people associated with this case that I could hypothetically see police looking at very hard, who might find occasion to have been in that basement beneath the Gambles store. Employees, customers, a helluva lot of people in Reed City went into that store on a regular basis. Some of them might be suspects. If they were, and their prints or DNA were found at the scene, there exists a problem as to when those prints were put there. There was also the matter of those "unidentified prints" Detective Pratt had mentioned.

Could be a random customer, could be the killer...

As he walked me out of the sheriff's office and I awkwardly shook his hand, my head was swimming. I found Detective Pratt to be as open as he could have been, and even though I steered clear of asking specifics that common sense would suggest he couldn't release, he offered more than I expected he would. But there were some hard facts to contend with. The DNA they had would never produce a smoking gun.

I hope they have a boatload of circumstantial evidence that along with the prints, hairs, and mitochondrial DNA, is *almost* enough to tip them over the edge. My fondest wish is that police are just waiting for that one thing...

Maybe, just maybe, all they're waiting for is one person with a small piece of evidence or information that seems inconsequential, but is the exact right piece to pull it all together. If that's the case, what Janette Roberson needs now is a hero; one person who may not even know what they know.

Or someone who knows *exactly* what they know and finally tells the right person.

WHO KILLED JANETTE ROBERSON?

On January 19, 1983
Janette Roberson was murdered in the basement pet department of the Gambles store in Reed City in the middle of the day.

Over thirty years later
this crime remains unsolved.

<u>If you have any information pertaining to this case please contact any of the following:</u>

Det. Sgt. Mike Stephens - Mt. Pleasant Post
(989-773-5951)
Chief Chuck Davis - Reed City Police
(231-832-3743)
CRIME STOPPERS ANONYMOUS TIP LINE
1-800-SPEAK-UP (773-2587)

[redacted]

State of Michigan
DEPARTMENT OF STATE POLICE
Lansing

RICK SNYDER
GOVERNOR

COL. KRISTE KIBBEY ETUE
DIRECTOR

September 18, 2014

MS JENI DECKER

RE: CR-95886-14 , ROBERSON

Dear MS DECKER

This notice is issued in response to your request received on 8/27/2014, asking for information under the Freedom of Information Act (FOIA), MCL 15.231, et seq.

Your request is granted as to existing, non-exempt records in the possession of the Michigan State Police that fall within the scope of the request. To process your request, the department estimates a FOIA processing fee of $5,828.73 to search for, retrieve, review, examine, and separate exempt material, if any. Please submit a check, made payable to the State of Michigan, to the address below, in the amount of $2,914.37, to cover the required deposit of the estimated processing fee. To ensure proper credit, enclose a copy of this letter with your payment.

Upon receipt of the deposit, the department will complete the processing of your request. You will be notified of the balance due before the mailing of the records, and of the statutory basis for the exemption of any records or portions of records and of your statutory remedial rights, if applicable.

Sincerely,

Renee Hultberg

Renee Hultberg
Assistant FOIA Coordinator
Michigan State Police

MICHIGAN STATE POLICE HEADQUARTERS • 333 SOUTH GRAND AVENUE • P.O. BOX 30634 • LANSING, MICHIGAN 48909
www.michigan.gov/msp • (517) 241-1934

The Ridiculous FOIA Response

About the Author

Jeni Decker lives on a farm in rural Michigan with a bunch of animals (human and canine), and her albino frog, Humbert Humbert. She is the author of:

I Wish I Were Engulfed in Flames
The Peacock Mirror
The Wisdom of Repugnance
Far From Happy
[Redacted] - *A search for truth about the murder of Janette Roberson*

~AND~

Rigor Mortis
Absente Reo
Gravoria Manent
de Profundis (*Coming Soon - 2015*)

Made in the USA
Middletown, DE
26 January 2017